Fighting Financial Fires

D1520355

Fighting Financial Fires

An IMF Insider Account

Onno de Beaufort Wijnholds

First published 2011 by
PALGRAVE MACMILLAN

Palgrave Macmillan in the UK is an imprint of Macmillan Publishers Limited, registered in England, company number 785998, of Houndmills, Basingstoke, Hampshire RG21 6XS.

Palgrave Macmillan in the US is a division of St Martin's Press LLC, 175 Fifth Avenue, New York, NY 10010.

Palgrave Macmillan is the global academic imprint of the above companies and has companies and representatives throughout the world.

Palgrave® and Macmillan® are registered trademarks in the United States, the United Kingdom, Europe and other countries.

ISBN 978–0–230–29267–3

This book is printed on paper suitable for recycling and made from fully managed and sustained forest sources. Logging, pulping and manufacturing processes are expected to conform to the environmental regulations of the country of origin.

A catalogue record for this book is available from the British Library.

A catalog record for this book is available from the Library of Congress.

10 9 8 7 6 5 4 3 2 1
20 19 18 17 16 15 14 13 12 11

Printed and bound in Great Britain by
CPI Antony Rowe, Chippenham and Eastbourne

Contents

List of Abbreviations   vi

Acknowledgements   viii

Preface   ix

Prologue   1

1   Tequila and *Tesobonos*: Mexico 1995   11

2   From Miracle to Panic and Back: The Asian Crisis   25

3   The Korean Christmas Crisis   51

4   Indonesia with Nukes: The Russian Crisis   70

5   Double Bailout for Brazil   80

6   The IMF Fails: The Argentine Drama   94

7   Turkey Stumbles   110

8   Lessons Learned, Not Learned or Ignored   119

9   A Global Firestorm   132

10 Europe's Turn   156

11 Saving the System   175

Epilogue   190

Notes   192

Index   203

Abbreviations

ABS	Asset Backed Securities
AIG	American International Group
BCBS	Basel Committee of Bank Supervisors
BIS	Bank for International Settlements
BOE	Bank of England
BOJ	Bank of Japan
BOT	Bank of Thailand
CAC	Collective Action Clause
CCL	Contingent Credit Line (IMF)
CDS	Credit Default Swap
CEE	Central and Eastern Europe
EC	European Commission
ECB	European Central Bank
EFSF	European Financial Stability Facility
EMU	Economic and Monetary Union (Europe)
ESCB	European System of Central Banks
ESF	Exchange Stabilization Fund (United States)
ESM	European Stability Mechanism
EU	European Union
FCL	Flexible Credit Line (IMF)
FDIC	Federal Deposit Insurance Corporation (United States)
FED	Federal Reserve System
FSA	Financial Services Authority (United Kingdom)
FSAP	Financial Stability Assessment Program (IMF)
FSB	Financial Stability Board
FSF	Financial Stability Forum
G7	Group of Seven
G20	Group of Twenty
GDP	Gross Domestic Product
GSE	Government Sponsored Entity (United States)
IMF	International Monetary Fund
IMFC	International Monetary and Financial Committee
LTCM	Long Term Capital Management
NGO	Nongovernmental Organization
NIE	Newly Industrialized Economy
OECD	Organization for Economic Cooperation and Development
OPEC	Organization of Oil Exporting Countries

PSI	Private Sector Involvement
SA	Substitution Account
SDR	Special Drawing Right
SDRM	Sovereign Debt Rescheduling Mechanism
SGP	Stability and Growth Pact (European Union)
STF	Systemic Transformation Facility (IMF)
WB	World Bank

Acknowledgements

This book has benefited greatly from the – often intensive – discussions I have had with a large number of persons, many of whom have been closely involved with the financial crises of the last fifteen years. I owe a debt of gratitude to the following individuals, who have either kindly agreed to be interviewed, read parts of the manuscript, or answered my many queries: Age Bakker, Bas Bakker, Fred Bergsten, Lorenzo Bini Smaghi, James Boughton, Jan Brockmeijer, Stijn Claessens, Antonio de Lecea, Graciana del Castillo, Bernd Esdar, Ambroise Fayolle, Michael Foot, Anne-Marie Gulde, HE Jianxiong, Willy Kiekens, Jeroen Kremers, Anne Krueger, Desmond Lachman, John Lipsky, Charles Lucas, Meg Lundsager, Julie McKay, Bertus Meins, Frank Moss, Aleksei Mozhin, Francesco Papadia, Georges Pineau, the late Jacques Polak, Murillo Portugal, Hans Prader, Francisco Ramon Ballester, Raymond Ritter, David Robinson, Wolfgang Schill, Nathan Sheets, Anoop Singh, Robert Solomon, Stephan von Stenglin, Jean-Claude Trichet, Nico Valckx, Jan Willem van der Vossen, Yuriy Yakusha and John Williamson. Any remaining errors are entirely of my own doing. I also wish to mention my appreciation for the many stimulating discussions I have had in recent years at both the International Monetary Fund and the European Central Bank, as well as at the Brookings Institution and the Peterson Institute for International Economics.

I also wish to thank my commissioning editor at Palgrave Macmillan, Taiba Batool, and other members of the Palgrave team involved in the publication of this book for their dedication and efficiency and to acknowledge the professional work of Newgen Publishing and Data Services during the production phase.

My wife, Chris Nicholson, contributed excellent language suggestions and provided me with moral support for which I am most grateful.

Preface

Michel Camdessus, the generally affable Managing Director of the International Monetary Fund, was furious. As an observer of his verbal explosion remarked later, "the adrenaline was coming out of his ears." Camdessus had summoned six of the IMF's Executive Board members to his private conference room to scold them for having refused to support a record large credit granted by the Fund to crisis-stricken Mexico the night before. I was among those invited, since I had been instructed by the Dutch authorities to join the directors from Germany, the United Kingdom, Italy, Belgium and the Nordic countries to be recorded as abstaining from supporting the provision of a credit of $18 billion to the Government of Mexico. While the twenty-four-member IMF Board's deliberations are confidential and individual members' positions are not revealed, the world media on February 3, 1995 widely reported that the jumbo credit for Mexico, strongly advocated by the United States and approved the previous night by a majority of the executive directors, had failed to receive the support of six of the Board's European chairs. The *New York Times* caption read "Western Allies Rebuff Clinton in Mexico Vote."[1] Because of the economic and political significance of the Fund's large-scale financial support of Mexico, it was hardly surprising that a leak occurred. But for the Frenchman Camdessus it was a galling experience that the European criticism leveled at him had become common knowledge.

Thus began my involvement with the dramatic series of crises which rocked the international financial system between 1995 and 2002 and then from 2007 onward. My tenure as a member of the Fund's Executive Board, and subsequently as the European Central Bank's observer at the IMF, happened to coincide almost exactly with these events. It was a fascinating and sometimes nerve-racking experience to have to deal with situations that constituted uncharted waters to both the management and the board of the IMF. There is little doubt that during this period the international financial system endured its most challenging and, from 2007, its most dangerous test since the end of the Second World War. The IMF, largely unknown to the general public before 1995, suddenly became a household name in many parts of the world. Despite its intention to douse the fires raging in the financial markets, many resented the Fund's role and especially its policy conditionality, thereby often greatly complicating its task. While its staffers would joke that IMF stood for "It's Mostly Fiscal" – a reference to the Fund's usual prescription of fiscal austerity – its critics would talk about the "International Misery Fund," or "I'M Fired" on the placard carried by one unfortunate Korean worker pictured in the media.

Only a small number of the many books and articles written about financial crises in recent years have been authored by individuals who were actually dealing with them. There are hardly any contributions from former IMF management or staff, and none that I am aware of from former executive directors.[2] Of those insiders who have told their part of the story, practically all have been former high American officials. This is not all that surprising, since the United States played a pivotal role, together with the IMF, in guiding the resolution of the various crises. However, although less visible, European monetary authorities and their representatives at the IMF, enjoying a considerably larger share of voting power and financial contributions in the IMF than the United States, were very much part of the process as well.

This book is meant to fill the gap left by the paucity of insider contributions, from both former IMF and European officials, on the highly challenging financial crisis management during the last fifteen plus years. The aim here is not to provide a Europe-centric view of what happened, but rather to give a more comprehensive treatment of the part played by the various players, including the embattled officials from the debtor countries during the emerging country crises, and the role taken on by the European Central Bank (ECB) and other protagonists in dealing with the global financial crisis that erupted in 2007. The description and analysis of the events that occurred during those years are first of all based on my personal recollections, supported by the notes I kept as events unfolded, as well as reports by my office of informal meetings in which I participated during my eight-year tenure on the IMF Board. Minutes of Fund Board meetings only provide information on the formal phase of the crisis resolution process. Surprises are generally absent from formal board meetings, as management tends to prepare the ground before presenting controversial credit requests before the Executive Board. The interviews I conducted with individuals who were at the forefront of the crisis management process have been a second important source for this book. I have also read widely on what others have had to say about emerging market and advanced country financial crises.

The book is organized as follows. In order to provide a historical background for the treatment of the various modern financial crises, the Prologue describes earlier major crises of the postwar era. These include the collapse of the US dollar of 1971–73, and the first oil crisis that followed on its heels, as well as the Latin American debt woes of the 1980s.[3] The less dramatic developments preceding the emerging country crisis of between 1995 and 2002 are covered, as well as the seeds that were sown for the calamitous events that followed. Subsequently the various systemic crises that erupted are described and analyzed, beginning with the Mexican crisis of 1994–95, followed by the Asian financial crisis (Chapters 2 and 3) and those that arose in Russia in 1998 (Chapter 4) and Brazil in 1999 and 2002 (Chapter 5), the debacle in Argentina in 2001–02 (Chapter 6), and the crisis in Turkey from 1999 to 2002 (Chapter 7). The main features of these crises and the lessons learned from them, and those not learned or ignored, are analyzed in Chapter 8. The worldwide financial firestorm that broke out in August 2007 is dealt with in Chapters 9 and 10. Chapter 9 briefly describes the near-meltdown of the financial system in advanced countries and the remedies being put in place. Chapter 10 focuses on the contagion that it spawned, especially in Europe. Finally, Chapter 11 is devoted to reforms that are needed to save the international financial and monetary system from collapsing at some time in the future.

Three main threads run through the book. The first is the leading role – in part politically inspired – played by the United States, together with the IMF, in dealing with international financial crises, generally with the support of other economically advanced countries. The second is the crucial role played by the IMF in managing balance of payments crises, often successfully but sometimes with unsatisfactory results. The third thread has to do with the nature of international financial crises. Such crises have differed in several ways, but demonstrate a number of common characteristics, including excessive risk-taking, herd behavior, a lack of transparency, supervisory shortcomings, and macroeconomic policy mistakes. Lessons have been learned, but often forgotten or ignored, so that the global financial system has remained fragile, requiring additional measures to save it from collapse in the future.

Prologue

Financial crises, like the poor, will always be with us. Kindleberger, author of the classic *Manias, Panics and Crashes*, described financial crises as "a hardy perennial."[1] The modern capitalist system, despite all its positive results, produces financial crises at a steady rate. Some of these are relatively harmless and limited to a single country or small region, while others are much more insidious and can cause great harm. Crises that pose a threat to the global financial system are labeled *systemic*. Since the end of the Second World War there have been a number of such inflammable crises, the most recent and most dangerous of which started in the summer of 2007. The modern history of financial crises is riddled with lessons learned, not learned, ignored, or forgotten. While the focus of this book is on systemic crises since 1995, it is instructive to recall in a succinct manner the experience with crises of a few decades earlier.

The breakdown of Bretton Woods

The so-called Bretton Woods system of fixed but adjustable exchange rates (also known as the par value system) lasted for about twenty-five years after the Second World War. The dollar was the pivot of the system, with other currencies pegged to it. This reflected the dominant economic position of the United States and the general desire to avoid repeating the chaotic monetary breakdown of the 1930s. The arrangement worked well until increasing imbalances in industrial countries' external positions appeared in the 1960s. The United States' balance of payments had swung into deficit, while European countries and Japan were accumulating sizable surpluses. These imbalances foreshadowed future problems in the international monetary system. Toward the end of the 1960s surplus countries became increasingly unwilling to accumulate more dollars, as they viewed the US's ability to run large balance of payments deficits indefinitely as contributing to inflation in their countries. Many of them, with France leading the way, converted their "excess" dollars into gold. By the early

1970s the par value system, of which the IMF was the guardian, broke down, and the Fund found itself dealing with a serious currency crisis. Pierre-Paul Schweitzer, an affable but assertive former French central banker, was the first IMF Managing Director to face a problem of global proportions. Advocating a devaluation of the dollar on television cost him his job in 1973, when the Fund's largest shareholder did not support a third five-year term for the Frenchman.

By 1971 the United States had come to the conclusion that a fixed relationship between the dollar and gold, and thereby between the dollar and other currencies, was no longer in the interest of the US. This sentiment was expressed most clearly by the then Secretary of the Treasury, John Connally, in stating, to the alarm of the US's main trading partners, that "the dollar is our currency and your problem." President Richard Nixon announced in August 1971 that foreign central banks could no longer convert their dollars into US gold, with the result that exchange rates were no longer fixed and currencies floated against the dollar. But, since most policymakers were reluctant to give up the adjustable peg system, attempts were made to shore up the system through a new configuration of fixed exchange rates. The new set of exchange rates, which became known as the *Smithsonian Agreement* as the final talks took place in the Smithsonian Institution Castle in Washington, was announced with considerable fanfare in 1973. The euphoria was short-lived, however, as markets soon demonstrated their lack of faith in the new parity grid through a renewed wave of dollar sales. This spelled the definitive end of the Bretton Woods system and called into question the role of the IMF. It also undermined the success of the special drawing rights (SDRs) in the IMF that were introduced at the end of the 1960s to supplement what was perceived as a shortage of international reserves.

While the Fund had been the centerpiece of the international monetary system under the Bretton Woods system, its role after 1971 as overseer of the system was seriously eroded. In a world of floating exchange rates between industrial countries, it was unclear what the IMF could do to remain involved with countries' exchange rate policies, assuming that they had such a policy. Moreover, while the Fund was charged with monitoring the adequacy of international reserves, the need for reserves would in theory be zero in a system of fully floating rates. (In practice, countries tended to manage the float, and at times intervened heavily in the market.) But the IMF management, together with the support of several important member countries, worked hard to ensure that the Fund remained relevant as the overseer of the international monetary system. At first it formulated guidelines for floating exchange rates, and subsequently incorporated in its Articles of Agreement a set of rules on how member countries should behave in a floating rate regime. This was followed in 1977 by a decision on surveillance over countries' exchange rate policies. But, as such decisions constitute "soft law," the

Fund's role was considerably diminished. What remained was the Fund's ability to wield considerable influence over countries that needed to borrow from it. If, for instance, the IMF felt it necessary for a borrowing country to devalue its currency, this usually happened. But for countries that did not need the IMF's resources, especially the large ones, the situation was quite different. Despite exhortations over the years to give the Fund's surveillance more teeth, the application of the 1977 decision was not very effective. Thirty years later, the decision was reviewed, its scope broadened, and its language sharpened, as described in Chapter 11.

The first oil shock

Almost immediately after having absorbed the turmoil following the breakdown of the Bretton Woods system, the international financial community was faced with a serious new challenge. Oil prices shot up at the end of 1973 as the oil exporting countries, organized in the Organization of Oil Exporting Countries (OPEC) cartel, cut back their production at a time when demand was rising in a booming world economy. The result was an unprecedented change in the balance of payments positions of most countries, with the oil exporters running large surpluses and oil importing countries suddenly facing much higher energy costs and, in quite a few cases, needing balance of payments support. The impact of the oil shock on the populations of these countries was akin to that of a hefty tax increase, leading to a combination of lower economic growth with a surge in inflation, posing a serious threat to the health of the world economy. Here, clearly, was a new global role for the IMF, in acting as an intermediary between oil exporters, which were running up large surpluses, and those oil importers that could not borrow on international financial markets. Stepping up to the plate, the Fund soon played a major role in facilitating what came to be known as the *recycling* of oil revenues.

After Schweitzer's departure, H. Johannes Witteveen, a bookish Dutchman, was elected as the IMF's Managing Director in 1973. Having been a minister of finance in the Netherlands and a professor of economics, Witteveen came with ample technical qualifications for the job. Moreover, it turned out that he was an adherent of Sufism, a mystic tradition within the Islamic faith which has as one of its tenets that many religions ultimately have the same basis. This also made him an attractive candidate for many developing countries. There probably were some doubts about Witteveen's firmness in dealing with demanding situations, but it quickly emerged that he was quite capable of stepping into the breach, dealing with the oil crisis with a combination of decisiveness and quiet diplomacy. Soon after taking office, the new Managing Director was traveling the world in search of contributions for the IMF's newly established *oil facility*.

The money borrowed from oil exporters was to be used to provide credits to those oil importing countries especially hard hit by high energy costs, a process known as recycling. The conditionality was light, since these countries' lack of foreign exchange was caused by circumstances beyond their control. Witteveen succeeded in borrowing $8 billion, a substantial sum in those days, from energy exporter countries. The facility was terminated in 1976 after having significantly eased the economic pain of oil importers.

Besides its direct role as financial intermediary, the Fund also served as a catalyst for recycling of oil money by the private sector, a role that enhanced its reputation. But the IMF's timely recycling initiative also came at a cost, as the oil exporting countries were accorded very large increases in their quota (capital) share in the Fund. This was considered necessary at the time to ensure sufficient future resources for the IMF's lending activities. While this was fine, a higher quota share also implied a larger share of the voting power. And, as the oil exporters' importance in the world economy as measured by factors such as gross domestic product and trade openness (the main elements on which quota share are normally based) did not increase in the following decades, the voting structure of the Fund became skewed. Moreover, and more importantly, official recycling helped foster a process of overzealous international lending by international banks. Internationally operating banks increasingly provided loans to cover balance of payments and budget deficits of a host of countries, going beyond their needs resulting from the oil shock. Thus began a process of *overrecycling* which eventually led to pervasive debt problems in developing countries.

The Latin American debt crisis

During the second half of the 1970s a large number of emerging countries became caught up in a borrowing frenzy. This was especially true of Latin America. With lending possibilities limited in industrial countries due to a period of near-stagnation, international banks engaged in a competitive race to provide lucrative loans to developing countries. Many sovereign borrowers built up unsustainable levels of external debt as they sought financing for chronic balance of payments deficits. As many of these international loans financed consumption rather than investment, they contributed very little to strengthening the economic structure of the borrowing countries. A recurring pattern in financial markets and the activities of banks is the tendency to lend excessively under competitive pressure; market share is of great significance to individual banks. Loan officers are incentivized to bring in loans and have little incentive to be concerned with risk. Risk managers tend to see their position weakened when a lending boom is underway. The result is often that lenders suffer from a herd mentality, leading to excesses and eventually to a restructuring of borrowers' debt and losses for the banks. The lending euphoria of the late 1970s and early 1980s was also influenced by the notion that sovereign debtors posed little credit risk, as countries could not go bankrupt, as famously averred by Walter Wriston, who headed Citibank at the time. But, since many of the loans extended to Latin American and some Eastern European countries were provided on the basis of adjustable interest rates, the surge in interest rates in the early 1980s (the Federal Reserve had pushed up rates in order to suppress accelerating inflation) caused the borrowers to face much stiffer debt service obligations. While the banks had shifted the risk of higher interest rates to the borrowing countries, they had unwittingly promoted another risk, that of default. This process of transferring one risk while incurring another risk is a recurring theme in the history of financial crises.

The global financial community was shocked when the Mexican government announced in August 1982 that it was experiencing difficulty in servicing its external debt. As happened on a few occasions later on, the IMF was slow in recognizing the extent of the problems building up in Mexico and other Latin American countries, concentrating more on the question of whether financial flows to developing countries were sufficient than on the dangers of overborrowing. But, once the seriousness of the situation became clear, the reaction of the Fund was swift. First, a financial lifebuoy provided by central banks was organized through the Bank for International Settlements (BIS), followed by a credit from the IMF with strong policy conditionality. Other Latin American countries, including the region's largest economy, Brazil, soon also experienced payments problems and asked for IMF support. As international banks hurried to reexamine their exposures to developing countries, they froze their credit lines to Latin American economies and Eastern European countries. During the years of overrecycling, banks had relaxed their internal standards of risk assessment, but, as the bad news on sovereign debt spread, in a typically herd-like fashion they abruptly cut off financing to emerging and centrally planned economies, without much differentiation. This process of *contagion* was frequently to cause problems in the future.

The IMF once again found itself in the spotlight, having to deal with a new crisis with potentially serious ramifications for the international financial system. While the Fund stood ready to support those countries that were facing a liquidity crisis, which if prolonged too long could develop into a solvency problem, it did not wish simply to bail out the creditors. After all, foreign banks had been engaging in imprudent lending and would have to suffer the consequences. But the banks were cutting credit lines, something that was individually in their self-interest, but collectively severely complicated the situation. What ensued was a classic collective action problem in which intervention from the public sector was urgently needed to untangle the mess. The IMF rose to the challenge.

The solution was to pressure the banks into pledging that they would maintain their exposure to sovereign borrowers. Only when a *critical mass* of commitments from banks had been obtained was the Fund willing to release the first portion ("tranche" in IMF parlance) of the credits it had negotiated with Mexico, Brazil, and others. The main architect of this approach was Jacques de Larosière, the energetic and shrewd former head of the French Treasury, who had taken over from Witteveen as the IMF's Managing Director in 1978. The dapper Frenchman employed an effective tactic for dealing with the world's most important commercial banks. He invited those with the largest credit exposures to send their representatives to a meeting with the IMF management. Ushering the bankers into a room, he exerted maximum pressure on them to provide assurances that they would contribute to solving the payments problems of Mexico and other distressed borrowers. Such action was usually supported by the central banks and banking supervisors in the home countries of the creditors. De Larosière succeeded again and again in attaining the sought-after *critical mass*, usually around 85 per cent of outstanding bank loans. By keeping the banks involved in the process, a collapse of the economies of the largest Latin American countries was avoided. The strong-arm tactics employed by the IMF proved to be successful, thereby greatly enhancing the reputation of the IMF as a crisis manager and effective coordinator of collective action.

While the critical mass approach proved its worth, the problems in most Latin American countries were so deep-seated that it took many years for their economies to recover. The international banks initially did their part, after strong "encouragement," by generally maintaining their exposure, and later renegotiated the outstanding debts. But the damage done by *dirigiste* and populist economic policies in Latin America in the 1970s and early 1980s was simply so extensive that it could not be repaired swiftly. Thus, the region experienced what came to be known as the *lost decade* in the wake of the Mexican crisis. It took further official intervention, initiated by the United States, to fully resolve the Latin American debt problem. The first initiative was taken in October 1985 and dubbed the *Baker Plan* after James Baker III, then US Secretary of the Treasury. It consisted of a three-pronged approach: an exhortation to debtor countries to follow sound macroeconomic and structural policies, a central role for the IMF in managing the adjustment process, and a reversal by the commercial banks of the drop in their net lending to Latin American countries.

The renewed debt strategy proved not to go far enough, and led to a new initiative for a comprehensive and sufficiently far-reaching solution. This time it was Baker's successor, Nicolas Brady, who put forward a plan that enjoyed widespread support in the international community. Agreement on Brady's proposal was speeded up by serious riots that broke out in Venezuela as a response to the government's attempts to implement IMF policy conditions, without which the country would likely face collapse. The main elements of the *Brady Plan* focused on obtaining sufficient relief for debt-ridden countries to ensure that their economic recovery was not held back by a lack of lending. Commercial banks had to agree to remove impediments, particularly sharing and negative pledge clauses in loan contracts, for negotiating debt reduction. The IMF and the World Bank agreed to a set-aside of funds to help countries buy back their bank debt at a discount. Both institutions also agreed to offer additional financial support to collateralize a portion of interest payments for debt or debt service transactions. This allowed debtors to issue so-called Brady bonds that incorporated lower interest rates and longer maturities. The Brady Plan was a success, removing an important obstacle in the functioning of the international monetary system and allowing heavily indebted countries to return to a path of satisfactory economic growth. In effect, it removed the *debt overhang* that saved overborrowing countries from prolonged economic stagnation. Moreover, commercial banks had to write down sizable amounts of their original loans in a manageable fashion, which, for a while at least, taught them a valuable lesson.

The Brady Plan, which included debt reduction for a number of emerging market countries facilitated by IMF resources, was an example of effective cooperation between debtor countries, the Fund, and commercial banks, with the blessing of the IMF's shareholders. The question remains, however, whether this approach did not foster higher than normal *moral hazard*, a situation in which an entity that believes it is shielded from a certain risk behaves differently from the way in which it would behave if it bore the risk itself.[2] It is important to distinguish between debtor and creditor moral hazard. On the *debtor* side moral hazard was probably quite modest. Any IMF credit creates some moral hazard in principle, but the – often stringent – policy conditions that come with Fund lending are likely to strongly discourage the borrower from repeating the experience. At the same time, there was a fair amount of *creditor* moral hazard, as expectations were likely to have developed that the banks would again benefit from the IMF's involvement in future crises, thereby limiting their losses. The question of moral hazard, not prominent at the time, came to play an important role in the approach to the emerging country crises of the 1990s, as well as regarding the abrupt drying-up of interbank liquidity in 2007–08, both of which are discussed in the rest of this book.

The IMF's relevance questioned

It is a common occurrence that, in periods of calm in the international financial markets, calls are heard for cutting back the activities of the IMF or even dismantling it. Such was the case in the late 1980s after the Latin American debt crisis had finally wound down. A lull in lending activity is always a difficult time for the Fund, as there is little knowledge among most politicians and the general public about the IMF, other than its role in managing financial crises. Its ongoing tasks of surveillance over its members' economic policies and the provision of technical assistance are not widely known and generate very little political interest. Moreover, the Fund's involvement in the dollar dilemmas of the 1980s and in the strains in the European Exchange Rate Mechanism (ERM) in the early 1990s was quite limited. These exchange rate crises were dealt with almost exclusively within the Group of Seven (G-7) and the European Union (EU).

In early 1985 the dollar appreciated to spectacular heights against the currencies of America's main trading partners, reaching almost four Deutsche Mark to the dollar. The main cause was high interest rates in the United States, due to a combination of tight monetary and expansionary fiscal policies, while interest rates in Europe were much lower. In September 1985 a secret meeting took place in the Gold Room of New York's famous Plaza Hotel. The main actors were the finance ministers and central bank governors of the major industrial countries. They agreed under the *Plaza Accord* that the dollar was overshooting and adding to the problem of the large balance of payments deficit of the US. After they announced in euphemistic language that "exchange rates should play a role in adjusting external imbalances," the markets promptly drove down the dollar. In the event the dollar threatened to fall too far by the beginning of 1987. The result was another secret meeting, held in Paris, leading to the *Louvre Accord*. This time the participants agreed on a set of ranges within which the main currencies should be kept. But this approach, dubbed "soft" exchange rate targets, was later abandoned. While these were important monetary events, they did not require IMF financing, so the Fund was only marginally involved in the Plaza and Louvre agreements.

The IMF was also not actively involved in the regional exchange rate turmoil that swept across Europe in the early 1990s. In the runup to the creation of the European Monetary Union (EMU), candidate members were required to adhere to the ERM. This mechanism was intended to prepare participating countries on the path to the adoption of a common currency. It required ERM members to keep their exchange rates *vis-à-vis* each other within a narrow range. This so-called parity grid came under serious pressure in 1992, with Italy and subsequently the United Kingdom throwing in the towel after massive central bank intervention failed to eliminate the severe pressure on their currencies. France narrowly escaped a similar fate. This was the time of the famous attack on the pound sterling by master speculator George Soros through his Quantum Fund, which netted a profit of $1 billion at the expense of the Bank of England and, indirectly, the British taxpayer. These events led to a speedy reassessment of the road to EMU and the establishment of ERM mark II, which allowed fluctuation margins of 15 per cent above or below parity between the exchange rates of its members. Calm returned to European foreign exchange markets and the common currency, the *euro*, was successfully adopted in 1998. Since the IMF was little more than an observer of deliberations on the most important exchange rate issues, its role as overseer of the international monetary system was further eroded.

But events were to take a positive turn in another direction for the Fund. The spectacular political events of 1989, starting with the demolition of the Berlin Wall and followed by the removal of the entire Iron Curtain and the dismemberment of the Soviet Union, came as a godsend for the IMF. All former Communist countries were in grave need of financial support, and even more of sound economic advice. Michel Camdessus, former governor of the *Banque de France*, who had taken over from Jacques de Larosière as the Fund's Managing Director in a job swap in January 1987, took up the challenge with alacrity. Once again the IMF was at the center of current economic and financial cutting edge developments. Aiding countries making the *transition* from centrally planned to *market economies* was a task to which the Fund was well suited. It had extensive experience with structural adjustment in developing countries, and also in a number of centrally planned economies, such as Hungary and Yugoslavia, which were already IMF members before the rupture of 1989. There was also the experience of Poland, which, in a bold approach, dubbed shock therapy, had made important strides away from the old system. To maintain progress on the transition process, the Fund established a temporary *Systemic Transformation Facility* (STF) to provide financing with limited policy conditions to ex-Communist countries. After the temporary facility came to an end, the countries of Eastern Europe and the former Soviet Union, with only a few exceptions, agreed on economic reform programs with the Fund based on regular policy conditions.

The process proved to be successful, as the formerly centrally planned economies, usually after a period of economic shrinkage, achieved increasingly positive results. Most Eastern European countries were well on the way, within a few years after their democratization, on the (long) road toward catching up with their Western brethren. Russia and its former satellites needed more time to embark on this process, but did achieve quite satisfactory growth rates over time. Most of the Eastern European countries joined the European Union after 2000, with the IMF playing an important role in preparing them for membership. Although good results were achieved, the systemic reform process has generally been less permanently established in the former Soviet Union, and many of these countries suffered serious payment problems after independence. In fact, during the transition process many of them experienced severe payment difficulties. Moreover, Russia underwent a serious financial crisis in 1998, as discussed in Chapter 4.

The IMF's effective involvement in the transition process, often initially taking place under difficult circumstances, placed the institution, once again, squarely in the limelight. Earlier talk of irrelevance was quickly silenced, and the institution was thriving, and expanding, in the first years after the Berlin Wall came down. Just as the Fund started to achieve its first successes in aiding the transition process, from Croatia to Slovakia and from Armenia to Ukraine, it was thrust into a new and highly challenging role. Starting in early 1995, and lasting over a period of some eight years, several important (and many less important) emerging countries experienced such severe financing problems that the international financial system came under threat on more than one occasion. This time the IMF's deep involvement turned out to be more controversial.

1
Tequila and *Tesobonos*: Mexico 1995

For almost a decade, beginning in late 1994, a large number of emerging market countries suffered violent economic convulsions that led to IMF rescue operations of an unprecedented magnitude. This series of crises was certainly not expected when I took up my position on the Fund's Executive Board on November 1, 1994. Two months later the Mexican crisis erupted, starting an era of crisis management by the IMF that constituted the most challenging time in its by then fifty-year history.

The 1990s had started off quite peacefully following the final winding-up of the Latin American debt crisis of the 1980s with the implementation of the Brady Plan. But, while there was an absence of financial crises, new imbalances were steadily developing, although undetected by the vast majority of observers. Latin American countries were again falling into their old habit of heavy external borrowing, now aided by the willingness of international bond markets to provide the money rather than by means of syndicated loans supplied by banks. Bond financing was rapidly replacing bank loans as the principal means to finance balance of payments deficits; syndicated lending had largely dried up, as the banks had had their fill of providing huge amounts of funds to sovereign borrowers. Moreover, many Latin American countries allowed their currencies to appreciate significantly in real terms in an attempt to combat domestic inflation, as the orthodox approach of tightening monetary policy was politically unattractive. Quite often the result was an overvaluation of the currency and a loss of competitiveness. On top of that, several emerging countries had weak domestic financial systems, which added to their vulnerability. Again, all of this was insufficiently recognized at the time, including by the otherwise diligent IMF staff. In retrospect, the situation was developing into an accident waiting to happen, but early warning systems were either absent or not working properly.

When I arrived at the Fund in 1994, I was surprised that in discussions on the world economic outlook Mexico was not mentioned as a country where things were not going in the right direction. Staff reports on Mexico earlier in the year had also not conveyed any warnings. Yet information that was coming out of meetings of central banks, gathering at their confidential monthly rendezvous at the Bank for International Settlements (BIS) in Basel, did give me the impression that all was perhaps not well. I had also been sensitized by remarks made in late 1993 by the highly respected economist Rüdiger Dornbusch at a conference I organize with others in Amsterdam.[1] Dornbusch noted that Mexico's imports were increasingly outstripping its exports (mainly oil) and that its external deficit was very high (5 per cent of GDP, soon to rise to 7 per cent). This, he said, raised questions about the sustainability of America's southern neighbor's exchange rate, the soundness of its banking system, and the level of foreign debt.[2] Why, then, did the IMF seem so unprepared when the crisis hit?

To his credit, IMF Managing Director Camdessus immediately launched an investigation into the matter after the Fund had dealt – effectively – with the Mexican crisis. An internal report produced by an eminent former senior staffer, Alan Whittome, reached some striking conclusions. The Fund's "deafening silence" in the run-up to the Mexican crisis was attributed to a number of failings. First, Fund staff and management had developed the habit of giving Mexico the benefit of the doubt. In fact, the authorities' assertions were accepted at face value. There was no insistence on timely provision of data. Contingency planning by Mexico would have been sensible, but the IMF also did not insist on this. Also lacking was sufficient attention to financial market developments, as well as the opinions of outside agencies and experts. Finally, the discussions between the Fund staff and Mexican officials lacked candor. The IMF's management promised improvements, and some changes could indeed be detected after 1995. However, when new crises struck in emerging countries some of the old problems resurfaced, as will be described in later chapters.

Living under the volcano

The history of Mexico is riddled with debt problems. Since it became independent in 1820 its debts have been either in default or undergoing restructuring for almost half of the time. There has also been a tendency for financial crises to erupt at the time of a change in government. Mexico's presidents enjoy a six-year nonrenewable term, and in 1976, 1982, and again in 1994 the transfer of power was accompanied by financial collapse. As described earlier, the very deep crisis of 1982 constituted the first wave of the Latin American debt crisis of the 1980s. The assassination in early 1994 of the presidential candidate of the Partido Revolucionario Institucional (PRI), the political party that had enjoyed a monopoly on power in Mexico for a very long time, triggered an erosion of confidence which ended in another deep crisis at the end of that year. Ernesto Zedillo, who was elected president as a substitute for his party's murdered leader, inherited an economy that was growing more unstable by the day. There had been some apparent successes in preceding years, as the use of a fixed exchange rate as an anchor (the peso was pegged to the US dollar) had helped to bring down inflation from an earlier peak of 150 per cent to 7 per cent in 1994. At the same time, Mexico was importing much more than it was selling abroad (its current account deficit reached 7 per cent of GDP in 1994), and this gap was increasingly financed by short-term capital, which by its nature is much more volatile than long-term inflows such as foreign direct investment. The government was borrowing heavily abroad and at increasingly short maturities, usually a telltale sign of mounting problems. In the course of 1994 it felt compelled to introduce a new borrowing instrument known as *tesobonos*. These were short-term government securities issued in pesos but paid back in dollars so as to cover investors' exchange rate risk. In addition, the Mexican banking system was inefficient, poorly supervised, and, as it turned out later, barely solvent.

Financial markets were starting to get nervous about the outlook for Mexico as 1994 progressed, resulting in increased swings in capital flows. The central banks' foreign exchange reserves began to fall rapidly from a comfortable level of $30 billion at the beginning of the year to $18 billion in May, of which only $8 billion could be used to prop up the peso. Unknown to the IMF and other observers at the time, the rest of the reserves were earmarked for other purposes. In the meantime, the stock of potentially costly *tesobonos* grew apace, reaching a peak of $50 billion. While issuing short-term paper helped to keep foreign capital flowing in, Mexican residents were taking their money out of the country in huge amounts. As the year progressed, the markets became quite jittery, even though the extent of the loss of reserves was not fully known. The Zedillo government presented its budget in early December, but, since the combination of tax cuts and spending increases was inconsistent with the target of overall budget balance, investors started rushing for the exit door. On December 20, 1994 the peso was devalued by 15 per cent, but capital kept flowing out. Two days later the government threw in the towel and the peso was decoupled from the dollar, eventually floating down by 70 per cent. Only then did Mexico approach the IMF with the message that it needed the Fund's help.

At the end of December 1994, the IMF's number two (officially called the first deputy Managing Director, to distinguish him from the two other deputies), Stanley Fischer,[3] and senior Fund staff informally briefed the Executive Board. Fischer mentioned that talks were underway between the Fund and Mexico, which was no big surprise. But the rest of the meeting was not very helpful, with the staff busy defending the Mexican authorities. This was my first whiff of clientelism at the IMF, which was particularly strong in its Western Hemisphere Department.

Meanwhile, the real action was taking place elsewhere, in Washington. United States officials, concerned about the effect an economic meltdown south of the border could have on the American economy and the prospect of vastly increased illegal immigration, were drawing up a rescue plan for Mexico.[4] It was also feared that what came to be known as the "Tequila crisis" could spread through Latin America, as had happened in 1982. Robert Rubin, the savvy Wall Street insider who had just been appointed Secretary of the Treasury, and his deputy, the brilliant economist Larry Summers, after conferring with Federal Reserve Chairman Alan Greenspan, put forward a proposal for providing guarantees of up to $25 billion on private sector loans to Mexico, in tandem with a credit from the IMF of around $8 billion. Despite the obvious political pitfalls, President Clinton swiftly agreed to the package. This inspired Rubin to supersize the loan guarantee to $40 billion. But the task of selling such an enormous support operation to politicians and the American public, who saw it as a massive bailout for Mexicans, proved to be a very hard slog.

European central bankers and treasury officials were also skeptical, although they were willing to go along with supporting a relatively large loan from the IMF, which they would in part Fund. But they did consider the "Tequila hangover" to be primarily an American problem, as mostly American interests were at stake, and therefore – in their view – financial support should come mainly from the US. They also did not buy the argument that this was a systemic crisis, threatening the global financial system. The Europeans considered that a collapse of the Mexican economy, about the same size as that of a smallish industrial country such as the Netherlands, would be incapable of seriously unsettling the generally favorable world economic outlook.

The US administration made a huge effort to push the loan guarantee proposal, which required Congressional approval. Some Republican leaders, particularly the newly elected House Speaker Newt Gingrich, expressed their support, but the perception that the Mexican scheme might well fail and cost the taxpayer a bundle was widespread. This prompted Gingrich to take the unusual step of asking Alan Greenspan to explain the plan to right-wing radio talk show personality Rush Limbaugh, who was heavily criticizing it.[5] However, this and other efforts failed to bring around the majority of the politicians and the public. And the complete turnaround by Alfonse D'Amato, chairman of the Senate Banking Committee, from initially supporting the Rubin–Summers proposal to becoming one of its most vocal critics was a serious setback. As the debate dragged on in the US political arena, the financial markets again became jittery about Mexico, leading Rubin to initiate discussions with the Federal Reserve (Fed) and the IMF on alternative solutions.

At the Fund, the Executive Board was regularly briefed by Camdessus and Fischer on the continuing Mexican saga. Camdessus warned board members that the consequences of a Mexican meltdown for the world economy could be serious. This line was strongly supported by the Brazilian Executive Director, Alexandre Kafka,[6] who suggested that a much larger Fund credit for Mexico was needed than the $8 billion that had been proposed, and which was the maximum that could "normally" be provided under IMF rules on access (300 per cent of a country's quota). On the opposite side were the Europeans, who objected to a credit for Mexico going far beyond this maximum (eventually $18 billion was provided, representing 700 per cent of Mexico's quota in the IMF). Adding to the Europeans' discomfort was Camdessus's request for additional credit lines to be provided, in large measure by central banks in Europe. And European directors were also dissatisfied with the limited information provided and lamented the absence of an early warning by the Fund staff on the trouble building up in Mexico.

At the US Treasury, the Rubin–Summers team decided to abandon the unpopular loan guarantee proposal and to opt for tapping the little-known *Exchange Stabilization Fund* (ESF) instead. The ESF, established in the 1930s when the United States left the gold standard, and intended for stabilizing the dollar exchange rate, amounted to $35 billion and could be utilized by the Secretary of the Treasury without Congressional approval. While it could not be used without the consent of the president, his support was quickly obtained once it became clear that Mexico's reserves were down to a mere $2 billion. Mexico's Minister of Finance, Guillermo Ortiz, warned Rubin and the IMF that without large-scale and rapidly disbursed financial support a default could not be avoided. Action followed swiftly, with the United States pledging a loan of $20 billion from the ESF and Camdessus proposing an IMF loan of $18 billion for Mexico. The Fund's Managing Director's announcement was audacious, as the amount was vastly in excess of anything the Fund had ever provided. Obtaining European support would obviously be a problem. Together with some smaller bilateral contributions, the total financial package amounted to $40 billion. It was expected that another $10 billion would be pledged in credit lines by central banks from industrial countries, via the BIS. The total of $50 billion, widely cited in the media, was enough to turn around market sentiment.

Not only was the financial package for Mexico by far the largest official balance of payments support in history; it was also unusual in that the modalities of the two main loans differed considerably. According to IMF rules, collateral is not required when granting credit, but timely repayment relies on economic policy conditions that are incorporated in the credit agreement. . By contrast, the ESF loan did require collateral, which took the form of future revenues from oil exports. In this way the United States was very well protected against incurring losses on its loan to Mexico. In the case of nonpayment, the IMF, and consequently its shareholders, among whom the Europeans were prominent, would be in a much weaker position. Moreover, the ESF loan carried a higher interest rate than that charged by the IMF and also included some policy conditions beyond the already demanding Fund policy prescriptions. All this made for a hard time selling the package, especially in Europe.

After President Clinton had given the go-ahead for the ESF loan, Camdessus immediately pressured the Fund's Executive Board to support his proposal for a loan that almost matched the US's contribution. This caused a fair amount of consternation in European capitals, where officials complained that they had not been consulted before the package was put on the table. On February 2, 1995, shortly before the Managing Director asked the executive directors to approve the jumbo credit for Mexico at short notice, I was accompanying an IMF staff team that was conducting an annual examination of the Dutch economy. I abandoned my rather leisurely attendance of the discussions and quickly made my way to the De Nederlandsche Bank (DNB, the Central Bank of the Netherlands) in Amsterdam. There I was told by the President, Wim Duisenberg, who later became the first head of the European Central Bank, that intense discussions were going on among European officials who were upset about the hasty actions of the IMF and the US and were contemplating a way to express their displeasure. Leading the charge of unhappy central bankers was Hans Tietmeyer, the outspoken head of the German Central Bank. As Duisenberg wanted me to be at the Fund to join European colleagues in giving a strong message to Camdessus, I got on the first plane to Washington.

Most IMF Board meetings on credit approvals are uneventful, as the outcome is almost always informally decided before such gatherings. But the meeting on Mexico's jumbo credit turned out to be lively. After a long discussion, during which most European board members expressed their objections, Camdessus, as chairman of the Executive Board, announced that the credit had been approved. No mention was made of any votes against or abstentions. Since European representatives had not explicitly requested to be recorded as withholding their support, Leo van Houtven, the Fund's secretary and responsible for counting the votes, had concluded that all was well. Immediately after Camdessus had closed the meeting, a number of European directors rushed toward the chairman to insist that they wanted to be recorded as abstaining, a somewhat milder form of opposition than voting against. Camdessus, relieved that the battle had been won (the abstentions, although irritating to him, did not change the outcome), said that, as he had already broken many rules, he would go along with this breach also. The next morning he was in a different mood, as the lack of support from six European executive directors[7] was widely reported in the media. Camdessus then called the meeting with the six of us described in the first sentences of this book. It would take a while for tempers to cool down after that day.

There was no disagreement among the Fund's shareholders on the *policy conditions* with which Mexico needed to comply. The main elements were a tightening of monetary policy, letting the peso float, strengthening the fiscal stance, cleaning up the banking system, and vastly improving the provision of financial data. More transparency was sorely needed, as it became clear that Mexico had not only been late in providing important data to the IMF, but had in some instances not been fully truthful. The most contentious issue in the negotiations related to the level of interest rates, which is a common sticking point when the Fund discusses an economic program with a potential borrower. Hiking interest rates is always and everywhere unpopular, but often a necessary medicine to improve the economic health of a country. Higher interest rates were sorely needed in Mexico in 1995 to restore confidence and ensure stability, especially by making it attractive for investors to buy and hold pesos. Real interest rates (inflation outstripping nominal interest rates) had been negative, discouraging saving and stimulating borrowing, while putting off foreign investors. In the end the Mexican negotiators had little choice but to accept the move to positive real interest rates, as time was running out. The policy package was a good one, but in the overall deal one important element was missing. No contribution by the private sector (banks and other lenders) was demanded by the IMF or the official creditors, although the banks and bond purchasers had significantly contributed to the crisis through their unrestrained lending to Mexico. This lack of burden-sharing carried the risk of creating expectations of future large rescue operations for overborrowing countries, and allowed banks and *tesobono* holders to escape without painful losses. *Moral hazard* became a prominent topic of discussion, also among the Executive Board of the IMF, but only a minority expressed real concern. At the time, management and staff of the Fund mostly played down the extent of moral hazard. After the arrival of Horst Köhler as managing director in 2000 this attitude changed, although some prominent staff members remained skeptical.

Initially, financial markets reacted favorably to the huge financial package backed up by tough policy commitments. But, in the following months, confidence ebbed again as investors felt uncertain about the release of further money from the IMF and the ESF. In contravention of the economic program, the Mexican Central Bank had been easing monetary policy prematurely. As more bad news surfaced, including the discovery that the Mexican banks were in worse shape than had earlier been thought, capital flowed out again and the peso fell. Michel Camdessus's public statements about the danger of the situation and the possibility that other countries could follow suit probably had the unintended consequence of making the markets even more nervous. The situation remained tense through most of 1995, but late in that year the first tentative signs of a turnaround appeared. The balance of payments was improving and the stock of *tesobonos* falling, bringing welcome relief to Mexico's debt-service payments. By early 1996, about a year after the rescue operation had been put in place, Mexico started emerging from the woods and was even able to make repayments on the US loan, which, like the IMF credit, had not been fully drawn down. As repayments to the IMF, which was charging less interest than the ESF, did not begin until later, European criticism emerged again. Conditions in Mexico continued to improve, however, and full repayment to both lenders was completed three years ahead of schedule. In 1999 Mexico approached the IMF again for a standby credit of around $5 billion, as it was concerned about the uncertainty that had taken hold in international financial markets after the Asian and Russian crises of 1997–98. The Mexican policymakers explicitly stated that they wanted to bolster confidence during the period of transition to a new government. This was a wise step in view of the tradition of financial mishaps almost every time a new president was elected in Mexico. In the event, the changeover of power to President Fox in 2000 went smoothly.

Despite all the difficulties encountered, the Mexican rescue was a success. Moreover, the "Tequila crisis" did not cause significant contagion in other Latin American countries. Default was avoided, the Mexican economy recovered fully, sound monetary and fiscal policy became the norm, and the health of the banking system improved dramatically. The leadership of the United States and the deep involvement of the IMF, but also the commitment and competence of the new Mexican government, were crucial in achieving this result. Michel Camdessus emerged from this episode with a greatly enhanced reputation. The former French top official, who was seen by many American politicians as a socialist with a Maurice Chevalier accent, had displayed resoluteness and impressive diplomacy, which – however grudgingly – came to be admired not only at the US Treasury but also on Capitol Hill. A fluent Spanish speaker, Camdessus enjoyed considerable popularity in Latin America, a region in which the IMF has seldom been viewed with enthusiasm. But most Europeans had a different view, feeling that the Fund's Managing Director was yielding too much to American pressure, although they respected his obvious skills.

Were the Europeans wrong in their criticism of the Mexican rescue? Yes and no. Yes, as they had tended to underestimate the damage that could have been done had the "Tequila crisis" spread, although Camdessus's warnings of a global financial meltdown were probably exaggerated and to be seen more as conveying a sense of urgency than as an objective assessment. No, in the sense that the unequal conditions under the ESF and IMF loans were unsatisfactory; there had been insufficient consultation by the United States with other industrial countries; European concerns about moral hazard sensitized others to the issue; and, finally, their pointed queries about the IMF's failure to see the storm coming led to a much-needed reexamination of the Fund's surveillance practices, that is, the way in which the Fund conducts checkups on the economies of its members.

A qualified success

While the first in the series of emerging market crises had caused a shock, the generally positive outcome reassured the markets and officials alike. This carried the obvious danger of a return to complacency and business as before. To some extent this was indeed what happened, although some lessons were beginning to be drawn by the main actors. It was the Mexican side that most took to heart the need to avoid a repeat of the events of 1994–95, and the private banking system the least. After the crisis Mexico's leadership, determined to break with the damaging tradition of recurring crises, embarked upon a new era in economic policymaking that not only ensured a smooth transition when in 2000 President Zedillo handed over power to Vicente Fox, but also led to a strengthening of its economic institutions. The central bank gained full independence, jealously defended by its new governor, Guillermo Ortiz, the former Minister of Finance, who had been the chief negotiator with the US and the IMF. In the years following the crisis Mexico's monetary and budgetary policies were generally exemplary. After a while inflation targeting was initiated, a generally successful policy tool first introduced in some industrial countries in the early 1990s while budgetary processes improved. Supervision of the banking system, which had been shoddy at best, was thoroughly overhauled. Foreigners were allowed to buy a considerable part of Mexico's banks, which furthered the cause of placing them on a sound footing. Domestic financial markets developed favorably, which, with inflation under control, made it possible for the government to issue long-term bonds in pesos, which would have been unthinkable in earlier years.

How did other parties involved in the crisis fare? The international banks and other financial players experienced the crisis mainly as a hiccup, which in

While sound macroeconomic policies remained in place over time, in large part thanks to Minister of Finance Agostín Carstens who later took over from Ortiz as Central Bank Governor, so-called structural reforms remained inadequate. Such measures are aimed at lastingly (or structurally) improving the capacity of an economy to generate economic growth; examples of structural reforms are more flexible labor and product markets, more effective competition, and improvements in the channeling of savings toward productive investments. Also important are measures to ensure an adequate level of public investment, which allows the government to provide such crucial services as education and infrastructure. For instance, the tax system, only partially reformed, still generates a disappointingly low level of revenue.

How did other parties involved in the crisis fare? The international banks and other financial players experienced the crisis mainly as a hiccup, which in the end hardly cost them any money. *Tesobonos* were fully redeemed, obviating the need for unpleasant write-offs. The Mexican rescue came to be viewed as a bailout for banks and bondholders which could lead to the expectation that similar action would be taken when other countries got into trouble. Moreover, reducing moral hazard by following the strong-arm tactics of De Larosière of the 1980s, putting pressure on international banks to maintain their exposure, had become less effective. Countries looking for foreign capital had become able to tap international bond markets, so that concentrating only on banks to engineer a "bail-in" was insufficient to attain a "critical mass." Herding numerous bondholders into a room was not a practical possibility, and bond-holder committees, which had existed in the 1930s, had not yet been formed. Bondholders would not become involved in rescue operations for emerging markets until later.

In the official sphere, the United States could look back at a successful operation, skillfully engineered by the US Treasury in close cooperation with the Federal Reserve and the IMF. American high officials did recognize, however, following European complaints, that they would have to consult better with their foreign counterparts, especially in the Group of Seven. Many Europeans came to realize that they had to become more proactive in dealing with financial crises, while trying to avoid moral hazard. For the IMF, whose central role in resolving the crisis had strongly raised its profile, there was a clear lesson on the need to be more alert to impending crises and to reexamine its surveillance practices.

Main causes of the crisis

In *summing up* the experience of the Mexican rescue of 1994–95, and also in drawing comparisons with other crises, *four main reasons* for the crisis can be identified. First of all, the real exchange rate became dangerously overvalued in an attempt to combat inflation without resorting to domestic tightening. Second, fiscal policy was too lax. Third, Mexico had built up a very large external debt, which made it vulnerable to a change in investor sentiment. Finally, serious weaknesses had developed in the poorly supervised banking system.

Was the impending crisis *detected in time*? While there had been some early warnings, for instance the one issued by Dornbusch, the overwhelming majority of investors and policymakers, including at the IMF, were caught off guard. The lack of transparency on Mexico's side and inadequate surveillance by the Fund, combined with the lending hubris of international banks and investors, contributed to this failure. All in all, a *lack of crisis prevention* caused the turmoil to be more severe than necessary.

When a crisis is not prevented, *crisis resolution* comes into play. Here high marks should be given to the United States and the IMF for taking resolute action and putting in place a large support package plus adequate conditionality. After some difficulties, the Mexican authorities cooperated well with the Fund and stuck to its policy conditions. In the parlance of the day, Mexican *ownership* of its program with the IMF was high. These factors combined to bring about a relatively swift resolution of the crisis. Its aftermath was characterized by rapid economic recovery, sustainable monetary and fiscal policies, a floating exchange rate, and a much stronger banking system. What remains lacking to this day is widespread and deep structural reform which would put the Mexican economy on a higher growth path, much needed in a country with an excess of jobseekers.

Lessons for emerging countries

First, for larger emerging countries a fixed exchange rate can easily lead to significant overvaluation, an erosion of competitiveness, and loss of reserves, all contributing to undermining confidence. A second lesson is that, without sound domestic economic policies, countries strongly reliant on foreign capital run a much bigger risk of a "sudden stop" of inflows. Third, a weak domestic financial system, even if it is not the immediate cause of a crisis, amplifies its spread. Finally, there is a clear need to mitigate the moral hazard associated with large financial rescue packages.

Not all *lessons were heeded*. The lesson on moral hazard was the least respected, particularly the role of the private sector, which hardly changed its international lending and investment behavior. Other lessons were better taken to heart, but as new crises emerged these were quickly abandoned. Established attitudes and practices are usually not changed easily, whether due to political reasons, recognition lags, or inertia. But, as one crisis followed another after 1995, new practices did emerge and a number of improvements were made in what became known as the international financial architecture. What remained a constant factor, however, were the political considerations that often influenced decision-making by the main players.

In the aftermath of the Mexican crisis a debate began concerning the *international financial system*, with a view to avoiding or mitigating major crises in the future and how to best resolve ongoing turmoil in financial markets. On the *prevention* side, proposals mostly focused on strengthening the IMF's surveillance over countries' economic policies. This is an old debate, continuing to this day, on which progress tends to be slow. At the time, I observed that the Mexican crisis had been a ruthless reminder of the limitations to the effectiveness of Fund surveillance. What could be done about it? The Whittome report had already exposed the main weaknesses. Ministers and central bank governors, in their gatherings in 1995, called upon the IMF to engage in a closer and more frequent policy dialogue with its member countries. Better data collection and more transparency were advocated and useful initiatives were taken. There was also an exhortation to pay more attention to countries' financing policies and the soundness of their financial sectors. All of this was useful, but could not, of course, guarantee the absence of future crises, not least because of patchy implementation of these laudable intentions.

A more ambitious suggestion circulating in the mid-1990s was to put in place an *early warning system* which would provide signals of impending crises. The system would consist of a number of core economic indicators of vulnerabilities to economic shocks. Whenever threshold indicators were exceeded in a country, the IMF was to urge it to respond in one way or another. This approach was to bring more objectivity to the surveillance process. While indicators of vulnerability were developed over time, and included in IMF country reports, an early warning system with explicit threshold values never got off the ground. A major objection was the likelihood of false alarms, which could well trigger unnecessary turmoil. Some prototypes of early warning systems were indeed found to grossly overpredict crises, while others remained silent even in the face of a thunderstorm.

The discussion on *crisis resolution* that took place in the period between the Mexican and the Asian financial upheaval provided some useful insights. While it proved to be too early to implement any of the measures proposed, and the Asian crisis hit the financial community before any firm conclusions could be drawn, the ideas developed proved to be a fertile base for later deliberations. A major consideration was to limit official financial support in dealing with major financial crises in order to mitigate moral hazard. This line was touted strongly by European officials, and I actively pursued it in my own statements in the IMF's Executive Board. The way I approached it was to distinguish four alternative approaches to financing countries with large balance of payments deficits. The first, and most simple, was *laissez faire*, where it is left entirely to markets to solve the problem. This I discarded as excessively risky and inconsistent with the central role of the IMF in the international monetary system. A second approach would be a full *bailout*, as took place in the Mexican case. But providing full IMF financing in order to avoid defaults (as happened in the case of the Mexican *tesobonos*) introduced excessive moral hazard. Under a third approach, financing would be provided in combination with an *orderly workout* to reduce an unsustainable debt burden. The best-known version of this approach was to have the IMF (or another organization) act as a sort of international bankruptcy court. The main drawback to this proposal was that it would give the Fund far-reaching powers and very likely draw it into very difficult legal proceedings. There could also be moral hazard problems on the part of the debtors, as they could anticipate the IMF coming to their rescue by imposing a moratorium whenever their debt got out of hand.

My own preference was for a fourth approach, which would entail an *informal international adjustment procedure.*

This informal procedure was to contain the following elements:

1. When a serious debt crisis emerges, with potential contagion to other countries, the affected country – in close consultation with the IMF – would announce a standstill with respect to its debt-service payments.
2. The country would draw up an economic adjustment program with the support of the IMF, backed by a Fund credit. This money should cover only part of the financing need of the country and not result in a full bailout of the investors.
3. Negotiations would take place with the country's creditors, with the Fund acting as an intermediary. The IMF could bring the main parties together, including representatives of the commercial banks and the bondholders.
4. The debtor and its creditors would agree to a workout resulting in debt relief. Debtor moral hazard would be mitigated by ensuring that the IMF policy conditions were strong, discouraging debtor countries from making this their preferred exit strategy.

This and other ideas were discussed in the IMF Board, but did not lead to any firm conclusions, although some elements were applied in dealing with subsequent crises. But the most important practical policy initiative that followed the Mexican crises turned out to be an *increase in the IMF's capital,* usually referred to as quotas. Quite soon after the eruption of the Mexican crisis, Michel Camdessus suggested that a substantial increase of the Fund's aggregate quotas was needed, allowing it to continue to provide large credits to countries in trouble. Camdessus launched his trial balloon at a retreat with IMF executive directors in early 1995. My reaction was immediately positive, as I could see the need to strengthen the Fund's liquidity in a world where financial conditions had become more uncertain and where IMF conditionality should ensure that borrowing countries would adopt sound policies. The least positive reaction, following a more formal proposal by Camdessus, came from the United States. This had a lot to do with the fact that the US Congress has to agree to an increase in the US's quota. Congress tends to be reluctant to increase funding for international organizations, which in turn makes the US Treasury reluctant to propose large increases. By contrast, the Europeans, and the developing countries who, as debtors, naturally favor more money for international organizations, were supportive of Camdessus's timely initiative.

There is irony in the fact that the United States, which had pushed hard for a very large IMF credit for Mexico, in the end only reluctantly went along with a sizable increase in total quotas, whereas the Europeans, who had expressed misgivings about the Mexican package, supported a much larger capital base for the Fund. During wide-ranging discussions in the IMF Board, in which positions ranged from hiking quotas by 25 per cent (the United States) to doubling them (the developing countries plus a few smaller European countries, including the Netherlands), it proved very hard to reach an agreement to be put to the IMF's supreme body, the Board of Governors. Final agreement was only reached at a special session of the Executive Board during the IMF annual meeting in Hong Kong in September 1997. The result was an increase of total quotas by 45 per cent, from slightly over $200 billion to close to $300 billion. This was certainly a good time to increase the IMF's financial ammunition, as the Asian financial crisis was beginning and would, only a few months later, keep the international financial community on tenterhooks as Korea became engulfed in a financial firestorm.

2
From Miracle to Panic and Back: The Asian Crisis

After getting through the Mexican crisis largely undamaged, international banks and investors in foreign bonds resumed lending to emerging countries at a fast clip in 1996. Private capital flowing into these countries reached $338 billion that year against a previous high of $201 billion in 1994 and a mere $75 billion in 1990. Much of this capital found its way to Asia, a large part of which was enjoying rapid growth. The economic image of developing Asia, especially its Eastern regions, had undergone a major transformation since the dismal economic performance of many decades after the Second World War. The two developing Asian giants, China and India, remained mired in poverty for a very long time, in sharp contrast to Japan. The situation was vividly depicted by the Swedish economist Gunnar Myrdal, who wrote an influential book with the title *Asian Drama*.[1] By the 1990s the prospects for the emerging Asian economies were vastly different, thanks to rapid economic growth, first generated by the *Asian Tigers*, including South Korea, Taiwan, Hong Kong, and Singapore, later joined by Malaysia and Thailand and, to a somewhat lesser extent, Indonesia, who were designated the *Newly Industrialized Countries* (*NIEs*). China, spurred forward by the movement toward a "socialist market economy" engineered by Deng Xiao Ping, was by then making enormous strides. In 1993 the World Bank released a widely quoted study entitled *The East Asian Miracle*, which looked into the causes of the successes enjoyed by a number of Asian countries.[2] The World Bank study concentrated on the NIEs. Their economies had outstripped all others in economic growth per head between 1965 and 1990, averaging 5.5 per cent a year, against less than 2 per cent in South Asia and Latin America. Asking what explained East Asia's success, the authors concluded that high domestic investment by the private sector and rapidly growing human capital were the main factors. High investment was supported by high levels of domestic financial savings. Such high savings were attributed to the right macroeconomic policies, which ensured positive real interest rates and low inflation, as well as policies aimed at increasing the soundness of the banking system. While the World Bank team's extensive study provided clear and convincing explanations of the Asian miracle, it did not address the potential risks that could be encountered in the future by rapidly growing economies. In the early 1990s the IMF did not perceive any serious future problems for the fast-growing economies of East Asia. This is not surprising, as the explosion of capital imports into East Asia, which would be a main cause of the financial crisis a few years down the road, was only in its early stages. And the World Bank's optimistic views on the soundness of the banking systems in the NIEs were probably based on insufficient evidence. What we know in retrospect is that weaknesses in the financial systems of a number of East Asian countries were important triggers for the financial crises they faced a number of years later.

A number of misunderstandings about the IMF's role in the Asian crisis have lingered. One of these is the claim that the Fund, just as in the case of Mexico, was caught unawares by the serious deterioration of the financial health of East Asia. This is only partially true. The staff of the IMF were aware at an early stage of the problems developing in Thailand in the course of 1997, but felt understandably reluctant to issue public warnings. By and large the IMF was also alert to deteriorating conditions in the Philippines and Malaysia, both of which narrowly avoided a real crisis, as well as in Indonesia, where the Asian crisis hit hardest. The Fund staff did, however, fail to detect the serious underlying weaknesses in South Korea, as will be explained later. In the years before the outbreak of the East Asia crisis in 1997, some warnings had been expressed in general terms. In 1995 , inspired by the Mexican experience, the Ministerial Committee of the IMF – then unhelpfully known, for historical reasons, as the Interim Committee, and later renamed the International Monetary and Financial Committee (IMFC) – warned against weaknesses in the financial systems in developing countries. This was followed by a gradual increase in concerns expressed by the management and staff of the Fund in their speeches and publications, especially in the *World Economic Outlook* (the Fund's flagship publication), not only about domestic financial vulnerabilities in Asian countries, but also about the risk of overheating and excessive appreciation of exchange rates. The huge capital inflows received by a number of Asian countries, from those seeking profitable investment opportunities in these fast-growing economies, were also highlighted from time to time as a risk factor, as short-term and portfolio capital (equities and bonds) could be subject to sudden reversal. However, these warnings were of such a general nature that they were largely ignored.

While the Mexican crisis was not universally seen as a threat to the international financial system, the East Asian crisis came to be recognized around the globe as a very dangerous firestorm that could cause first-degree burns among banks and other financial players. The problems first came to the surface in the early summer of 1997, when the currencies of Thailand and the Philippines faced strong downward pressure as capital fled these countries. Other Asian countries' currencies subsequently came under attack, especially the Malaysian ringgit, the Indonesian rupiah and the Hong Kong dollar. What made the crisis especially acute was that in the fall of 1997, while the stresses in those countries that had been previously targeted were mostly still ongoing, Korea was infected by the stampede of capital heading for the exit. Korea's economy had grown spectacularly in previous years and had become the eleventh largest in the world, implying that its collapse would have widespread repercussions. Moreover, in a climate of great nervousness in international financial markets, the process of contagion became virulent.

Countries such as Brazil, Russia (which was already borrowing from the IMF), Ukraine, South Africa, Turkey, and some smaller emerging market borrowers such as Hungary and Ecuador were also experiencing the fallout of the unrest caused by the pullout of investors from East Asia. Doubts were also expressed as to whether China would be able to withstand the pressure. Taking into account what happened to the Chinese economy in the following years, with its mounting balance of payments surpluses, acting on these doubts would have been the wrong response. China, which was less vulnerable than most other countries to speculative attacks because of the many restrictions that existed within the economy, was not the only emerging country that avoided serious injury to its economy during the late 1990s. The Philippines had a narrow escape, but benefited from its close collaboration with the IMF, with which it had been running an economic program – and thereby had access to its credit – virtually continuously for decades. Malaysia, whose economic fundamentals were better than those of most Asian countries, shunned the Fund and imposed capital controls which insulated it long enough to ride out the storm. The Malaysian Prime Minister, Mahathir Mohammed, emerged as one of the most outspoken critics of the IMF, lambasting its policy prescriptions, particularly as regards liberalizing capital flows. At the annual meeting of the IMF in Hong Kong in September 1997, he debated the American financier George Soros in an acrimonious encounter at a seminar organized by the Fund.

Outside Asia several countries were experiencing the effects of contagion, and many underwent hard times sooner or later. Pakistan, Russia, Ecuador, and Ukraine defaulted on some of their debt obligations, while Brazil got into serious trouble in late 1998. For Turkey the crunch came about a year later and lingered for many years. Rather surprisingly, South Africa escaped a full-blown crisis and was able to get through a rough period without official external support despite the fact that it held only quite limited official reserves. In fact, its reserves were negative on a net basis, as the Central Bank had earlier supported the rand by selling dollars in the forward market. These dollars had to be delivered sometime in the future and therefore could not be counted as part of the country's reserves. Understandably, the Central Bank kept quiet about this. But, as South Africa was also able to increase the maturity of its foreign debt through negotiations with its bank creditors, it remained outside the crisis zone. Still, the country remained vulnerable to contagion, partly because it had earlier relaxed some of its capital controls. During this period, secret discussions took place between South Africa and the IMF on a confidence-inspiring economic program supported by money from the Fund. But President Mandela, who was in favor of this collaboration, was unable to convince the Executive Committee of the ruling African National Congress. This was the end of the story, and the matter was never heard of again.[3] Nonetheless, South Africa got through difficult times without suffering major damage thanks to skillful handling of its monetary and fiscal policy.

The baht takes a bath

The first domino to fall in East Asia was Thailand. The "smooth as silk" country had performed exceedingly well between the mid-1980s and the 1990s, growing on average by almost 10 per cent a year while keeping inflation under control. A number of challenges subsequently emerged and grew into unsustainable imbalances, which were initially largely ignored. The current account of the balance of payments ballooned to 8 per cent of GDP, significantly larger than the 5 per cent level considered sustainable according to an often-applied rule of thumb. This was in part a reflection of an overvalued exchange rate. The baht, like many other currencies in Asia, was pegged to the US dollar, which started strengthening in 1995, resulting in an erosion of Thailand's competitiveness. At the same time, more foreign capital was flowing into Bangkok than was needed to cover the external deficit. Some of this money was directed to poorly conceived investments. Furthermore, the Thai financial system was characterized by a large number of badly run and weakly supervised banks, as well as an abundance of so-called finance companies. These were shadow banks that applied an unsound business model: providing risky loans to unsound borrowers and funding themselves by issuing notes to the public as well as borrowing wholesale at short maturities from "real" banks, also in foreign currency. On top of all this, the Thai economy was burdened by a dose of what came to be known as *crony capitalism*.

In contrast to the experience with Mexico, the IMF was well aware of the dangerous situation developing in Thailand, although it probably underestimated the severity of the underlying problems. Still, in the course of 1996 the IMF staff expressed concerns about the size of Thailand's short-term foreign debt and questioned the wisdom of maintaining a rigid peg of the baht to the dollar. On the Thai side, however, the tendency was to ignore or deny the warning signals that were becoming ever stronger. Moreover, the Thai policymakers were refusing to provide the IMF with confidential data on their foreign exchange reserves and banks' bad loans. This uncooperative stance continued for a long time, making it difficult to uncover how bad things really were.

Toward the end of 1996, and early in the following year, pressure on the baht grew rapidly. Market participants, including hedge funds, were on the attack, as they saw the pegged baht as posing a one-way risk, much like the pound sterling in 1992. By late spring it was becoming clear to the IMF that the dam was likely to burst, and the IMF advised the Thais to act on the exchange rate. The US authorities were also alert to the situation, not least because of their strategic interests in the region. This was even more the case for Japan, which was loath to see an Asian country in serious trouble and was also worried about the large exposure of Japanese banks to Thailand. In Europe, where Thailand was not seen as a strategic partner and there were no former colonial ties, there was as yet little interest in what was happening in East Asia. Still not happy with the role they had had to play in the Mexican crisis, European governments and central banks were not eager to get involved. This was quite noticeable to me when I met with Dutch policymakers in Amsterdam in early June 1997 to discuss IMF matters, as I did on a regular basis. When I suggested adding Thailand to the agenda, in view of some ominous information I had obtained in Washington, my request was met with some surprise. I suggested that there was a risk of contagion if the baht were to take a dive, but received little response.

Events in Bangkok came to a head as the Central Bank was finally forced by a new Minister of Finance, Thanong Bidaya, to reveal the true extent of Thailand's usable reserves. It turned out that, while the balance sheet of the Bank of Thailand (BoT) showed a healthy level of $30 billion in reserves, only a small fraction of this stock of dollars was usable. What had happened was that the BoT had been supporting the baht by selling dollars for future delivery in large amounts. Since such transactions were not recorded in its balance sheet, the Central Bank could keep up the façade that there was ample ammunition left to defend the baht. But now, with this disconcerting information, the new minister realized that time had run out and that the dollar peg had to be abandoned. When the announcement was made on July 2, 1997 the baht immediately fell deeply against the dollar. Shock waves soon rippled toward other Asian countries, resulting in attacks on the currencies of Hong Kong, Malaysia, the Philippines, and Singapore. Not long afterward attention became focused on Indonesia, and the rupiah plummeted.

Like policymakers elsewhere, the Thai government and the BoT were very reluctant to turn to the IMF for help. The experience is akin to delaying going to the dentist with a toothache because of the unpleasantness of the treatment that will follow. Waiting too long just makes things worse, of course, and the patient may well end up having to undergo truly unpleasant root canal treatment. And so it went in Thailand. First there was an attempt to obtain credits from China and Japan. When this did not work, the Thai officials had no choice but to approach the IMF with its feared policy conditions. In the meantime, BoT Governor Rerngchai resigned. The ex-governor had previously been head of the Central Bank's library, and his elevation to the top position was a typical case of "Buggins' turn." His central banking skills were quite modest, according to someone closely involved with the crisis. A commission formed later to look into the Thai financial debacle came down harshly on Rerngchai. A court subsequently ordered him to repay the losses incurred on Thailand's reserves to the tune of $4.6 billion. Some observers saw this verdict as mainly symbolic and the former Central Bank governor as a scapegoat for the failure of a host of policymakers in dealing with the baht crisis.

The IMF was on the Thai case at an early stage. The Fund's number two, Stanley Fischer, visited Bangkok several times on secret missions and gave the authorities strong advice. The IMF staff mission chief, David Robinson, flew to Thailand no less than a dozen times in a single year. This intensive contact culminated in an agreement between the Fund staff and the Thai negotiators in late July 1997. The program was approved a few weeks later by the Executive Board without incident. Its centerpiece was a combination of tax increases and spending cuts amounting to 3 per cent of GDP, which would bring the budget into surplus and, together with the cheaper baht, make a big dent in the current account deficit. In addition, important measures were to be taken in the financial sector, which was in a very poor state. After much discussion, the IMF staff had reversed their position on the granting of general guarantees by the government on bank deposits. Initially the Fund stuck to its traditional view that such guarantees were undesirable, as they generated moral hazard. But, as the gravity of the situation became clearer, the staff on the ground in Bangkok changed their minds completely and were able to convince Fund management that protecting households' and corporations' bank deposits was crucial for avoiding a run on the banks.

The economic package contained bitter medicine, especially its fiscal component. In addition, Thailand was required to be more transparent in its provision of data. The US Treasury, which was intensively involved in the resolution of this crisis as it was in all emerging country crises, insisted that the BoT reveal the true state of affairs regarding its reserves. But the Thai negotiators only reluctantly went along with these conditions in order to obtain a financial package of $17 billion, quite large in relation to the country's economic size. The IMF put up $4 billion (500 per cent of Thailand's quota), the Japanese government pledged the same amount, and other Asian countries provided $6 billion. The remainder came from the World Bank and the Asian Development Bank. What stood out was that the United States itself did not offer a bilateral contribution, despite support for such action by officials from the State and

Defense Departments as well as the National Security Council. Robert Rubin, who as Treasury Secretary opposed a bilateral US loan, wrote later that he probably gave too little weight to the symbolic importance of joining the package.[4] He also revealed that he had considered a US contribution from the Exchange Stabilization Fund (ESF), which had been tapped for the Mexican rescue, but was concerned that this time there would be even more trouble from Congress and more restrictions placed on the use of the ESF.

While the Thais were unhappy with the US's absence from the bilateral lenders, the size of the package was fine with them, as it was considered to be large enough to restore confidence. But things did not quite work out that way initially. Going public with the true reserve data at the same time as the IMF credit was announced proved to be problematic. Markets reacted violently, pushing the baht to new lows. There was poor adherence to the IMF program in the months following its adoption, and markets became concerned that the Thai government was not serious about implementing the program. In the meantime, the Thai economy had gone from a state of overheating into serious contraction, turning the fiscal austerity required by the Fund into overkill. In a pragmatic fashion not always recognized by its detractors, the IMF eased its policy requirements on the budget. Still, it took a change of government in Thailand to really turn things around. The cleaning up of the financial sector was a crucial element in this process, with the new Minister of Finance, Tarrin Nimmanhaeminda, playing an admirable role.

Although the foreign exchange crisis abated in 1998, the Thai economy shrank by over 10 per cent that year. While it caused a lot of pain, this shock therapy proved to be effective in turning around the economy rather quickly. As in the case of Mexico, a very sharp but fairly short-lived contraction was rather quickly followed by a restoration of confidence which jump-started the economy. By 1999 GDP was growing at over 4 per cent again, in subsequent years rising to over 6 per cent on average. When a group of IMF executive directors, of which I was the spokesperson, visited Thailand in October 2001, we encountered a country on the mend. The new government led by the populist Prime Minister Thaksin Shinawara[5] inherited a much improved economic situation.

After the crisis the Thai economy embarked upon a somewhat slower, but sustainable, growth path. When economies mature, the hectic growth of the takeoff years often eases, while still remaining satisfactory. The greater stability which this produces makes the economy more resilient to future shocks. Understandably, critics of the Fund have questioned whether a dramatic contraction such as that experienced by Thailand was necessary. With perfect foresight, the IMF would have no doubt constructed its program differently and placed less emphasis on fiscal adjustment. But the Fund was handicapped by the unwillingness of Thai officials to provide it with all relevant information, including on the mess in the financial system. This meant that the IMF staff had to operate without sufficient reliable information. In fact, when the depth of the recession became clearer, fiscal policy conditions were relaxed. There can be no doubt that Thailand came out of the baht crisis stronger than before: its economy became more resilient with the sweeping away of inefficient and sometimes corrupt practices; its institutions (including the Central Bank) were strengthened and its competitiveness restored.

In *recapitulating* what happened in Thailand in 1997–98, the following developments stand out. The crisis was mainly due to maintaining a fixed and increasingly overvalued exchange rate, exacerbated by excessive capital inflows and a seriously unhealthy financial system. This time the IMF saw the trouble coming and gave timely, if not perfect, advice, which was, however, ignored for a long time. As often happens, the Fund was called in only when the fire had already reached the roof. Cooperation with the IMF by the Thai authorities, who were shocked by the rapid reversal of their economy, was initially weak. Transparency, touted in IMF ministerial communiqués following the negative experience with Mexico, was totally inadequate. However, once serious negotiations got underway, an economic program and a large financial package were rather quickly put together. Both the overall amount of the IMF credit and its share in the total financial package were considerably smaller than in the case of Mexico. Also, the fact that Asian countries provided the biggest contribution soothed potential European concerns that they would be asked to contribute disproportionately to the bailout of a country in which their strategic interest was negligible.

The spectacular reversal of capital movements in Thailand was not caused – as is sometimes suggested – by an insistence from the IMF on liberalizing capital transactions. There is no evidence that this was the case, and the staff who were at that time dealing with Thailand emphatically deny any earlier pressure from the Fund with respect to lifting capital controls. What had occurred was that the Thai authorities had been promoting Bangkok as an international financial center before the crisis broke. They had hoped that Bangkok would become a regional financial hub and had abolished some capital controls in the process. But this had not been at the insistence of the Fund. Not surprisingly, the baht crisis put an end to Bangkok's ambitions as a regional financial center.

Whether the Thai rescue significantly increased creditor *moral hazard* is not clear. Private banks and investors once again escaped serious pain, but it is likely that the Japanese commercial banks, which were heavily exposed to Thailand, were persuaded by the Japanese authorities not to pull out their money in haste. While there is no reliable information in this regard, it would not be surprising if moral suasion had been exercised as a *quid pro quo* for the large contribution by the Japanese government to the financing package. More important, and glaringly clear, was the *contagion* that the Thai crisis generated. After Thailand, more dominoes would fall over while others wobbled precariously. The extent of the contagion was initially underestimated by most observers, but as panic swept across East Asia the stability of the entire international financial system was called into question. In this climate, the process of liberalization of capital movements and the attempt to provide the IMF with wide-ranging jurisdiction over its members' capital transactions abruptly came to a halt.

Suharto's swan song

The collapse of the Indonesian economy in the fall of 1997 was the steepest and longest-lasting in all of the Asian countries caught up in the financial tsunami of the late 1990s. The Thai baht's sharp devaluation in early July unleashed tremendous unrest in East Asia. Indonesia was affected much more strongly than close neighbors such as Hong Kong, Malaysia, the Philippines, and Singapore. Capital flows to Indonesia were suddenly reversed, driving down the rupiah precipitously. The causes were in part economic and in part political. Although Indonesia had enjoyed solid economic growth in recent years, its performance had not been as stellar as those of Korea and Malaysia. At the same time, endemic corruption and uncertainty surrounding the political situation that would develop after the departure of the seventy-six-year old President Suharto, a classic Asian strongman, made foreign investors as well as local capitalists (often unpopular ethnic Chinese) wary. While Indonesia held great economic promise, fear that progress could easily be stalled was pervasive. To put it differently, the *country risk* associated with Indonesia was considered to be higher than that of its neighboring countries.

The annual meetings of the IMF and the World Bank which took place in Hong Kong in September 1997 were more than a nod to Asia. They represented something of a coming out by China into the international financial community and coincided nicely with the imminent handover of Hong Kong by the British to China. The atmosphere at the meetings, among both the officials and the private sector "special guests," consisting mainly of bankers, was festive – given the spectacular setting and the lavish treatment they enjoyed – but also somewhat apprehensive. The Thai crisis was causing tension in other countries in the region, though practically nobody felt that a full-blown crisis would soon sweep through a large swath of East Asia. Most bankers and officials recognized the possibility of contagion, even beyond the confines of Asia, but were inclined to play down such risks. I remember mentioning in a discussion in Hong Kong among Dutch officials and bankers that a country like Turkey could also be vulnerable to attack. The reaction of one prominent Dutch commercial banker was that he had talked to the main Turkish banks and that they had assured him that all was well. But the Turkish banks proved to be in poor shape at the time, as described in Chapter 7.

The main official business at hand at the meetings in Hong Kong was not how to deal with the looming crisis, not yet fully recognized as posing a grave danger to the world economy, but to agree on a package of measures relating to the IMF itself. These were to find a compromise on the size and composition of an increase in the Fund's capital, to decide on adding new SDRs to global reserves, especially to accommodate the former Communist countries which had not shared in earlier allocations of SDRs, and, finally, to provide the IMF with jurisdiction – and far-reaching powers – over international capital transactions. In the event, although all three elements of the package were agreed at the time, only the first came to fruition. It can be argued that only the sizable increase in IMF quotas (45 per cent) really mattered, so that with hindsight the meeting was still a success, despite the fact that the United States later did not ratify the decision on SDRs, and the international community walked away from capital account liberalization after the Asian crisis.

The Indonesian crisis, while not totally unexpected, erupted right after the Hong Kong meetings. The rate of the rupiah soon deteriorated spectacularly, falling quickly from 2,500 to the dollar to 8,000 as foreign capital dried up and wealthy Indonesian residents voted with their money. Eventually the exchange rate was to drop to a level of 16,000 rupiahs to a dollar. Adding to the gloom in Asia at the time were the peat fires that were burning in many places in Indonesia and Malaysia and causing very limited visibility. The visibility of what was actually happening in the economy was initially equally limited, once again greatly complicating the work of the IMF and World Bank staff members who had been called in to help.

The disastrous collapse of the exchange rate, which rapidly caused inflation to surge and confidence to erode, in turn causing economic activity to spiral downward, made the world pay attention. Although Indonesia's economic size was not large enough to threaten the world economy on its own, banks and bondholders were also starting to shun investment in countries in Latin America and Eastern Europe. Many financial institutions apply certain fixed ratios to their exposure in various categories of assets. In this case banks tended to reduce their exposure to other emerging countries, such as Brazil and Hungary, in tandem with cutting back on loans to Indonesia.

A bit of history

Looking at Indonesia's development over a longer period helps to explain why it was hit so hard in 1997–98. After Indonesia gained independence in 1949, it went through a long period of slow development, not unlike India at the time. It depended heavily on foreign aid and was unable to attract foreign private capital in significant amounts. Indonesia's charismatic postwar political leader, Sukarno, was more interested in finding a place for Indonesia in the movement of nonaligned nations and playing a role on the world stage than in fostering the economy. He was ousted in 1966 in a bloody coup by General Suharto, who used the opportunity to squash the powerful Indonesian Communist party. Suharto followed a pro-Western course, and his populous, moderately Islamic country became quite popular with American and European leaders. Moreover, Indonesia was an oil exporter, seen to be playing a moderating role in OPEC. Suharto's economic advisors tended to be trained at Western universities, advocating pro-market policies which began to pay off after a number of years. By the early 1990s economic growth was quite buoyant, averaging 7 per cent a year, while inflation was generally kept under 10 per cent. Domestic savings reached a healthy level of around 34 per cent by the mid-1990s, slightly lower than in Korea, but some 10 per cent of GDP higher than in the Philippines, where economic growth was commensurately lower. The state budget was roughly in equilibrium and the external debt service of Indonesia a manageable 21 per cent of exports of goods and services.

Behind this rather bright picture lurked a darker reality. A number of distortions and imbalances, not always visible, constituted a weak element in the economy. Official institutions, such as the Central Bank and supervisors of the financial system, tended to be weak and prone to political influence. In combination with the existence of widespread crony capitalism and corruption, with the Suharto family deeply involved, these weaknesses constituted a considerable risk to the economy. By the mid-1990s the positive macroeconomic picture also became increasingly clouded by an inappropriate exchange rate regime. Indonesia, like Thailand up to July 1997, had pegged its currency to the US dollar. This had been fine when capital movements were small, but caused problems when large amounts of foreign capital flowed into the country. In order to maintain the peg with the dollar, the Central Bank bought up large amounts of dollars, which after conversion into rupiahs pumped up Indonesia's money supply, in turn stimulating consumption and investment. After this had gone on for several years, the economy started to *overheat*. To their credit, the IMF staff flagged this development in their 1995 report on the Indonesian economy. The Fund's advice was to tighten both monetary and fiscal policy. And, in case higher domestic interest rates were to lead to excessive inflows of capital, the exchange rate was to be allowed to move upward. This contradicts the accusation later leveled at the IMF that it had not warned against the danger of large short-term capital inflows which could reverse quickly. The report of the staff also mentioned that weaknesses existed in the financial sector, as reflected by the high level of nonperforming loans in the banking system. However, the extent of the rot in the financial sector and the poor shape many corporations were in, often due to their large and unhedged exchange rate exposure, were not fully recognized. But here too the staffs of the Fund and the Bank were faced with a high degree of opacity and an unwillingness of Indonesian officials to provide the full, not pretty, picture.

The IMF gets involved

On October 31, 1997 the IMF negotiators reached an agreement with their Indonesian counterparts on a comprehensive economic program and a large financial support package. The IMF was to put up $10 billion and the World Bank and the Asian Development Bank pledged $8 billion between them, an unusually large amount for balance of payments support by development banks. In addition, a number of Indonesia's allies, which included Japan, the United States, Australia, Malaysia, and Singapore, were to provide up to $18 billion in case the money from the multilateral institutions proved to be insufficient. The nature of this *second line of defense*, which would also be deployed in some support operations elsewhere, remained somewhat vague. Nonetheless, the support package was reported by the world media as amounting to $36 billion. Together with a few colleagues on the Executive Board of the Fund, I expressed some doubt about the wisdom of announcing as large an amount as possible, when the two elements of the overall package were not fully comparable. I also worried about announcing ever larger packages, which would mean that in order to satisfy market expectations future support operations would have to be even bigger. This is indeed what happened when the Korean crisis struck, requiring a very large second line of defense, the actual availability of which was of a somewhat dubious nature.

The economic program of Indonesia contained a number of stringent macroeconomic conditions, in IMF jargon known as *performance criteria*, essentially targets to be met in order for the next credit tranche to be released. Additional conditions were set to address serious weaknesses in the financial system. On top of that, an unusually large number (some 150) of conditions of a structural nature were to be met. There were two main problems with the program. First, while its conditions in the area of monetary and fiscal policy were appropriate in the light of the information on the economy available at that time, the financial sector interventions proved to be insufficient. Second, the numerous structural performance criteria, many of which dealt with the breaking up of monopolies, required more action from the Indonesian side than could be delivered in the time frame required. This was not merely a matter of weak administrative capacity, but largely due to resistance from the Suharto clan and their close friends. Many of the monopolies were serving the special interests of the president and his immediate family, and they were not prepared to give up their extraordinary privileges and sources of ill-gotten income. In IMF parlance, there was *insufficient ownership* of the program.

The trouble with the program started after sixteen insolvent banks had been closed at the insistence of the Fund. While drastic, this action turned out to be insufficient. Fearing that more banks might subsequently be closed, depositors withdrew their money from other unsafe banks and placed it in state-owned banks, in the belief that these were less likely to be closed. The result was that the inherently unhealthy financial system was exposed for what it was, leading to a *crisis of confidence*. There was no immediate announcement of a blanket guarantee of bank deposits, which probably would have mitigated the turmoil. As in the case of Thailand, there was much discussion within the IMF, including its Executive Board, on whether such a guarantee would simply generate moral hazard and reward undeserving depositors such as the Suharto clan and their cronies. When – with the blessing of the Fund – a guarantee was announced, amounting to a maximum of around $5,000 per account, the measure proved inadequate to restore confidence. Another problem was caused by excessive borrowing in foreign currencies by private corporations, which were facing ruin as the rupiah dropped like a stone. Foreign banks, which provided the money, should have been involved earlier to negotiate an orderly workout. Eventually an agreement of this kind was reached, but in the meantime economic activity had been dealt a severe blow. While the international organizations should, in retrospect, have pushed for a speedier debt restructuring, they generally lacked sufficient information to reach a better outcome, as their counterparts in Djakarta were initially displaying little cooperation.

As regards *monetary policy*, implementation of the program was poor. A tightening of monetary conditions was called for in order to support the exchange rate, which was threatening to go into free fall. The Bank Indonesia, whose independence was nonexistent, did not respect the monetary targets under the program but continued to provide huge amounts of liquidity to the banks even if they were technically insolvent. The fact that several banks were controlled by friends of Suharto no doubt played an important role in the central banks' stance. There was also strong resistance against raising interest rates, even though rates were negative in real terms. This was a common reaction among the countries hit by the emerging market crises in the 1990s. A painful trade-off arises in these circumstances between the urgent need to stabilize the exchange rate and the deflationary effect of higher rates on the real economy. This issue was extensively debated at the time, as will be seen later. As to *fiscal policy*, the program required a degree of tightening in light of the overheated state of the economy, which appeared to be continuing when negotiations took place on the policy requirements. As the economy deteriorated much faster than expected, the Fund adjusted its stance on fiscal policy. Under the revised program agreed in the spring of 1998, a budget deficit of 4 per cent of GDP was accepted.

Much of the focus of the Indonesian program related to *structural measures*. Many interested parties, including the United States, whose involvement in the negotiations was extensive, and the World Bank, whose expertise in this area is preeminent, pushed for strong measures of a structural nature. The result was a whole shopping list of measures, which included actions to be taken that were desirable as such, but not crucial to the success of the program. For instance, one of the requirements was to abolish the monopoly on cloves (used in the cigarettes that are popular in Indonesia). It is hard to see how freeing up such a tiny sector of the economy would have had any discernable macroeconomic impact. The United States, backed by most other G7 countries (with the exception of Japan), insisted on including a raft of structural conditions in the program in a determined attempt to eradicate crony capitalism in Indonesia. This stance contributed to politicizing the Indonesian program to an unusually high degree, with Suharto perceiving the pressure from the IMF and the United States as directed against him personally.

Revision of the program

It became clear in early 1998 that the economic program was not working and that, besides some problems of design, a lack of ownership was leading to poor implementation. The United States and the international financial organizations were concerned that a failure to turn Indonesia around could have not only serious economic consequences, with a high risk of contagion, but also undesirable political ramifications. As Suharto was rightly seen as the main obstacle to improvement, a series of initiatives were taken to push him in the desired direction. President Clinton called him, and subsequently Larry Summers, then the number two at the US Treasury, was dispatched to Djakarta. Germany, which had built up a strong relationship with Indonesia after the departure of the Dutch, also reached out to Suharto. There are indications that Japan – whose economic and political interests in Indonesia are substantial – discreetly approached the Indonesian leader as well, but with a milder message. These efforts bore no apparent fruit. However, when Michel Camdessus, the Fund's ever-ebullient Managing Director, flew to Djakarta in early 1998, he was able to come to terms with Suharto. A revised program was announced and personally signed by the president.[6] There were unfavorable omens, however, as it was rumored that Suharto had declared to his inner circle that he would wage a "guerrilla war" against the very program he had officially supported.

Not surprisingly, success again remained elusive. By now the population was becoming increasingly restless as unemployment shot up, import prices soared as the rupiah continued to weaken, and opposition leaders were starting to stir things up. In this explosive climate opposition leaders became increasingly vociferous. Megawati Sukarnoputri, daughter of former President Sukarno, daringly stated that if the mess continued "then striped prison uniforms should be sewn for the economic criminals who have destroyed our nation and our economic future."[7] In the meantime, Suharto was still not delivering fully on his promises, and when he sometimes did so it happened in a strange way. An oil producing nation, Indonesia maintained very low domestic prices for oil products. The IMF had insisted on raising the price of fuel gradually so as to move away from subsidizing the use of energy. It had also emphasized the need to provide targeted support to low-income groups rather than providing subsidies, only a fraction of which would reach the poor. In a surprise move, Suharto drastically increased the price of fuel products, going considerably beyond the pace envisaged in the program. This enraged the population and serious riots broke out. A standard complaint against the Fund is that its programs often cause riots, especially when subsidies on food, energy, or transportation are cut. Such "IMF riots" have damaged the reputation of the Fund, as they are generally viewed in isolation as reaction against unnecessarily harsh measures. But, when pushing for lowering subsidies, the IMF routinely advocates putting in place a social safety net for the poorest segment of the population. Direct and targeted income support tends to be the preferred option. Unfortunately, governments often do not follow this approach.

There has been considerable speculation over Suharto's bizarre behavior, one of the theories being that, by infuriating the public with a steep rise in fuel costs, he was aiming to discredit the Fund. Be that as it may, the social and political climate in Indonesia at that point was so inflamed that Suharto stepped down in May 1998. Some saw the demise of Suharto as a deliberate ploy by the United States to oust the undemocratic and corrupt Indonesian president through the means of onerous IMF conditions. This led to the accusation that the United States was once again using its dominant position in the Fund to achieve its own economic or, in this case, political objectives. Asian countries would, in later years, continue to display considerable resentment over the treatment by the IMF and the United States of the crisis-stricken countries. Japan, while not directly affected by the crisis, expressed similar criticism in various forums, including through its articulate Executive Director on the Fund Board, Yukio Yoshimura. There was also talk at the time of establishing an *Asian Monetary Fund*, an idea attributed to Eisuke Sakakibara, the then Japanese Deputy Minister of Finance. The Asian Fund was to operate as a substitute for the IMF in Asia, providing financial assistance to countries with balance of payments problems with little or no conditionality. The G7, led by the United States but not including Japan, came out strongly against this proposal and it never took off, except for the establishment a number of years later of a swap network among Asian central banks known as the *Chiang Mai Initiative*, named after the city in Thailand where it was launched.

Another example of American behind-the-scenes maneuvering took place in April 1998, shortly before Suharto's departure. The United States, through its representative on the IMF's Executive Board, Karen Lissakers, was seemingly engaged in delaying tactics by unexpectedly criticizing the newly revised program that Stanley Fischer, the Fund's number two, had just negotiated with the Indonesians. Lissakers complained that insufficient attention was being paid to the social aspects of the Indonesian situation. She questioned whether an increase in fuel prices, which, she pointed out, would also increase bus fares, was at all necessary. The American Executive Director also commented on the poor working conditions in Indonesia. As the United States was not known for questioning the need for cutting subsidies or raising the issue of working conditions, at least not in the IMF, some of us were greatly surprised. We were even more surprised when Hubert Neiss, the main staff negotiator, indicated that the matter of working conditions still had to be settled before the revised program could be set in motion. When asked whether the Fund was now also going to get involved in working conditions in its member countries, Camdessus strongly denied this. As became clear to me later, the American strategy was to bring up new issues so as to delay adoption by the Board of the revised program for Indonesia for as long as the US Congress had not fully debated the proposed increase in IMF quotas agreed on in Hong Kong. American high officials first wanted to see Suharto leave before feeling secure about congressional approval of a large IMF quota increase. Considerable hostility toward the Fund from conservative members of Congress had to be overcome. Among these was Trent Lott, the influential senator from Louisiana, who stated: "I would like to get rid of the head of the IMF. He is a socialist from France."[8]

The new president, former Technology Minister B.J. Habibie, who took the helm on May 21, 1998, had been close to Suharto, and expectations for a rapid turnaround of the Indonesian situation were muted. Gradually, however, the situation began to improve under the third version of the economic program, and the currency returned to a more sustainable level in the vicinity of 8,000 rupiahs per dollar. Economic recovery was slow in coming, however, and GDP fell by a shocking 13 per cent in 1998, coupled with an increase in the general price level of 77 per cent. In August 1998 the new Indonesian team, led by Coordinating Minister Ginanjar, reached agreement with the IMF for a new credit under its *Extended Facility*, which has a repayment period of up to ten years.

Not until 1999 could a modicum of growth be detected, while unemployment kept on growing. From 2000 on, however, a steady recovery set in, and Indonesia embarked upon a growth path of around 5 per cent a year. Much of the gradual restoration of confidence was related to an easing of political tension. In a climate of extreme political uncertainty, measures that would normally foster a return of confidence do not work. A good example in the case of Indonesia was monetary policy. It was clear to any politically neutral econo-mist that Indonesia needed to maintain high interest rates to avert the threat of hyperinflation through a too rapid expansion of the money supply and a free fall of the currency. However, at the height of the uncertainty surround-ing the position of Suharto, it was unlikely that any economic policy change would help to restore confidence. I therefore took the position, in an exchange of views in the IMF Board at the time of Suharto's last stand, that it seemed better to wait until the political situation had become clearer before insisting on further monetary tightening.

The monetary policy debate

Part of the monetary policy debate in Indonesia focused on the idea of intro-ducing a *currency board*. In February 1998 President Suharto announced that he favored introducing a currency board, which would effectively place monetary policy on an automatic pilot. This was a surprise move by an increasingly des-perate president, seeking a quick fix for his problems. The idea was not without merit, however. It had been introduced to Suharto by an American econom-ics professor, Steve Hanke, who had earlier stated at a congressional hearing that a currency board was the only certain way to stabilize the exchange rate. Currency boards, which tended to be applied only in very small economies lacking the capacity to run their own monetary and exchange rate policies, had come into vogue in the mid-1990s. In 1991 Argentina, in a radical move to eradicate its recurring bouts of hyperinflation, introduced a mechanism which closely mimicked a currency board. In 1998 the strains that would later undo Argentina's framework were not yet visible, and its currency board was gener-ally considered to be a success.

Initial reactions to Suharto's monetary gambit ranged from strong skepti-cism to mild interest. The governor of Bank Indonesia did not like the idea and was summarily fired by the president. The IMF staff were publicly non-committal, but at an informal briefing of the Fund Executive Board the gen-eral assessment was that it would be premature to adopt a currency board in Indonesia. Much of the discussion focused on the preconditions that had been identified to ensure a successful operation of a currency board. These included a well-functioning banking system, an adequate level of international reserves, and a sustainable external debt service. While most directors agreed with the Fund staff that these conditions were not met, I pointed out that in the case of Bulgaria, which I knew well as it was one of the countries that I represented at the IMF, the currency board had been introduced despite a dysfunctional banking system. As regards meeting the other conditions, the answers were not obvious either: reserve adequacy was hard to judge, and corporate debt restruc-turing was already underway in Indonesia. My suggestion was, therefore, for the Managing Director to say "not yet" rather than a flat "no" in the letter he intended to send to Suharto. Camdessus took this approach, and also cleverly made it into a polite *nyet* by stating that he would be the first to recommend a currency board if the various preconditions were met, which of course was unlikely, especially with respect to the banking system. He emphasized to members of the Executive Board that, if markets were to test an Indonesian currency board with a rate fixed at, say, 5,000 rupiahs per dollar, poor implementation of the program could cause the Central Bank's dollar reserves to be quickly depleted. And in a worst case scenario the exchange rate could possibly plummet to 30,000. Although extreme, this possibility, together with a later warning by Stanley Fischer that in such a populous and decentralized country as Indonesia, with its widely separated islands, administrative capacity was likely to be inadequate to operate a currency board successfully, made me give up my brief flirtation with the currency board option.

Messages from President Clinton and German Chancellor Kohl, as well as the IMF, convinced Suharto after a while that he could expect disbursements from the IMF to dry up if he were to introduce a currency board. Professor Hanke, who had enjoyed his fifteen minutes of fame, was deeply disappointed and resentful, and attributed the American position to trying to get rid of Suharto. At the end of June 1998, two months after his loss of guru status, Hanke made clear at a conference in Croatia that he remained totally committed to currency boards, which he believed should be adopted on a much wider scale. He ascribed the fact that this had not happened to politicians' wish to meddle in monetary matters. The fact is that no new currency boards have been established since the Indonesian debacle, although Ecuador and El Salvador have opted to go a step further by adopting the US dollar as their currency.

But the real *debate on monetary policy* centered on the trade-offs involved when monetary policy is tightened in reaction to a plunging exchange rate. Critics of the IMF maintained that pushing up interest rates sharply was undesirable, as it led to a contraction of demand, which could be very large if combined with a tight fiscal policy. In addition, the weakness of the financial system would complicate the process of restructuring the banks. And, as the initial economic program for Indonesia prescribed macroeconomic tightening, these arguments were seen by many as persuasive. But the monetary tightening initially envisaged was simply not implemented by Indonesia, and the fiscal conditions were relaxed when it became clear that the downturn was much more severe than had been projected. These developments were often not taken into account in the frequently heated and sometimes emotional discussions about the right course for Indonesia's economic policy. This was also the case with respect to the strong arguments the IMF had for insisting on monetary tightening in Indonesia and elsewhere. The need to halt the disastrous collapse of the exchange rate was considered to be of overriding importance.

This was most effectively achieved by higher interest rates, an approach I fully supported. Failing to halt a free fall of the exchange rate would have risked hyperinflation, which, as shown by the experience of other countries, such as Germany in 1923 and Bolivia in the 1980s, would have caused a total collapse of the economy. On top of that, the rapidly falling rupiah hugely complicated the plight of Indonesia's corporate sector, which had borrowed extensively in foreign currencies and mostly at short term. The plunge of the rupiah was also having undesirable fiscal consequences, as the domestic price of government purchases paid for in foreign currency shot up.

The Fund was not blind to the trade-offs, as documented in a report by the IMF's Independent Evaluation Office, which mentions that a vigorous internal debate took place on this issue.[9] This is certainly accurate as regards the Executive Board. Throughout the Asian crisis, several intensive exchanges of views on the best course for monetary policy in a crisis took place among the directors. At one such meeting it was suggested that a middle course between a tight stance, aimed at supporting the exchange rate, and an easy stance, geared at avoiding a weakening of domestic demand, would be optimal. My reaction was that in a serious crisis, such as Indonesia was experiencing, following the middle ground did not work, as a number of currency crises in Europe in the 1980s and 1990s had demonstrated. Central banks had to be seen by market participants as fully committed to defending the exchange rate through monetary means if they wanted to be successful. While this implied high interest rates, restoration of confidence in the exchange rate would allow monetary policy to be relaxed again. If well executed, such a monetary squeeze, also known as a *bear squeeze* as it could severely punish those who were shorting the currency, would be short-lived, thereby mitigating the negative effects of high rates.

This philosophy generally prevailed in the Fund. At the same time, there was widespread recognition that it was not useful to push for a tightening of monetary policy at times when a crisis had become mainly political in nature. The fact that the Indonesian rupiah had tumbled by about 80 per cent at the apogee of the crisis, against a depreciation of some 30 to 40 per cent in the case of other crisis-stricken Asian countries, strongly suggested that political uncertainty was a major factor in Indonesia at the time. But, after the resignation of Suharto, the conditions were in place to pursue a quick stabilization of the rupiah, followed by a loosening of monetary policy once the exchange rate was seen as holding at a level around 8,000 to the dollar.

Also crucial in determining the right stance of monetary policy in a crisis is the mix of interest rate hikes and *intervention in the foreign exchange market*. In theory it is possible to halt a slide in the exchange rate by the Central Bank by purchasing its currency against dollars (or yen or euros as the case may be). But this will, in most cases, require massive amounts of dollars, which are unavailable to all but the most reserve-rich countries. Beyond ideological aversion to such intervention by free marketeers, who believe that unfettered markets always deliver the best outcome, there are strong arguments for generally refraining from intervention in countries with sophisticated foreign exchange markets. For emerging market countries, however, the situation is different. Their currency markets are mostly "thin," with a relatively modest turnover and a much higher risk of excessive volatility. Foreign exchange intervention is therefore generally more effective in emerging countries. In fact, most of these countries practice *managed floating*. During the Asian crisis, intervention in support of falling currencies was widespread. But a number of free market enthusiasts pushed for prohibiting intervention under IMF programs. Together with a number of colleagues, I took a less rigid stance, but warned that intervention alone without supporting policies was unlikely to be effective. When a currency comes under strong pressure, simply selling large amounts of dollars will only temporarily prop up the exchange rate. This is precisely what happened in Indonesia in the final months of 1997, when, after spending some $5 billion of reserves (about a quarter of total official dollar holdings), the rupiah strengthened only briefly before falling back to earlier levels.

Gradual progress

By the middle of 1998 Indonesia was beginning to find its bearings again. But complications remained. The following little-known episode illustrates how skillfully the, then much criticized, Managing Director of the Fund operated in an environment fraught with difficulties. In order to finalize the IMF support for the new extended arrangement, financing assurances were needed from other sources, including bilateral official creditors. Among these was the Netherlands. The Dutch Minister for Development Assistance, Jan Pronk, succeeded in muddying the waters and delaying completion of the agreement. Pronk had felt offended when, in 1992, President Suharto had broken off the aid relationship between his country and the Netherlands following criticism by Pronk of the Indonesian actions in East Timor, whose population was fighting for independence from Indonesia. Pronk now saw an opportunity to get even by withholding his agreement as the Dutch minister responsible for the participation of the Netherlands in a rescheduling of government debt through the Paris Club.[10] He justified his stance by claiming that, since there was no Dutch–Indonesian aid relationship, there was no way he could sign off on any deal with Indonesia. This position caused a general impasse in the whole exercise of providing much-needed additional money for Indonesia. It was summer, and Michel Camdessus was taking a well-deserved break from the hectic work on the Asian crisis. I called him at his vacation home in Bayonne, France, and explained that Pronk would only be willing to move if President Habibie directed a request to the Dutch government for a resumption of the aid relationship. This was clearly a delicate matter, and at the same time a challenge fully suited to Camdessus's diplomatic skills. He listened attentively, asked a few questions, and said he would draft a letter for Habibie to present to the Dutch government, which he did single-handedly from his vacation home, and faxed the letter to his staff and to me for comment. He also got in touch with the usually gruff Pronk and was able to resolve the matter amicably with the Dutch Development Minister. There followed an exchange of letters between President Habibie and the Dutch Prime Minister Wim Kok, agreeing on a resumption of the Dutch–Indonesian aid relationship. To the outside world the message was simply that there had been technical difficulties with the new financial package for Indonesia and that they were now resolved. But Camdessus's swift action meant much more to my countrymen and me, as it led to a rapprochement between the Netherlands and Indonesia after a long period of frosty relations.

The Indonesian outlook continued to improve in 1999 and beyond, but it took quite some time for the problems in the banking system to be resolved. Indonesian banking supervisors were dragging their feet. Not until late 1999 did the Indonesian Parliament release for publication a long-awaited report on the scandal-ridden Bank Bali. This cleared the way for the IMF to pay out a new slice of its augmented credit, which had been put on hold. At the same time, the IMF's tenacious chief negotiator, Hubert Neiss, stated in Djakarta that change was needed at both the Indonesian Central Bank and the Indonesian Bank Restructuring Agency, the latter having been specifically established to deal with the raft of failed banks. A month after IMF payments to Indonesia were halted again in March 2000, two ministers closely involved with the economy were fired by President Wahid, who had in the meantime succeeded the tainted Habibie. In another confidence-inspiring move, a high-level committee to combat corruption was put in place. A few more incidents between Indonesia and the Fund followed, but step by step the situation improved and foreign investors started taking a fresh look at the Indonesian economy. The widely scattered archipelago was regaining its luster with a structurally sounder economy, a largely cleaned-up financial system, restructured foreign debt, and a restored buffer of reserves, reaching a comfortable $30 billion in 2002. And, whether or not this had been intentional, Indonesia had been transformed in the course of the crisis from a corrupt dictatorship to a democratically run country. But the price was high; the public cost of restructuring the financial sector was $85 billion, or a staggering 51 per cent of GDP.

Success or failure?

The Indonesian rescue operation was undoubtedly the most criticized element of the IMF response to the Asian crisis. Part of the reason for the frequent critical judgment of outsiders, as well as of insiders from Asia, was the depth and duration of the crisis. The social cost was seen as too high, and avoidable with alternative policies. For some, especially from East Asia, the politicization of the Indonesian crisis and the perceived excessive Western intervention were troubling. Prominent among the critics was Joseph Stiglitz, whose position as chief economist of the World Bank from 1997 to 2000 gave his opinion additional weight. Stiglitz's sharp attacks on the IMF (and the US Treasury) at the height of the Indonesian crisis, whether correct or otherwise, contravened earlier agreements between the Bretton Woods Institutions not to publicly voice criticism between their institutions. His diatribes were seen as disloyal by the Fund and damaging to its attempts at restoring confidence. It has been suggested that part of the conflict had its roots in an initial lack of smooth coordination between the staffs of the IMF and the World Bank on financial sector reform, an area which both regard as part of their core activities. Stiglitz, who had gained further stature by winning the Nobel prize in economics in 2001, later wrote a book in which he spelled out his criticism of the IMF.[11]

Clearly the frequent stinging criticism of the Fund complicated the IMF's role in the Asian crisis and in Indonesia in particular. Michel Camdessus was becoming a reviled figure for many. The normally feisty and socially conscious IMF Managing Director was starting to show the strains of his highly public role in the Asian crisis, but was to take more punishment over the Russian crisis which emerged just as the situation in Indonesia was showing the first signs of improvement. As a member of the Executive Board of the Fund, I supported the IMF's approach to the Indonesian crisis. It remains my opinion that the general thrust of the program was correct, but that in hindsight some aspects could have been handled better, especially the reform of the financial sector, the excessive emphasis on other structural reforms, and the tardy involvement of foreign banks in the restructuring process. But the fact remains that one important reason for the struggle to get the Indonesian recovery going was the intransigence of Suharto and his coterie, who felt threatened in both their dubious financial dealings and their status. When we look more closely at the Fund's crisis management in Indonesia, the following conclusions can be drawn.

Indonesia's economic problems were recognized by the Fund staff at a relatively early stage. IMF country reports issued before the emergence of the crisis indicated that, despite the favorable macroeconomic results, a number of weaknesses existed. The questionable state of the financial sector was flagged, as well as the existence of governance issues, implying widespread corruption. But these problems were probably underestimated and, moreover, described in the generally diplomatic language the Fund staff tended to use in those documents that were widely available.

Bitter medicine

Was the program design adequate? Taking into account the revisions that were made to the program, the answer is again by and large yes. At the time the program was initiated (November 1997) the latest data pointed to a still relatively strong economy, leading the staff to make forecasts that were too optimistic. Moreover, the Indonesian negotiators were careful not to show any alarming figures. The upshot was that the initial requirement of a small budget surplus, although somewhat lower than for 1996–97, was too tight. However, as mentioned earlier, subsequent revisions allowed for fiscal deficits. In complaining about IMF "Hooverite" policy prescriptions, Stiglitz failed to mention this; in fact, the April 1998 revision of the Indonesian program allowed for a fiscal deficit of almost 4 per cent of GDP. Another accusation by Stiglitz was that the Fund's prescription of a tighter monetary policy and higher interest rates was all wrong and had made an important contribution to the serious contraction of the economy. In actual fact, for quite a while there was no tightening of monetary policy as the Indonesians simply did not comply with this request, something Stiglitz also did not mention. Furthermore, discussing the stance of monetary policy, Stiglitz looked only at the contractionary effects of higher interest rates and made no mention of the danger of hyperinflation in Indonesia. A free fall of the exchange rate, which was a constant threat, would have made imported goods impossibly expensive for the population and caused great hardship, an argument that the former World Bank chief economist neglected to mention.

Financial sector reform was addressed too weakly in the beginning. More than just sixteen banks holding only 3 per cent of all deposits should have been closed straightaway, but the Indonesian side was not ready for such drastic action. Had the Fund insisted, it is possible that Suharto would have signed off but then failed to comply, as he did in several other instances. Eventually, after Suharto's departure, a more drastic restructuring of the banking system did take place, with the active support of the IMF and the World Bank. In hindsight it is clear that the initial deposit guarantee scheme was much too limited, but it was later extended to a blanket guarantee arrangement. The initial timidity reflected a lack of clarity as to the seriousness of capital flight out of Indonesia, as well as doubts that existed in a number of quarters (some within the IMF, some among large shareholders of the Fund) about the desirability of such schemes. As in the case of Thailand, the Indonesian debate was settled in favor of a blanket guarantee once the extent of the crisis was fully understood. But earlier drastic action would have ensured a less ruinous run on the banks. By the same token, earlier intervention in the deeply troubled corporate sector, which was heavily indebted to foreign banks, would have had a mitigating effect on the crisis. The problem was that with Indonesia's limited administrative capacity it was well nigh impossible to move swiftly on all fronts. But the opportunity to involve Indonesia's foreign private sector creditors in a timely manner was truly missed. The foreign banks were, as is usually the case, dragging their feet to engage in discussions over debt work-outs. Such *private sector involvement* (PSI) should have been encouraged by the supervisors and regulators of the foreign banks, but they were reluctant to do so, often for fear of later being accused of undue intervention. This was a particularly strong consideration in the United States. In Europe there was a much greater willingness to engage in moral suasion, but since the authorities did not want to place their own banks at a disadvantage they held back. Experience with the involvement of the foreign banks in Indonesia's rescue suggests that considerable moral hazard was generated.

Regarding the structural *reforms* required from Indonesia, there is now wide agreement that they went beyond what was strictly needed. Under the revised programs, detailed requirements on breaking up monopolies, most of which had no significant macroeconomic impact, as well as the push for privatization proved to be a distraction reducing the focus on the main objectives. Two shopping lists, one put together by the World Bank, the other drawn up by the United States, however well intentioned, overburdened the program. They included such microconditions as dismantling the clove monopoly (of which one of Suharto's sons was a major beneficiary). The problem of overburdening Indonesia was recognized by some in the IMF staff, particularly by Anoop Singh, who led missions to Indonesia at the time when the crisis was winding down. At an Executive Board meeting on Indonesia in June 2000, Singh argued that some structural conditions should be handled by the World Bank in the future, noting that this view had not yet been discussed with the Fund's management. Stanley Fischer, who chaired the meeting, reacted as if stung by a wasp, emphasizing that management had not yet expressed itself on this matter. But Singh's position, which was shared by many members of the Executive Board, was to prevail.

The Indonesian crisis was clearly more difficult to overcome than most others. A *core problem* was a lack of ownership on the Indonesian side. President Suharto, his greedy family, and their hangers-on had much to lose from a strict implementation of the program. The president on several occasions reversed his position and was in fact waging a "guerrilla war" against the IMF. The situation became highly politicized, with Suharto feeling that the Fund was seeking his ouster on behalf of some of its major shareholders. It did not help that representatives of the US Treasury were mostly present in the vicinity of the IMF negotiators in Djakarta, creating the impression that the United States was in fact calling the shots. Press articles describing the trio Robert Rubin, Larry Summers, and Alan Greenspan as "the committee that saved the world," while containing an important kernel of truth, strengthened this feeling.

The severity of the crisis and the extent of the contagion from the Thai collapse were initially underestimated, requiring adjustments to the design of the program and delaying the recovery. Moreover, the pervasiveness of the weaknesses in the banking system was not fully apparent in the early stages of the Fund's involvement. Lack of transparency and outright fraud and corruption also complicated dealing with the financial sector. At the same time, the IMF staff lacked experience in matters such as closing insolvent banks, guaranteeing deposits, and corporate debt restructuring. Involvement of the World Bank was important here, but coordination between the institutions initially left much to be desired. As often is the case, unproductive sibling rivalry was part of the explanation.

Finally, the IMF program with Indonesia initially lacked ownership not only within the country, but also outside Indonesia. Asian countries generally perceived the Fund's role in Indonesia as unnecessarily harsh, imposing conditions that it had not required in other cases, such as Mexico. While there was some truth to this accusation, political considerations of Asian solidarity were also at play. Charges of lack of sensitivity to social conditions and pressure to liberalize capital movements were often not based on a careful examination of all the facts, but contributed to creating a climate in which it was more difficult for the IMF to operate. Here, too, a valuable lesson was learned, namely that *communication* has to be an important element of crisis management. In subsequent crisis episodes the Fund attempted to increase its outreach to interested parties outside official circles. This proved to be a difficult exercise. While some politicians and NGOs, although usually still critical, acknowledged that they had benefited from the IMF's improved external communication, other groups in fact ratcheted up their rhetoric and increasingly partook in massive demonstrations against the IMF and the World Bank. This activity reached its height in 2000 at their annual meetings in Prague, but virtually ceased after the events of September 11, 2001.

Slow recovery

It took four years for Indonesia to return to its precrisis output level, which had plunged by 13 per cent in 1998. Subsequently it embarked on a healthy growth path of around 6 per cent. While less than before the crisis, this growth rate is well in line with Indonesia's capacity. A return to the overheating seen before 1997 has been avoided and inflation has been kept reasonably well in check, although remaining somewhat higher than in other countries in the region. The exchange rate, while floating, has not fluctuated excessively. Indonesia has also succeeded in building up its reserves to a comfortable level (to around $60 billion at the end of 2008, more than twice the size of its short-term external debt). It did not benefit much from the commodity boom of the late 2000s, however, as it has ceased to be a net exporter of energy and as a consequence gave up its membership of OPEC in 2008.

Indonesia emerged from its lengthy crisis with a stronger economy, much improved institutions, and a functioning democracy. The financial sector has become quite resilient, and fraud and corruption have been significantly reduced. Social indicators also point to considerable improvement, although poverty reduction has made only slow progress, with around 16 per cent of the population remaining below the poverty line.

3

The Korean Christmas Crisis

While the Indonesian crisis was the most intractable of the Asian mishaps of the late 1990s, the Korean crisis was the most dangerous. It did not last long, but caused great anxiety, not only in Asia but across the globe. The Korean economy was the eleventh largest in the world, considerably bigger than those of Thailand and Indonesia. It was also an important trading partner, not only of Japan and other countries in the Far East, but also of the United States and Europe. Its banking system was quite advanced and was closely connected to important financial centers. A financial and economic meltdown in Korea would not only have created severe problems in East Asia, but carried a large potential for further contagion elsewhere in Asia, as well as in Eastern Europe and Latin America. It was even feared that the burgeoning Chinese economy, which was becoming an important engine of economic growth in Asia and beyond, would be seriously affected. Finally, an economic collapse of South Korea could have endangered the geopolitical balance on the Korean peninsula, possibly emboldening the rogue North Korean regime to launch an attack on Seoul.

The Korean economic miracle

In modern times few countries have been as successful as Korea in improving their standard of living. While Japan and Western Europe enjoyed impressive recoveries after the Second World War, their economies had already been quite advanced before hostilities started. South Korea succeeded in achieving a staggering tenfold increase in its national income over a thirty-year period starting in the mid-1960s. Although it had emerged from the Korean War deeply impoverished, a combination of sheer hard work, good education, and foreign capital and know-how, as well as sound macroeconomic policies, delivered an average annual growth rate of over 8 per cent. In addition, the long-lasting American military presence contributed to providing comfort with respect to political risks to investors, both domestic and foreign. The Korean people are imbued with an astonishing work ethic, which translates into the largest number of hours worked per person in the world. I was deeply impressed by what I saw when I spent ten weeks in Korea in 1978, which was then still in the early stage of its industrial development.[1] Since then Korea has not only gained in economic strength, but also achieved international recognition for its economic performance. In 1996 it became a member of the Organization for Economic Cooperation and Development (OECD), an influential club of industrialized countries, and was made a member of the Group of Twenty (G20), which is made up of the leading industrialized and emerging countries, when it was founded in 1999.

Korea's rapid growth, which relied heavily on exports, took place in a very competitive environment. What was not very apparent to outsiders was that the Korean manufacturing sector was generally operating with low profitability and high financial leverage. Its corporate governance structure, dominated by *chaebols* (Korean-style business conglomerates), was flawed and often characterized by crony capitalism. There were also serious weaknesses in Korea's financial system which only came to light once the crisis struck. But of more immediate importance in 1997 was that the exchange rate regime, based on pegging the *won* to the US dollar, was not appropriate for a country that had rapidly freed many capital transactions. Moreover, hidden from sight – including from the IMF – was much too low a level of usable reserves and a large short-term external debt, which made Korea vulnerable to financial shocks.

An accident waiting to happen

At a conference held a few years after the Asian crisis had blown over, former World Bank Chief Economist and future number two at the IMF, Anne Krueger, argued that the Korean crisis had been a disaster waiting to happen, because of the role played by the *chaebols*, who combined economic dominance, low profitability, and high leverage.[2] Others, with hindsight, identified factors such as weaknesses in the financial sector, the pegged currency, and the accumulation of short-term external debt as harbingers of serious trouble. But were these problems identified and the crisis foreseen by the IMF and the World Bank or other observers? The short answer is that the crisis sweeping Korea in the fall of 1997, and especially its depth, took practically everybody by surprise. Still, this does not provide a legitimate excuse for the failure of the Fund to foresee anything of the kind of events South Korea experienced at the height of the Asian crisis. Sadly, the lessons from the Mexican crisis, as put forward in the Whittome report, were not heeded. Why this happened is not easy to pinpoint, but many agree that within the IMF the culture in the Asian Department, as in the Western Hemisphere Department, deviated from the more rigorous surveillance practiced by the staff of the European Department. Similar to the *clientelist* mentality that used to be displayed in dealing with Latin American countries, staff in the Asian Department tended to avoid strong views in their country reports. But in the case of Korea the problem went further.

Fund staffers working on Korea before the crisis broke in November 1997 allowed themselves to be misled by their untransparent Korean interlocutors and failed to take on board Whittome's strong advice to probe deeply and use external sources of information. This led to the Executive Board of the IMF being told in an informal briefing on Asia in late October 1997 that the situation in Korea, while not without problems, was not a cause for serious concern; macroeconomic policies were well on track and the current account deficit was manageable. While the repercussions in the financial sector caused by problems in the corporate sector were identified as an issue, no sense of urgency was conveyed. Yet at that very moment things were already unraveling in Seoul. Some ten days earlier Taiwan had abandoned the peg of its currency to the US dollar and allowed it to float downward. This had set off a renewed frenzy among market participants. But little attention was paid in the Fund to what happened in Taiwan, mainly because it was not a member of the organization and therefore did not undergo the Fund's usual annual examination. Hong Kong did receive regular IMF missions although it was not a member (its colonial overseer, the United Kingdom, was very much in favor of annual consultations), enabling the Board to be better informed about what went on there. The Hong Kong dollar, pegged to the US dollar through a currency board arrangement, suffered a severe speculative onslaught soon after the Taiwanese move. The Fund Board was well apprised of this situation and, like staff and management of the IMF, noted with relief that the astute Hong Kong Monetary Authority had succeeded in repulsing the attack, raising short-term interest rates briefly to as high as 300 per cent in the process. But, in a development similar to that which played havoc with the European Monetary System in the early 1990s, markets continued to probe weaknesses in other currencies. By early November 1997, markets were starting to seriously test the won, in part because of increasing worries about Korea's financial system. Several *chaebols* had been allowed to go bankrupt, which was a departure from the earlier implicit government guarantee protecting these entities. This suggested that the banks which had been liberally lending to them could also get into serious trouble.

The specter of default

By mid-November a full-blown crisis was underway, and the IMF was by then fully alert to the situation. Michel Camdessus paid a secret visit to Seoul on November 16, 1997, during which an IMF credit was discussed. Upon his return to Washington, Camdessus confidentially briefed the Executive Board at a breakfast meeting. He stated that Korea was still in *denial* about the seriousness of the situation, while the depreciation of the won was continuing and the Central Bank had ceased its purchases of won against dollars, as its reserves were being rapidly depleted. While the dollar holdings of the Bank of Korea were officially valued at $30 billion, it now turned out that a large part was not usable in interventions as the money had been placed with overseas branches and subsidiaries of Korean banks. It was not possible to repatriate these funds, as they were needed to repay expiring short-term debt of the banks. It became clear that, if the drain on the reserves continued at the same pace, the Central Bank's dollar holdings would be depleted before the end of the year. An additional shocking discovery had been that Korea's foreign debt was much larger than previously thought and consisted mainly of short-term borrowing by Korean banks. According to initially produced Korean data, $65 billion would have to be repaid in the coming year if these loans were not renewed (rolled over). In actual fact, however, as much as $115 billion was falling due. Korea's lack of transparency matched that of earlier experiences with Mexico and Thailand, but that was no consolation for us at the IMF. We were simply shocked by the *liquidity crisis* that was looming. As I was sitting next to Camdessus at the briefing, he whispered to me that Korea would now soon turn to the Fund and that a large financial package would be needed. This information was most probably already known at that time by my American colleague, and possibly by those from other G7 countries, but for me it was very helpful to be in the loop at an early stage. It was clear to me that I would soon have to approach the Dutch decision-makers. Like their more influential German counterparts, they were concerned about moral hazard. Huge support operations in the absence of burden-sharing by foreign banks, who had lent liberally to Korea and had helped cause the problem, was therefore a hard sell. While several continental European countries were concerned about moral hazard, it was the German *Bundesbank*'s outspoken governor, Hans Tietmeyer, who tended to lead the charge against what he saw as an overrelaxed Anglo-Saxon attitude toward this risk. Both the Dutch and Swiss authorities fully shared this opinion. While I also worried about the creditor moral hazard of jumbo rescue operations, I felt that, given the risk of contagion, the size of the Korean economy, the fact that this was a liquidity but not a solvency crisis, and Korea's good track record, it would not be a good idea to resort to the position we had taken in the Mexican case. Moreover, we Europeans had gone along with large rescue packages for Thailand and Indonesia.

It took a while longer for the Koreans to actually "invite" the IMF to send a negotiating mission to Seoul. In the meantime the foreign banks were heading for the exit, mainly by refusing to roll over their short-term loans to Korean firms. The result was a further decline in the value of the won, despite some renewed sales of dollars by the Central Bank from its now precariously low reserves. The specter of default was by that time spooking many observers. The dramatic events that followed have been described "blow by blow" by Paul Blustein,[3] and the international discussions and crucial internal debate in the United States on whether to let Korea go under or try to save it, by Robert Rubin.[4] My own recollections are predominantly those of a member of the IMF Board for whom the five weeks following November 26, 1997, when an IMF staff mission arrived in Seoul, were the most riveting and enervating during the eight years that I served on the Fund's Executive Board.

From denial to sullen agreement

Korea was part of a group of countries (*constituency*) represented on the Board of the IMF by Australia, whose ebullient representative, Greg Taylor, suddenly had a lot on his hands. His Korean Alternate, Okyo Kwon (later to become his country's Minister of Finance), was new in his position and was clearly shocked by the events that had suddenly thrust him into the limelight. Taylor did his best to help the Koreans, but found it far from easy to get them to face reality. The newly appointed Korean deputy Prime Minister and chief negotiator, Lim Yeul Chang, held strong, if not always constructive, views.[5] In the 1980s he had been an alternate executive director on the Fund's Board, where he was known for frequently observing that something "was not in Korea's interest." Like quite a few Korean politicians and high officials, Lim seemed to suffer from a state of denial. For a proud nation like Korea, which had so success- fully advanced from a postwar state in which people even resorted to eating bark from trees to joining such a prestigious group of advanced countries as the OECD, the idea that it was close to bankruptcy was almost unfathomable. But relentless pressure from the IMF, and even more from the United States, as well as the cold figures of rapidly declining rollover ratios and empty reserve coffers, helped to turn around the Korean negotiators, or so it seemed. Lim first tried to obtain a large bilateral loan from Japan, and then from the United States, so as to bypass the Fund. After he got nowhere, he had no choice but to deal with the IMF.[6]

The urgency of the Korean crisis was compounded at the end of November 1997 by the failure of Yamaichi, a prominent Japanese brokerage firm. The Japanese economy was mired in a long period of weakness following the col- lapse of the "bubble economy" a few years earlier. Japanese banks were strug- gling with a large portfolio of nonperforming loans, and a default by Korea, to which these banks had a large exposure, could have brought some of them down. In this climate of great nervousness and fears of domino effects in the international financial system, I had to travel to a few of the countries that I represented at the IMF Board. My main destination was Ukraine, which as recently as 1991 had gained independence and was still experiencing great difficulties in its transformation to a market economy. For a variety of reasons, it was the last of the former Soviet republics to return to the level of production that it had achieved before independence. Ukraine was an important country with a population of close to 50 million, strategically located as the "underbelly" of Russia and in dire need of economic advice and financial support. Its relationship with the Fund was difficult, resembling the experience we were having with Indonesia. Ukraine's programs with the Fund tended to veer off track rather soon, and frequent attempts had to be made to get the country back on track. While my experienced Ukrainian Alternate, Yuriy Yakusha, was the one who mainly dealt with his country's economic policymakers, I felt it necessary from time to time to visit Kiev to play the role of "honest broker" between the Ukrainians and the IMF staff and management. Moreover, in early December 1997, Ukraine was suffering from the effects of both the Asian crisis and the crisis brewing in Russia. The fixed exchange rate was under strain and Ukraine's reserves were being run down. The situation had been aggravated because high-yielding Ukrainian treasury bills that had been purchased earlier by Korean and Brazilian banks were now being sold by them, as their own liquidity position had seriously deteriorated. After finding my way to the ornate building of the National Bank of Ukraine, I complimented the then Governor, Viktor Yuschenko, later to become president of his country, for pushing up interest rates and increasing reserve requirements in defense of the *hryvnia*, Ukraine's young national currency. At the same time, I remarked that continuing to defend the exchange rate at the existing level did not seem viable. Yushenko acknowledged that the National Bank's international reserves were running low, but argued that there were other sources of funds that could be tapped. This turned out to be borrowing from foreign banks at punitively high interest rates.[7] After a few more discussions with Ukrainian officials, whom I could not talk out of their borrowing plans, I cut short my visit when told that a record IMF loan for Korea was going to be put before the Executive Board on December 4. As I was driven to Borispol airport in a giant black Zil automobile over icy roads in the early morning of December 3, I was under the impression that the Ukrainian Airlines aircraft in which I was to fly to Frankfurt, from where I would travel on to Washington, was a Boeing 767. Arriving at the airport, I learned that the plane would be a Russian-made Tupolev and that if I agreed to get on I would receive a 50 per cent discount, an offer I could not resist.

Because of dithering by the Korean negotiators, the IMF staff had only three weeks to design a program, a very short period in view of the complexity of the situation. However, on December 4, 1997 the Executive Board unanimously supported a record $21 billion loan for Korea, even though this represented almost 2,000 per cent of its quota (under normal conditions the Fund did not lend beyond 300 per cent of a country's quota, but could do so under "extraordinary circumstances"). The whole package came to $55 billion, another record. The World Bank was to put up $10 billion and the Asian Development Bank $4 billion, and another $20 billion was pledged by a large number of industrialized countries as well as by a few Asian countries as a *second line of defense*. The modalities of the bilateral loan commitments still had to be worked out, something that later proved to be complicated. The policy conditions agreed with the Koreans were quite tough, which was appropriate, but like some colleagues I had doubts about their ownership of the program.

A novel element was that Korea's borrowing from the Fund came from two different lending facilities: a regular standby arrangement for three years and a larger one-year loan, constituting about two-thirds of the total, from the newly established facility called the *Supplemental Reserve Facility* (SRF). The new facility was put together very quickly, since the crisis was one of capital outflows rather than of a trade deficit. Whereas in the past the vast majority of countries asking the IMF for financial assistance were losing reserves because their imports were significantly and persistently outstripping their exports, the Asian financial crisis was due to capital inflows from abroad drying up (known as a *sudden stop*), often in combination with capital flight from within the country. Capital crises, by their nature, could be corrected more quickly than large current account deficits. "All" it took was a restoration of confidence to bring about a cessation or reversal of capital outflows. The new facility, therefore, had a shorter maturity than the IMF's regular credit facility. It was also more expensive (the surcharge over the interest rate applied under the regular facility went as high as 350 basis points), on the grounds that only middle and high-income countries would undergo capital crises. The SRF proved to be a useful instrument, and was also used in later crisis situations.

Stumbling toward catastrophe

The hunch that ownership would be a problem with the Korean IMF program proved to be correct. This sentiment was shared by the markets, who continued dumping the won. Part of the problem was that presidential elections were due to be held on December 18, 1997. The other element was the continuing atmosphere of national humiliation, which proved to be a hindrance to cooperation. For instance, a spokesman for the presidential candidate of the Grand National Party (the party then in power, but ousted in the elections of the 18th) stated after the agreement of December 4 that the IMF's demands were "nothing but rude acts that encroach upon the autonomy of a sovereign state."[8] Many observers also were of the view that it was the United States, rather than the IMF, that was negotiating with Korea. The presence in Seoul of a high US Treasury official, David Lipton, did nothing to dispel this suspicion, and in fact the United States successfully pressed for a number of measures that were clearly in its interests to be included in the program. In line with these sentiments, it soon emerged that, while the Korean side had agreed to raise interest rates in order to support the currency, there had been considerable resistance to such action. Although this had also been the case in other Asian countries, there was a twist to it in the case of Korea. It turned out that, according to Korean law, 25 per cent was the maximum that could be charged as interest. Since a credible defense of the won was likely to require short-term interest rates higher than the legal limit, strong pressure had to be exerted to change the law. The Koreans also did not fully stick to the "rules of the game" agreed with the Fund on financial sector issues. While they did deliver on closing nine merchant banks (unregulated savings and loan banks akin to the Thai finance companies), they then proceeded to restructure and recapitalize two large commercial banks, a decision that clashed with what they had agreed to earlier in the so-called letter of intent.

In an attempt to turn the situation around, Michel Camdessus pressured the three presidential candidates into producing letters in which they pledged to support the Korean program with the Fund. But soon doubt emerged regarding the credibility of the letters. Kim Dae Jung, the frontrunner by a narrow margin and later elected president, made public remarks which cast doubt on his commitment. All of this only made the bankers and other market participants more nervous, ensuring that the rollover ratio (the ratio of short-term lending to Korea extended for the next period as a percentage of the total) continued to fall. By mid-December the ratio was down to around 30 per cent. Usable reserves slumped to a mere $6 billion. Talk of default became widespread. At a special meeting of the IMF Executive Board on December 16, 1997, covering the world economic outlook, I asked for an assessment by the staff of the consequences of a Korean default, but I was not surprised that I did not get a clear answer. In the meantime, both the IMF staff and the US Treasury were confidentially discussing what options were left to deal with the Korean crisis, including default. As Christmas approached the news became worse and worse. On December 22, the won fell by another 10 per cent against the dollar, making a total depreciation of 57 per cent for the whole of 1997. The Korean stock market also took another pounding, while the interest rate on three-year corporate bonds reached 30 per cent. Board members were also informed by the stalwart IMF staff negotiator Hubert Neiss that the rollover ratio had fallen to an alarmingly low level of 18 per cent.[9]

Crunch time on Christmas Eve

Amid an atmosphere of high tension, the crisis was finally brought under control on December 24, 1997. The decisive factor was a pledge by the commercial banks to roll over their credits to Korea. Finally, the United States (Rubin and his team) had concluded that without involvement of the private sector a default was inevitable. On Christmas Eve the rollover ratio was down to a shocking 10 per cent, making it impossible for the Korean banks to repay all their maturing short-term debts. One month previously, at a discussion of high officials from the G7 countries, the need to let the banks share the burden of rescuing Korea had been put forward by Jürgen Stark, the State Secretary of Finance of Germany. But the United States, and also Britain, dismissed the idea. In the IMF Executive Board similar suggestions were made by my German colleague, Bernd Esdar, and myself. Camdessus's answer was that the G7 did not want to go that route, arguing that "it is not the way we do business anymore." This was a reference to the practice of the 1980s when Jacques de Larosière had strong-armed banks to keep up their exposure to problem countries. It was no longer a viable strategy, according to the detractors of bailing in the banks, as the sources of borrowing by emerging market countries now included large amosunts of bonds. The argument was correct in general terms and the problem was in later years addressed in a different way, but it hardly applied to Korea, whose government had practically never entered the international bond market. It was not clear whether Camdessus and Fischer had actually pushed for private sector involvement in the case of Korea, but once the breakthrough took place they welcomed it, as, suddenly, did most of the earlier skeptics.

Robert Rubin gives a fascinating account of how the various options of dealing with Korea were weighed within the US Administration.[10] The possibilities ranged from accepting default, to increasing the size of the financial package, to announcing a voluntary *standstill*, in which case the creditor banks would pledge to fully roll over their short-term claims and extend the maturities of their other loans. The US Treasury approached the – eventually preferred – third option with great circumspection. Rubin states that the (American) banks probably would not have considered the bail-in route at an earlier stage, as they had not understood how dangerous the situation was.[11] But there was also a collective action problem, as no bank wanted to get the short end of the stick by rolling over more than the others. In such circumstances moral suasion is called for, since forcing the banks into action can be problematic. This is especially the case in the United States, where banks might be able to successfully sue the authorities for losses they incurred as a result of official intervention. No doubt Rubin's background as an investment banker made him very reluctant to twist the banks' arms hard. After a number of meetings with Wall Street bankers as well as contacts with treasury and central bank colleagues abroad, who generally had fewer qualms about putting pressure on their banks, the banking community recognized that it was in its self-interest to play along. In fact, the banks ended up doing quite well by receiving an attractive rate of interest on the loans they had rolled over or on which they agreed to a longer maturity.

The second line of defense

A curious development took place regarding the so-called second line of defense, which was to be used in case the IMF loan proved to be insufficient to save Korea. The initial size of this backup line was a hefty $20 billion, to which a few billions were added later on as some smaller countries also agreed to participate. As it turned out, the line was there – but it was not there. Much effort was put into getting the technical details, such as the term sheets of the various participants, drawn up in time. Executive Board members from the countries participating in the second line of defense conferred regularly, often sitting at a rickety table among ancient metal cabinets in the filing room of our American colleague's office. We were under pressure to get the job done, as it had been announced that the second line of defense would be activated when the crisis was at its height. The thinking behind activation was not only to provide Korea with additional money to restock its falling reserves, but also to inspire confidence by demonstrating that the advanced countries stood squarely behind Korea.

As time passed, additional technical issues were raised by the United States. Some of my colleagues and I, who had experienced some difficulty in convincing our capitals to release part of their contributions under the second line, were getting worried. After a while it dawned on me that a tactical maneuver was underway and that the United States was reluctant to use the backup line. Domestic politics seem to have been at play, particularly concern that Congress might balk at activation. The delay in disbursing the money was, of course, bad for confidence, but the last-minute bail-in of the banks took the sting out of the crisis. In the end the second line of defense was never used. What had been meant as a showpiece of international cooperation in support of Korea proved to be something of a chimera. Not surprisingly, an operation of this kind was only repeated for Indonesia, but was not pursued in subsequent crises.

A remarkable recovery

The Korean crisis proved to be a severe hurricane that struck hard but moved away rather quickly. After initial rescue efforts faltered, the program and the financing sources were adjusted. This still failed to do the trick, and only after the banks were brought in did the crisis abate. The Koreans reacted swiftly to restore their economy. After initial widespread demonstrations, most of the public stood behind the adjustment effort. Not only did consumers tighten their belts, but they also contributed impressively to a program to donate personal jewelry and precious metals for the national cause. What is particularly striking is the turnaround in Korea's balance of payments: after a deficit of $23 billion on current account in 1996 and $8 billion the following year, a surplus of $40 billion was recorded in 1998. While exports declined only slightly, imports were compressed by a third in that year, but rebounded by 28 per cent in 1999. Thanks to a halt in capital outflows and the placement of $4 billion in government bonds on the international market, Korea's virtually depleted international reserves surged to $52 billion in 1999 and topped $200 billion by 2005. While the economy contracted by almost 7 per cent in 1998, it bounced back by 11 per cent the very next year, and subsequently growth hovered at around 5 per cent, a respectable rate for an advanced economy like Korea. After the battle for Korea was over, there were no further attacks on the currencies of Asian countries. The world heaved a sigh of relief, but in Korea a search for scapegoats was on. Such had been the trauma of the near-collapse that several players on the Korean economic team were jailed for a while. Having to go cap in hand to the IMF, and, in addition, bowing to specific demands of the United States, was generally experienced by Korean politicians and the public as a national humiliation never to be repeated. In order to avoid having to approach the Fund in the future, except for advice, Korea embarked on a massive buildup of its foreign exchange reserves. Such a policy of *self-insurance* against liquidity crises was emulated by several other Asian countries.

Overall, the Korean crisis was successfully contained, although the rescue operation proved to be a cliff-hanger. The handling of the crisis was frequently criticized, and the IMF was on the receiving end of some particularly vituperative remarks by outside "experts." Two examples may serve to illustrate the views expressed. On the political right, Jude Wanniski, a maverick economist and longtime advisor to former Republican politician Jack Kemp, who was strongly opposed to any kind of bailout, called Camdessus the most dangerous man in the world.[12] On the left, the well-known Indian economist Padma Desai accused the Fund of misdiagnosing the problems, "encouraging a disaster-prone policy gamble of capital account liberalization," going against "received Keynesian wisdom" on fiscal policy, and a number of other failings.[13] Perhaps the most influential criticism came from Harvard University Professor Jeffrey Sachs, who described the IMF as too powerful, untransparent, and giving wrong policy advice.[14] He was particularly critical of what he saw as draconian policy prescriptions on monetary and fiscal policy. In conclusion, Sachs stated that the IMF should have less power, but without spelling out how that should be achieved except for having the Fund publish all facts about its operations so that public debate of its policies would be facilitated. He also felt that the IMF Executive Board needed to do a better job of overseeing the Fund's functioning and not be a mere rubber stamp for proposals from staff and management. Sachs advocated consulting outside experts in the early stages of IMF operations. A few days later, the Fund's second in command, Stanley Fischer, replied to these allegations (without mentioning Sachs by name).[15] This was part of a new initiative, supported by the Executive Board, to let the Fund directly address some of its critics. Fischer went through the list of criticisms, explaining the need to first restore confidence in the Asian economies, referring to the need for financial sector reform and tight (but not too tight) monetary and fiscal policies. IMF credits, he argued, are not given to finance a continuing capital outflow, and high interest rates are therefore unavoidable. Letting the exchange rate go would not be a sound option, as depreciation in the order of 30 to 50 per cent, seen at that point in Asia (the fall of the won would turn out to be greater before it was halted), would go beyond any calculation of the initial overvaluation. Moreover, it would cause severe problems for companies that had borrowed abroad and, most importantly, excessive devaluations would endanger the world economy by spreading to other countries. In the same edition of *The Financial Times*, the IMF's Director of External Relations came to the defense of the Executive Board in an attempt to rebut the rubber-stamp charge.[16] He described in glowing terms how the situation in the Fund was "probably unique as regards the massive extent of day-to-day, hands-on direction the Executive Board provides and the firmness with which it holds management and staff fully accountable to it." While, as a member of the Fund's Board, I experienced a warm feeling upon reading this uplifting prose, I could not suppress a smile when thinking of the times the Managing Director warned us that he would call our ministers, or would threaten to resign when some of us were being, in his view, too assertive.

Surveillance deficit

There is general agreement that the IMF staff's surveillance of the Korean economy in the years before the crisis erupted was inadequate. It failed to probe deeply when analyzing the Korean economy, and should have done a better job in identifying problem areas. And, with respect to the Fund's handling of the Asian crisis in general, the verdict must be that its performance in cleaning up after the storm was much better than in issuing early warnings of serious potential problems.

The main shortcomings in the IMF staff's periodic examinations of the Korean economy related to the exchange rate, the external debt and international reserves, the financial sector, the quality of data provision, and the liberalization of capital transactions. Regarding the exchange rate, the overvaluation of the pegged won was not identified as a serious problem, thereby overlooking the significant potential for a dangerous downward spiral at a time when other Asian countries were already facing strong pressures on their currencies. There was insufficient insight into the extent of Korea's external short-term debt, which turned out to be much greater than initially reported. The sizable borrowing by Korean banks through their foreign offices was not identified. The Korean side, whose lack of transparency greatly complicated the IMF's work once it was asked to develop a comprehensive program at short notice, was partly to blame. But the staff should have probed deeper, following the experience with Mexico, and also neglected to make adequate use of external sources of information, such as market indicators (spreads) and the BIS's international banking statistics. As regards the size of Korea's usable reserves, more assertive questioning would have been desirable, although the lack of openness displayed by the Korean side may have been such that it would have been very hard to flush out the true state of affairs. Concerning the financial sector and the role of overleveraged *chaebols*, certain problems were identified by the Fund staff, but these were not considered to be potentially unmanageable. Finally, the treatment of Korea's policies with respect to capital flows was not up to standard.

Liberalizing capital movements

Much of the criticism of the Fund's handling of the Asian financial crisis was directed at its approach to capital account transactions. The Korean case was seen by many as a particularly egregious example of a misguided bias in favor of eliminating controls on capital transactions. A close examination of the facts does not support this claim. While the IMF had earlier encouraged Korea's move toward liberalizing capital flows, it never made such liberalization a condition of its financial support for Korea, or for any other country. The overall package, as described in the Memorandum of Economic Policies presented by the Korean side, did include the intention to allow some forms of capital inflows, which were, of course, desirable during an outflow crisis.[17] It is true that the United States strongly advocated lifting capital controls, which the Korean side did not appreciate. Some of the American proposals (allowing hostile takeovers and opening up foreign investment in retail trade) were felt by the Fund staff to be unhelpful.

The IMF's *Articles of Agreement* do not allow it to require countries to lift capital controls. This would have been different if the amendment to the Fund's Articles to give it jurisdiction over capital movements, as agreed upon in principle at the IMF's annual meeting in 1997 in Hong Kong, had not been scuppered in the wake of the Asian crisis. During the 1980s and 1990s the move toward liberalization of cross-border capital flows, which had already started earlier in the United States, the United Kingdom, and the European Union, gathered momentum. The rationale behind the removal of capital controls was rooted in the theory that free capital mobility would lead to a channeling of savings to the highest-yielding uses in all parts of the world. This increased efficiency of the allocation process, together with a higher degree of risk diversification, was seen as enhancing global welfare. In addition to the analytical arguments, experience with capital controls in industrialized countries was increasingly negative as their effectiveness eroded over time. The possibilities for circumvention of controls increased as global financial markets expanded rapidly and the introduction of new and sophisticated instruments proliferated. Finally, policymakers felt that freeing up capital movements had a disciplinary effect on monetary and fiscal policy.[18]

While trade liberalization was generally acknowledged to enhance world welfare, there was no general acceptance of the notion that free cross-border flows of capital would on balance be beneficial to all. This applied particularly to emerging countries, which were increasingly following the earlier example of industrialized countries in deregulating their domestic financial systems and allowing greater freedom of capital inflows and outflows. By the 1990s many emerging economies were moving along the path toward full or comprehensive freedom of capital transactions. At the same time, opposition to lifting capital controls was voiced, particularly in the academic community. There are two main arguments against capital account liberalization. First, freeing capital flows makes countries more prone to financial crises, especially at the short end of the spectrum. Second, the existence of information asymmetries in international financial markets can undermine the efficient allocation of savings. Moreover, the empirical evidence on the benefits of free capital movements is not overwhelming. For instance, a sophisticated model finds that, for a typical developing country, a move to complete freedom of capital flows leads to a permanent increase in domestic consumption of about 1 per cent.[19] But it should not be overlooked that most of those in favor of liberalization warn that a hasty and poorly sequenced lifting of capital controls is dangerous. At the same time, not all skeptics are dead set against greater capital mobility, but all are particularly concerned about the effects of premature liberalization. Nondogmatic supporters of phasing out capital controls tend to agree that a number of conditions have to be in place for liberalization to work: well-functioning and developed domestic financial markets, and adequate supervision and regulation of those markets. Freeing capital flows in a country with a weak and poorly supervised banking system is asking for trouble. It is also important to realize that in many cases financial crises that have erupted were caused not so much by the process of liberalization, but by an abrupt deregulation of the domestic financial system that preceded it or took place at the same time.

These issues were discussed at length in the Fund, including its Executive Board, during the 1990s. The initial impetus was the desire of Michel Camdessus to allow the IMF to play a central role with respect to international capital transactions. Rawi Abdelal sees Camdessus's effort as being part of a grand design by prominent French socialists to codify the liberalization of capital transactions.[20] He avers that pressure from the United States was not a major factor. My interpretation is different. While Camdessus was obviously strongly motivated to extend the role of the Fund, the push for opening up capital markets worldwide was strongly supported, and mostly led by the United States. Furthermore, Abdelal's opinion that the American executive director in the Fund (Karen Lissakers) acted largely on her own in her initial support of Camdessus's proposal is not credible. The executive director appointed by the United States is among the least independent of all board members, having to closely toe the line set out by the US Treasury. Camdessus's initiative to give the Fund jurisdiction over capital account transactions, in addition to its powers over current transactions, had the backing of most industrialized countries. But other countries displayed skepticism and only agreed to accept the codification of capital account liberalization in the IMF's statutes as the price to pay for a large increase in the Fund's capital. While both proposals were endorsed at the Fund's annual meeting in 1997, the United States and the United Kingdom (represented by the politically savvy Gus O'Donnell on the Fund Board)[21] hastily withdrew their support for IMF jurisdiction over cross-border capital movements after the Asian crisis, effectively killing the proposal.

In subsequent years the sentiment against the removal of capital controls in emerging countries grew stronger, especially in the wake of large inflows of capital to such countries as Brazil. These pushed up their exchange rates to unwanted levels despite sizable purchases of dollars. As many countries did not want to follow China's example of accumulating massive amounts of dollars in their reserves, having already reached comfortable levels and not wishing to be too exposed to abrupt movements in the major reserve currency, they looked for alternatives. Lowering their interest rates to discourage foreign purchasers of their currency, they introduced certain restrictions on inward capital flows. Brazil and Korea followed this route in 2010. This approach had already been practiced many years ago with some success by Chile, although it abandoned the measure at a later stage, as it had lost its effectiveness over time. It is popularly believed that the IMF has been ideologically opposed to capital controls, which, even if true, overlooks the fact that the Fund took a neutral position with respect to controls on *inward* flows in the past. Nevertheless, in an apparent attempt to dispel the widespread impression of Fund hostility to all manners of capital restrictions, the Fund staff, no doubt with the blessing of the Managing Director Dominique Strauss-Kahn, produced a paper arguing in favor of controls on *inflows* of capital in certain circumstances.[22] But a lack of historical perspective seems to have led part of the media to describe the paper as a complete reversal of an earlier IMF stance.

To return to the situation at the time of the Asian crisis, it can be asked whether the IMF pushed Korea, and other Asian countries, into premature liberalization of cross-border capital transactions. While this is often claimed, a close inspection of the evidence does not justify such a conclusion. The IMF's Independent Evaluation Office concludes in a comprehensive study on capital account liberalization[23] that the Fund did encourage a number of countries to open their borders to capital movements, and sometimes acted as a "cheerleader" for liberalization. But the report firmly concludes that it found no evidence of the use of leverage in order to pressure countries into liberalizing faster than they themselves wanted to go. What can be said is that the IMF did not always sufficiently emphasize the risks that are inherent in liberalization, and that it could have been more forceful in stressing the need for having a sound financial infrastructure in place before freeing up cross-border flows. There was sometimes also a lack of consistency in advice to countries on the sequencing of liberalization measures. Getting the sequencing wrong can have serious consequences; for instance, if a country decides to first open up short-term capital outflows, which carry a large potential for volatility and therefore can have a sudden impact on the exchange rate and foreign exchange reserves, it can unnecessarily create the conditions for a serious crisis. Long-term capital flows provide a much more stable element, especially direct foreign investment, which also does not increase the recipient country's debt.

It was precisely a failure to get the sequencing of capital account transactions right that unnecessarily endangered Korea's external position. In a nutshell, Korea proceeded along the road to liberalization by freeing short-term capital outflows and maintaining restrictions on long-term inflows instead of the other way round. The reluctance to move on the long side of the market is partly attributable to a fear that foreigners could gain too large an influence in the Korean economy, for instance by buying up large amounts of Korean stocks. A particular example of poor sequencing occurred when short-term borrowing was liberalized a few years before the crisis struck. Overseas borrowing by banks surged, leading to large inflows and pushing up the rate of the won. Rather than reversing the measure and eliminating its unintended consequences, the Korean response was to free investment abroad in stocks and bonds. Had restrictions on long-term borrowing abroad been lifted before, or even simultaneously with, those on short-term loans, the banks and the *chaebols* would have drawn in long-term capital rather than volatile short-term funds. Korea's external debt profile would have been healthier, and the onslaught on the won most probably less onerous. Add to this that Korean supervision and regulation of the financial system was weak, and a formula for serious trouble is easily detected. In an intriguing twist of history, Alan Greenspan was among those who publicly criticized the Korean government for its subpar performance in this area. The Fed chairman was quoted as saying on December 2, 1997 that much of the blame for the financial turmoil in several Asian countries could be attributed to their governments failing to adequately supervise their banking systems.[24] Flash forward ten years, and Greenspan himself is attacked for regulatory failures by the Fed under his watch.

Adjusting the policy mix

The economic program worked out in great haste in Seoul was aimed at restoring confidence by means of a swift adjustment of Korea's macroeconomic policy mix. The combination of an expansive monetary and fiscal policy with a pegged exchange rate and low reserves was misguided. Not surprisingly, the initial adjustment effort did not succeed and had to be tweaked after a few weeks in light of the time pressure under which the IMF staff and their Korean counterparts had to work. Some of the criticism leveled against Fund programs is that they have to be adjusted frequently, as some of the initial assumptions turn out to be invalid, or some data are misinterpreted, or some matters of importance are overlooked. But in crisis situations the economic picture can change very rapidly, and adjustment of the program later on is also a sign of flexibility. In fact, as regards fiscal policy, the IMF staff had to urge the Korean side in late December 1997 to ease its stance of sticking to a balanced budget as the depth of the economic downturn became clear.

The insistence by the IMF on a tight *monetary policy* to defend the exchange rate against serious overshooting was controversial. Near-consensus existed in the Fund's Executive Board on the need for high real interest rates, while recognizing that if they were maintained too long the damage to the domestic economy would become too great. While in retrospect it can be argued that monetary policy could have been eased somewhat sooner, in early 1998, there was a legitimate fear on the IMF side that the exchange rate might fall again, as confidence was still fragile. But, since the period of high interest rates did not last for more than a few months, the decision to pursue a tight monetary policy for a short period of time was the right one. And yet high interest rates alone were not enough to reverse the downward spiral of the won. What was urgently needed was the direct participation of foreign banks by agreeing to an orderly rollover of their short-term claims. Without this involvement the Korean crisis would have turned into a veritable disaster, and contagion to other emerging countries would have been even greater than it turned out to be.

There was not much difference of opinion on the approach to financial reform. Korea had slowly embarked on this path in the years before the crisis, and the Fund's conditionality generally dovetailed with the Korean aims. At the same time, several of the *structural conditions* other than those on financial matters raised questions. Were they all really necessary, and was it not better to leave these to the World Bank to address? As in the case of Indonesia, which went even farther, the Korean program was overburdened with too many structural measures which were not critical to the success of the program.

These included accounting standards, bankruptcy procedures, liberalization of the market for corporate control, and introducing greater flexibility in the labor market. While all of these measures were useful, and aimed at reducing the economic power of the *chaebols*, the rush to include them in the IMF program was a mistake. The program also contained some elements which were seen to be included at the insistence of Japan (eliminating the Korean import diversification program) and the United States (greater foreign participation in the Korean financial system). Since they were clearly not crucial to the success of the program, it would have been better to leave them out and let other organizations deal with them in a more thorough manner. Incidents of *political interference* with the IMF and its policy conditions have been damaging to the institution, but continued to surface in later crises.

The bankers' easy exit

There can be little doubt that the way the Korean crisis was handled strengthened the belief among banks that if push came to shove they could count on being rescued by the IMF and the large creditor countries. Yet there was a difference this time – the banks were asked to make a contribution as well, but without making a real sacrifice. As rolling over their short-term loans was clearly in their collective self-interest, the banks' sharing of the burden was cosmetic rather than real. Moreover, the private sector involvement in the Korean rescue consisted of not only rollovers but also a lengthening of maturities against a favorable interest rate. The banks actually made a profit on the whole operation, which can only have encouraged them to keep taking considerable risks in their lending to emerging countries. The consequences would soon speak for themselves.

While the Korean experience contributed to *creditor* moral hazard, the opposite was the case for *debtor* moral hazard. The Korean IMF program contained tough policy conditions and made quite an impression on the rest of the world. It can only have led to countries becoming even more reluctant to approach the Fund. To some extent this is unfortunate, as turning to the IMF at an early stage of trouble can significantly reduce the pain of adjustment. Delaying the inevitable intensifies the economic malady and necessitates stronger doses of medicine with unpleasant side effects. But, since political considerations often involve delaying inevitable adjustment, and borrowing from the IMF is often seen as a shameful sign of failure, the reluctance to call Washington is usually only overcome when all other alternatives have been exhausted.

On September 9, 1998, the IMF Executive Board held its biannual discussion of the world economic outlook, an exchange of views that is based on an in-depth analysis by the Fund staff and is subsequently published without substantive changes. Considerable attention was paid at the meeting to the

Asian crisis, as it was the first occasion for board members to discuss the dramatic events that had taken place. Just a few weeks earlier Russia had decreed a default, and this latest turn of events also influenced the discussion. The roles of the various protagonists were evaluated and judgments expressed on the behavior of governments and central banks in the affected countries, the IMF, and creditor countries. What was vastly *underplayed* was the role of private financial institutions in the buildup to the cataclysm. This bothered a handful of board members. I emphasized that institutions such as foreign banks, hedge funds, and mutual funds had made overborrowing by Asian countries possible, leading to unsustainable levels of external debt. I drew a parallel with the private sector's aggressive search for yields leading up to the Latin American debt crisis of the 1980s. The policy conclusion was that, since private financial agents bore some responsibility for what happened in East Asia in the late 1990s, they should also play a role in the resolution of the difficulties. This implied that more should be demanded of the banks in future bailouts than in the case of Korea, where they did not suffer any real pain, only anxiety attacks.

4
Indonesia with Nukes: The Russian Crisis

The rapid recovery of Korea and the improved situation in Indonesia in the spring and early summer of 1998 helped to calm financial markets. Market indicators, such as bond spreads and appetite for risk, improved and exchange rates remained reasonably stable. There were still problems in some emerging countries, but a sense that the worst was over was taking hold. This feeling was short-lived, however, as in the second half of 1998 three events combined to shock the world financial system once again. The first jolt came on August 17, when the Russian government announced a partial default. Soon afterwards, Wall Street was shaken when Long-Term Capital Management (LTCM), a large hedge fund, had to be rescued. Following this, with markets, governments, and central banks already in a state of heightened nervousness, a serious deterioration of the situation in Brazil took place. The IMF played a major role in getting both Russia and Brazil back on their feet. Once again, the Fund was attacked, although this was limited to its handling of the Russian crisis; the Brazilian crisis generated little controversy.

After its turbulent transition from a communist dictatorship to a fledgling democracy in the early 1990s, Russia gradually integrated into world financial markets. It became a member of the IMF in 1992, and was soon receiving visits from management and staff of the Fund and the World Bank with the aim of supporting Russia in its transition from a command economy to a market economy *à la Russe*. The United States and other Western countries, particularly Germany, showed great interest in this process in view of Russia's overwhelming strategic importance. At the height of the Russian crisis in the summer of 1998, the need to continue to engage with Russia, despite its often recalcitrant attitude, was seen to be justified by its importance as "Indonesia with nukes." While Russia's global economic significance was limited (its economy was not much bigger than that of Indonesia), its huge arsenal of nuclear weapons strongly focused the minds of policymakers and politicians in the West. It was feared that a collapse of the Russian economy could lead to domestic upheaval, posing serious political risks, and could even endanger security on a global scale. The result was that Russia was treated with kid gloves, when it needed a "tough love" approach as had been applied to Indonesia.

The buildup to the crisis

After Russia joined the IMF in 1992 it soon started discussions with the Fund on financial support and policy advice. Prior to the IMF's involvement, the young reformist Russian Prime Minister, Yegor Gaidar, had invited Harvard professor Jeffrey Sachs to act as an advisor on transforming Russia into a viable market economy. The first remedy advocated was a form of shock therapy, starting with a radical liberalization of prices. This was implemented more or less successfully. The other major pillar of this therapy, privatization, consisted of mass distribution of shares, which was reasonably structured, followed by a messy privatization of state-owned enterprises. Production was seriously disrupted (GDP was halved between 1990 and 1996), leading to massive unemployment, while a small group of entrepreneurs, who became known as the *oligarchs*, were able to acquire huge swaths of industry at extremely low prices. It has even been claimed that the rushed and seriously flawed privatization in Russia contributed significantly to a disastrous deterioration in the health of Russians.[1] Although the IMF was not directly involved in the privatization process, it could have spoken out more forcefully against the speed of implementation. The World Bank, however, can be held more responsible here, since privatization is part of its core business rather than that of the Fund.

Gaidar did not last very long, as the reformist element in Russia was weakened by the stormy reaction to some of the measures taken by the government. President Yeltsin replaced him with Viktor Chernomyrdin, who was initially decidedly nonreformist, but gradually adjusted his views. During the mid-1990s several economic programs, backed up by financial support, were agreed between Russia and the IMF. The focus was very much on macroeconomic policies, with particular emphasis on bringing down rampant inflation (which was running at more than 300 per cent as late as 1994) and lowering the huge budget gap. The success of these programs was mixed. Agreement was usually reached without too much difficulty on monetary policy, but great problems were encountered in bringing down the budget deficit. Raising tax revenues was one major obstacle. The lack of willingness by oligarchs and others to pay taxes, various dubious exemptions, and the inability to collect outstanding taxes all made it hard to achieve desirable fiscal outcomes. Fundamental to these problems was the tension between the government and the *Duma*, the communist-dominated Russian parliament, which resisted most attempts at reform. Just how badly the Russian state operated at the time was generally not fully understood, according to Martin Gilman, who represented the IMF in Moscow during much of the 1990s.[2]

To say that politics played an important role in the IMF's dealings with Russia is an understatement. While Fund management and staff were, in true professional manner, politically neutral, the IMF's main shareholders were anything but. "Indonesia with nukes" thinking permeated the way the G7 dealt with Russia. And its favored vehicle for supporting Russia was the IMF. This led to many situations in which Russia was given the benefit of the doubt, and credit disbursements made, when its policies were not sufficiently in accordance with its program with the Fund. As for Russia's politicians, already resentful in having to deal with the "kids" of the IMF (as Russian Prime Minister Yevgeni Primakov, who took over in the fall of 1997, dubbed the IMF team), they were not inclined to follow IMF prescriptions closely, anticipating that the G7 would continue to show leniency. John Odling-Smee, a former high British official who had in 1992 become Director of the Fund's new European II Department dealing with the former Soviet Union countries, emphasized in a retrospective paper[3] that the IMF's influence in Russia had been limited not only because Russia considered itself an important country that could not be pushed around, but especially because the United States and the rest of the G7 constantly showed forbearance when confronted with Russia's policy failures. My experience chimes with Odling-Smee's conclusion that the Fund's work in Russia was from time to time seriously undermined by the United States and its main allies. While some members of the IMF's Board from time to time expressed misgivings about the favorable way Russia was being treated, none went so far as to oppose extending new credits, especially since executive directors from the G7 countries were bound by their governments' position. Moreover, directors from developing countries always tend to support proposals for IMF lending. In my own case, although belonging to neither group, I felt constrained by my representation of Russia's southern neighbor, Ukraine, which itself was struggling to stay on track in its various Fund programs.

IMF lending to Russia on a large scale started in 1995, followed in April 1996 by a medium-term arrangement of $10 billion, most of which was disbursed over time. Considerable criticism of the largesse accorded to Russia was expressed. The Fund's Managing Director, Michel Camdessus, was sensitive to these views, recognizing in an interview that the 1996 loan would be seen by many as support for President Yeltsin or a waste of money. But he added ominously that "nothing more important could be done today for the prosperity of the entire world."[4] As related earlier, Russian implementation of the economic programs agreed with the Fund turned out to be spotty, but credit tranches continued to be paid out under pressure from the highest political circles, including President Clinton and German Chancellor Kohl. As for IMF management, it believed that staying in close contact with the Russian leaders would help to create ownership of the programs negotiated with the Fund. Michel Camdessus, as the head of the IMF, maintained a close relationship with Prime Minister Chernomyrdin, which included going bear hunting together.[5] But the surprising chemistry between Chernomyrdin, a shrewd former Soviet party boss with limited education, and Camdessus, the epitome of a highly educated, smooth French diplomat who was also a devout Catholic, was not always seen as an advantage. John Odling-Smee, the senior IMF staff member dealing with Russia, who had to tag along at the bear-hunting outings, saw a downside to the personal relationship between the Russian Prime Minister and Camdessus, recalling that his then boss became increasingly willing to accede to pleas for further payouts despite failures by Moscow to meet important policy conditions.[6] After Chernomyrdin was suddenly dismissed by Yeltsin in early 1998, the relationship with the Russian leadership became cooler.

Whereas in 1997 it looked as if Yeltsin was finally getting a grip on the internal political turmoil in his country, and his appointment of two reformers (Anatoly Chubais and Boris Nemtsov) as deputy prime ministers raised hopes of a new beginning, the situation looked decidedly worse toward the end of the year as large-scale capital flight, which had earlier plagued Russia, reappeared. Fallout from the Asian crisis played an important role, as did a large drop in the price of oil, strongly affecting Russia's major export and putting pressure on the rate of the ruble. Russia had earlier adopted an exchange rate band which required it to support its currency when it threatened to move beyond the outer limits. When selling dollars from its reserves did not do the trick, the Russian Central Bank was obliged to raise interest rates to as high as 150 per cent. But the loss of confidence was such that the ruble remained under strong pressure.

Collapse

Despite continuing support by the G7 and the IMF, it became increasingly clear that a catastrophe was in the making. A major contributing factor was the intransigence of the *Duma* in refusing to go along with fiscal measures necessary for restoring confidence. It looked as if Yeltsin would once again have to resort to issuing a decree to adopt the package of measures, which was not to the liking of the Fund, as it reflected a serious lack of ownership. But soon a new package of credits, totaling $22.5 billion, was announced; the IMF was to provide $15 billion, the World Bank $6 billion, and the Japanese Export-Import Bank $1.5 billion. On July 20, 1998, Anatoly Chubais, who had in the meantime been designated Russia's chief negotiator with the Fund, made a special appearance in Washington in which he tried to convince skeptical executive directors that the new program had a good chance of success.[7] That very evening, after a long meeting, the IMF Executive Board rubber-stamped the deal the G7 had worked out.

After a brief respite of relative calm, the *Duma* refused to interrupt their recess to implement the fiscal measures that the Russian government had agreed with the Fund. Market reaction was strong, forcing the Russian Central Bank to further deplete its reserves in defending the ruble. Western countries, as well as Japan, which also had a strong interest in keeping Russia from collapsing, conferred intensively on what to do next. Some wanted to finally pull the plug and refuse further financial support; others were more hesitant. The IMF's second in command, Stanley Fischer, who was very much involved alongside Camdessus in most of the Fund's large rescue operations, suggested that an additional $20 billion be provided to Moscow. This time the money was to come directly from the G7 countries, given their geopolitical concerns. This idea was shot down, the consensus among the large industrial countries, including the United States, being that enough was enough. On the European side there was a particularly strong concern that the markets were involved in a "moral hazard play," buying large quantities of high-yielding Russian short-term debt (Gosudarstvennoye Kratkosrochnoye Obyazatyelstvo, known as *GKOs*), in the belief that they would be bailed out in the event of a mishap. This was not surprising in view of the earlier rescue operations for Mexico and Korea, which had left private financial institutions largely unscathed. Offers by Russia to convert *GKOs* held by foreigners into eurobonds with longer maturities, and taking on the exchange risk of borrowing in dollars, met with limited interest from investors.

With capital continuing to flow out of the country, the IMF credit frozen, and international reserves down to less than $10 billion, Russia stunned the world on August 17, 1998 by announcing that it was devaluing the ruble, and, which was much more shocking, defaulting on its foreign debt. This was not the first time that a major crisis had erupted during the vacation month of August, but it did catch the markets off guard. Investors complained that the Fund had let them down, used as they were to being bailed out. This attitude is aptly conveyed by the Dutch saying "stop me before I cause an accident" – the careless party trying to put the blame on others. It was a telling moment for financial markets, as this was the first time since the breaking of the Mexican crisis that bankers and bondholders had not been rescued by a major support package led by the IMF. The significant losses they incurred dealt a strong blow against moral hazard. And, while it was a desirable outcome that there would be no more "moral hazardplay" featuring Russia, the Russian action in dealing with its precarious debt position had been crude and raised fears of emulation elsewhere. A default had been announced without any attempt to come to a workout solution with the holders of *GKOs*, an unheard-of action by a sovereign borrower in modern times. A week after announcing the moratorium, the Russians made it known that *GKOs* would be converted into a "bouquet" of government paper with much longer maturities and interest rates of 30 per cent, falling to lower levels in future years. Since the new securities were – as before – denominated in rubles, except for a "sweetener" of 5 per cent paid in cash, the "bouquet" did not smell very good to foreign investors, who were used to receiving much higher interest rates on Russian paper.

With world opinion and financial markets turning very negative toward Russia after its abrupt actions, a secret attempt was made in late August 1998 to limit the damage. Chernomyrdin had (briefly, as it turned out) reappeared on the scene as acting Prime Minister and was eager to improve the situation.[8] He immediately asked for a secret meeting with Camdessus. Aleksei Mozhin, Russia's shrewd veteran Executive Director at the IMF, who was closely involved in this initiative, explained later that the meeting had been held in the Crimea to avoid unwanted media attention.[9] As the rendezvous took place on Ukrainian territory, Ukraine's president, Leonid Kuchma, received the *incognito* visitors and regaled them over a long dinner. At midnight Chernomyrdin and Camdessus finally got down to business. In a meeting lasting until five o'clock in the morning, the Fund's leader made a radical proposal. Russia was to introduce a *currency board*, which, by imparting severe discipline on economic policy (if the rules of operating a currency board were strictly followed), could restore confidence. Chernomyrdin, who was taking copious notes, seemed to be convinced. Camdessus was able to point to the successful operation of a currency board in Bulgaria and Argentina.[10] But the proposal was met with skepticism by the Russian Central Bank, who worried that the scheme would be very resource-intensive in such a vast country as Russia, highly dependent on energy exports, and that lack of control over the budget constituted a serious risk. The proposal, which never became public, did not gain traction, as Chernomyrdin vanished from the scene soon after returning from the Crimea.

With the world oblivious of the Crimea effort, gloom had descended on world financial markets. The Russian debacle had led to sharply falling stock prices, and spreads over US Treasury bonds had ballooned for borrowers as diverse as emerging countries and US corporations, especially those whose low credit ratings had given rise to the term "junk bonds." In this climate of extreme risk aversion, confidence was further eroded when it was reported that the large American hedge fund LTCM was on the brink of collapse. Despite using highly sophisticated mathematical models, the "rocket scientists" employed at LTCM had not reckoned with the possibility of unusual configurations in the markets such as occurred during the Russian crisis. Since LTCM was highly leveraged, it was feared that a forced liquidation of its assets would resemble a fire sale, entailing huge losses and a drying-up of credit in the financial markets. These concerns led to a rescue operation by major Wall Street banks, which had been summoned to a meeting at the Federal Reserve Bank of New York by its president, the amiable and much respected former diplomat and commercial banker Bill McDonough. The Fed did not get directly involved, preferring a market solution for solving the problem. Although a serious market disruption was avoided, concerns about moral hazard resurfaced. The LTCM meltdown also raised the issue of how to deal with similar cases in the future. Should a basically irresponsible player like LTCM be allowed to go under in the future, or would the risks to the financial system be too great? And, more importantly, what could be done to prevent such situations from arising again?[11] In the event, little, if anything, was done in the following years to ensure this. The problem was to reappear with a vengeance exactly ten years later.

Getting tough

A somber and nervous mood prevailed at the IMF and World Bank annual meetings in October 1998. The senior officials and bankers converging on Washington to discuss developments in the world economy and the international financial system, and, of course, to do business, worried that the Russian example of taking unilateral action against creditors could have a demonstration effect. Further sovereign defaults would have serious consequences for the international financial system and damage the world economy. Intensive discussions were also held among IMF, Treasury, and Central Bank officials on reforming the international financial architecture to avoid a repetition of the bad experiences of the Asian and Russian crises. These talks did lead to some limited changes, as described in Chapter 8.

The crisis had a strong impact on the Russian economy, which shrank by more than 5 per cent in 1998. Fueled by a colossal depreciation of the ruble, whose value against the dollar had fallen by 70 per cent by February 1999, inflation soared to 85 per cent. Fortunately, after the crisis the Central Bank of Russia pursued a fairly tight monetary policy, which helped to prevent hyperinflation from taking root. While the return of the much-criticized Viktor Gerashchenko to the helm of the Russian Central Bank caused some apprehension, he did not repeat his earlier policy mistakes. Fiscal policy was also fairly solid, the lesson that large deficits cause serious problems having apparently been learned. And Prime Minister Primakov was able to get the *Duma* to accept a much improved budget for 1999. These positive developments enabled Russia to negotiate a new IMF credit of around $5 billion in July 1999. But little of the money was actually made available, as Russia failed to meet some of the structural conditions of the program, and the stance of the Fund had become much tougher than before. This was due in no small part to a drastic change in the attitude of the G7 toward Russia. In this connection Mozhin mentioned the second war in Chechnya, concern about Russian corruption, and the US presidential campaign as important factors. Al Gore, the Democratic candidate, had in the past strongly supported IMF programs in Russia, but was vulnerable to attack by the Republican candidate, George W. Bush, on this score.

In the meantime the Russian economy was undergoing a rapid recovery, with growth picking up to the tune of 6 per cent in 1999 (and even 10 per cent in 2000) and inflation coming down to more comfortable levels, falling to 20 per cent in 2000. This rebound,[12] supported by an improvement in the balance of payments and higher oil prices, made the Russian leadership more confident in its dealings with the IMF and Western governments. Russia no longer needed IMF money, as it was rapidly building up its severely depleted international reserves. By 2002 reserves amounted to almost $50 billion, and in subsequent years they continued to grow, aided by further increases in oil prices and capital inflows, reaching a staggering peak of close to $600 billion in mid-2008.

Good advice, weak enforcement

In general the IMF staff were well aware of developments and risks in the Russian economy after it became a Fund member. At the same time the transformation of a large country, whose economy had been centrally planned for over seventy years, posed particular problems of analysis and policy prescriptions. In general the Fund staff rose admirably to the challenge, aided by studies from other institutions such as the World Bank and by academics. IMF staff and management, as well as the Executive Board, had sufficient information in the runup to the crisis to know that the way the Russian economy was managed was very risky. In my own notes I opined at the time that the program the Fund had negotiated with Chubais and his team in 1998 was the most risky we had ever undertaken. As to the outside world, foreign banks and other investors were riding the risk versus reward curve, often speculating that they would be bailed out if and when the bubble burst. What was not anticipated by the Fund and national officials in creditor countries was the crude manner in which Russia took action once it became convinced that it could no longer service its debt. In later years the Fund staff made useful efforts to gain a better understanding of political economy, but it is doubtful whether this would have led to a better anticipation of Russian unilateralism if it had been done earlier.

IMF programs with Russia were generally adequately designed, though sometimes on the lenient side. Lack of implementation was the real issue, with the Kremlin counting on receiving the benefit of the doubt time and again. Were it not for Odling-Smee's extensive description of this politically inspired process, a lot less would be publicly known about it. It is a pity that the excellent Independent Evaluation Office of the IMF never undertook an evaluation of the

Fund's dealings with Russia. After all, the Russian debacle was one of the IMF's biggest failures, even though the G7 had much to do with this outcome.

On *monetary policy* there was general agreement between the staff and the Central Bank of Russia, which was gradually enjoying an improved reputation. The conduct of *exchange rate policy*, on the contrary, was problematic, with the Russian leaders clinging for too long to a fixed rate. Still, it was difficult for the Fund staff to make the case for abandoning the peg, as they found no clear evidence of overvaluation of the ruble on the basis of developments in the balance of payments. In retrospect, however, a timely devaluation would likely have allowed the economy to recover at an earlier stage. This moment would have been in the fall of 1997, before the Korean crisis struck with full force. While the Fund tried hard to improve Russia's *fiscal policy*, the task proved to be an uphill battle, with implementation falling woefully short. The IMF staff enjoy extensive expertise on expenditure controls, tax systems, tax administration, and the like, but, given the Russian intransigence and the lenient attitude of the G7, much of the staff's efforts were wasted. As regards *structural policies*, the Fund wisely provided little input, with the World Bank playing a bigger role in this area. Again, political constraints precluded satisfactory progress.

All in all, the IMF's involvement with Russia was questionable, not so much because of serious mistakes made by the Fund staff, but because it became clear that special treatment was accorded to "Indonesia with nukes." Any collapse leads to finger-pointing, and the Fund was a convenient scapegoat. The whole episode damaged the reputation of the IMF. Particularly harsh criticism was leveled against Michel Camdessus, who as the Fund's Managing Director was seen as the principal architect of the strategy leading to the Russian debacle. As was explained, much of the blame belongs to politicians in the West, but it can be argued that Camdessus should have resisted these political pressures more strongly. At the same time, it is quite possible that, had he done so, large shareholders in the IMF would have worked to push him out. Whatever the precise truth in this matter, the usually affable Camdessus became noticeably prickly in the period following the Asian and Russian crises. He soldiered on through one more crisis, but resigned in early 2000.

If there is one benefit that emerged from the Russian collapse, it is that it dealt a blow against moral hazard. Banks, hedge funds, and other investors had come to expect the IMF and its main backers to ride to the rescue once again. Although they had experienced some nervous episodes, especially at the time of the Korean meltdown, they had escaped largely unscathed from the main emerging market crises of the 1990s. In those instances such as the defaults of Ecuador, Pakistan, and Ukraine, where investors experienced large *haircuts*, losses were modest in relation to their overall investments in emerging markets and did not have much of an impact on their behavior. But foreign investment in Russia, especially in *GKOs*, was of a different order of magnitude, and the losses they caused led to more cautious lending practices by private sector creditors toward emerging countries in general. This is illustrated by a decline in net private capital flows to emerging and developing countries from $93 billion in 1998 to $59 billion the following year. It took until 2002 for these flows to recover strongly. While a more cautious stance concerning lending to countries with weak policies is positive, investors often do not distinguish sufficiently between the soundness of the various emerging countries and tend to pull back across the board when confidence wanes. The IMF does not have specific tools to remedy such pullbacks, but national authorities in lending countries can exert moral suasion to prevent their banks from suddenly refusing to continue rollovers and providing fresh loans to countries following sound policies. However, central banks and treasuries have been reluctant to do so, as they want to avoid being blamed if these loans turn sour. After the emerging market crises of the 1990s, many countries sought to protect themselves against such sudden stops by building up their international reserves.

5
Double Bailout for Brazil

In the course of the acute crisis year 1998, Brazil was increasingly feeling the heat of the general erosion of confidence in emerging countries. Contagion from the Asian and Russian crises was spreading fast and reached Brazil in the summer of that year. It came as no surprise that Latin America would be next in line to be attacked, and in that sense the developments in Brazil were less dangerous than the largely unanticipated attack on Korea. Brazil, whose economy was roughly the same size as that of Korea, enjoyed sound leadership under President Fernando Henrique Cardoso, who seemed to be more open to reform than the policymakers of troubled Asian countries. The *Banco Central do Brasil* had also built up a healthy stock of foreign exchange reserves (some $70 billion in the immediate precrisis period), providing a relatively high degree of insurance against sudden capital outflows.

The country of the future?

Brazil has long been regarded as a country with a bright future, given its enormous natural resources and large population. But time and again periods of rapid growth have been followed by serious setbacks, usually in the form of hyperinflation or severe debt problems (Brazil defaulted on its debts during the Latin American debt crisis of the early 1980s). Cynics remark, therefore, that Brazil is "the country of the future and always will be." During the 1970s Brazil enjoyed a period of rapid growth and looked set to develop as dynamically as Korea, with which it shared a roughly equal standard of living. But by 2003 Korea's income per head had reached $18,000, while Brazil's population earned only $7,500 on average. While many explanations can be given for this widening gap, one major difference between these countries is their level of investment. For Korea the ratio of private investment to GDP, which exceeded 30 per cent for a long time, still stood at 25 per cent in 2007, while Brazil's investment ratio hovered around a modest 15 per cent.

Since Brazil's bouts of hyperinflation proved to be very unhealthy for the economy, in 1994 President Cardoso and the Central Bank Governor, Gustavo Franco, embarked upon a radical plan to eradicate this scourge.[1] Under the Real Plan, as it came to be known, a new currency called the *real* – initially set to equal one US dollar – was introduced. Backward-looking indexation of wages and prices was eliminated in an ingenious way without resorting to wage and price freezes. The real proceeded to appreciate, and inflation, which still amounted to almost 1,000 per cent for December 1994 over December 1993, came down rapidly to 22 per cent the next year and subsequently decelerated further. But the battle was not completely won, as Brazil's inflation rate stayed significantly higher than that of its main trading partners. The result was a gradual erosion of Brazil's competitive position, reflected in a deficit on the current account of the balance of payments which at its peak reached 4.5 per cent of GDP. Here was another example of the serious side effects of fighting inflation by means of exchange rate appreciation, which had been popular for a long time among Latin American policymakers.

With its large current account deficit, Brazil was quite dependent on capital imports. It did receive significant amounts by means of foreign direct investment ("the country of the future"), but in addition borrowed heavily in international capital markets, at times to the tune of $50 billion a year. This made the country quite vulnerable to sudden stops in the flow of foreign capital. External debt was high and increasingly short-term. As it became more difficult to borrow large sums abroad, the government issued increasing amounts of debt bearing a *de facto* exchange rate guarantee. This was another case of applying a dangerous practice that had previously been tried elsewhere, particularly in Mexico before 1995. And, as in Mexico, the Brazilian government was operating a fixed exchange rate regime which it was determined to defend to the bitter end.

The onslaught

While Brazil enjoyed large inflows of foreign capital during the first half of 1998, the picture changed dramatically after the Russian default in August of that year. During September the Central Bank was losing reserves at a rate of $1 billion a day, before it radically raised interest rates from 29 to 49 per cent in defense of the real. Calm briefly returned to the foreign exchange market, but a sharp drop of the Brazilian stocks heralded a new bout of trouble. The IMF, worried about contagion sweeping through the whole of Latin America, issued a statement in support of Latin America. The intention was to make clear that the Fund would step in on a large scale if that proved necessary. Rumors started to circulate that Brazil needed $30 billion to close its payments gap. As the IMF's resources had become considerably depleted in the course of providing credit to crisis-ridden emerging economies, additional funding would be required to provide this kind of money. One source would be to draw on the special borrowing arrangements that the IMF had negotiated with member countries with strong reserves.[2] Another source would be to ask for bilateral loans from countries with ample reserves to supplement an IMF credit. In the event both avenues were pursued.

In mid-September 1998 the IMF's Executive Board was informed confidentially that Brazil's reserves were already down by $20 billion and had fallen below the level of its short-term foreign debt. Stanley Fischer, who was directing the Fund's dealings with Brazil, was asked whether an approach had been made for IMF financial support. While no official request had been made, Fischer noted that "a courtship ritual" of informal meetings was being conducted. The Brazilian side was clearly waiting for the presidential election of October 4 to be over before making a move. After President Cardoso had been comfortably reelected, talks with the IMF intensified. While the Brazilian policymakers seemed to be thinking in line with the Fund on monetary and fiscal policy, the exchange rate emerged as a major sticking point.

During the Russian crisis the IMF had too long supported the position of Moscow on maintaining a *fixed exchange rate*, leading to a serious overvaluation of the ruble. On the European side, doubts were sometimes forcefully expressed in the Fund's Executive Board. Warnings were sounded about the viability of Brazil's exchange rate system. I stated on several occasions that continuation of an overvaluation of the exchange rate, generally estimated at between 25 and 35 per cent, would condemn Brazil to years of slow growth. And the Canadian Executive Director, Tom Bernes, emphasized that a program with Brazil was doomed without an adjustment of the real's peg to the dollar.[3] But the Brazilian economic team, led by the charismatic Finance Minister Pedro Malan, was adamant in its opposition to regime change. It argued that a sizable devaluation of the real would risk returning to a high rate of inflation. Gradual depreciation by means of a crawling peg was considered sufficient to maintain competitiveness. The United States' position was, as usual, crucial. US Treasury thinking on this "enormous issue" demonstrates considerable ambivalence. On the one hand, it was felt that floating the real could well be crucial for the success of a program with the Fund, whereas on the other hand the Treasury was "hesitant to push the issue too hard."[4] Despite what Rubin describes as unfavorable odds, it was decided to go along with a program which would not require an exchange rate adjustment. In Russia the reason for this lenient position had been the concern about nuclear weapons. In the case of Brazil it was purportedly the fear that in a fragile world economy a devaluation of the real would add to market unrest. But several IMF Board members, myself included, had the feeling that the US did not want to cross Brazil, by far the most important country in South America, and was therefore willing to take a chance on the outcome. Further evidence of this stance can be deducted from President Clinton's reaction to the Treasury's proposal, as related by Rubin.[5] While Clinton was prepared to go along with a large rescue operation for Brazil, he observed that, while he had had no qualms in endorsing the Mexican rescue in 1995, he was more worried this time, adding that the Brazilian program "just seems chancier to me." The position of the IMF management and staff was also to take a gamble and hope for the best, probably having in mind that, if needed, a future devaluation could still save the program.

Another European concern was that private sector involvement would be inadequate. European officials, both in their capitals and at the IMF, argued that if a large official package were agreed, including significant bilateral lending, the international banking system should share the burden. European banks had a surprisingly large exposure to Brazil. At the end of 1997 foreign banks had loans of $76 billion outstanding to Brazil, more than half of which was due to European banks as against no more than 20 per cent to American banks. European central banks and supervisors, therefore, had a large stake in ensuring that a rescue operation for Brazil would work and that the banks under their jurisdiction did not stand in the way of a solution. While the banks made the right noises concerning their willingness to cooperate, their actual actions did not bear this out. Rollover rates were declining steadily in the latter part of 1998. And it did not help that opinions were divided among policymakers in the United States. The IMF remained mainly passive and restricted its role to monitoring banks' exposure and reporting on rollover rates.

Half-baked policies

After President Cardoso's reelection, the Brazilian negotiators were still dithering, this time waiting for sensitive gubernatorial elections in several states to be concluded. In the meantime Brazil's international reserves continued to dwindle and by the end of October were down to $44 billion, of which $ 6billion was not usable (the part of reserves held in support of Brazil's Brady bonds). It took until November 13, 1998 for an agreement on an IMF credit plus bilateral contributions from creditor countries to be announced, and December 2 for the standby agreement to be approved formally by the Executive Board. The total package amounted to no less than $45 billion, with the Fund providing $18 billion, of which $12.6 billion came from the more expensive Supplemental Reserve Facility, and the World Bank and the Inter-American Development Bank each providing $4.5 billion. In addition, large bilateral loans were pledged by the United States, the large European countries ($5 billion each), and smaller European countries ($3 billion), with the rest coming from Japan and Canada. The size of the bilateral contributions was to a large degree a reflection of the exposure of the creditor countries to Brazil. An important difference from previous bilateral lines of credit was that in the case of Brazil it was not a "second line of defense," as had been agreed for Korea, but a *pari passu* arrangement, meaning that as tranches of the IMF credit were disbursed there would be simultaneous drawdowns of bilateral credit lines.

The economic program agreed with the IMF was sound as regards *fiscal policy*, which was its centerpiece, the objective being to stabilize the ratio of public debt to GDP at 47 per cent in 2000 with the ratio declining thereafter. To achieve this, the budget deficit was to be reduced by 4 per cent of GDP, implying a primary government surplus (i.e. excluding interest payments) of 2.6 per cent of GDP. Moreover, the fiscal adjustment was front-loaded so that early results could be expected. A less positive element of the fiscal package was that it would significantly rely on an increase in the financial transactions tax, generally considered to have undesirable side effects. While *monetary policy* requirements under the program were not controversial (the usual ceiling on the provision of credit by the Central Bank was a performance criterion), the decision to leave the exchange rate unchanged was rightly criticized and would soon lead to serious trouble. Here the United States did all parties a disservice by supporting Brazil's refusal to float the real. According to closely involved staff members, the exchange rate was discussed intensively with Brazilian officials, who adamantly refused to sever the (crawling) peg with the dollar.[6] As in other cases of exchange rate overvaluation, IMF management gave in. With the Brazilian banking system in reasonably good shape, the economic program's *structural benchmarks*[7] were mild, in contrast to what had been the case in Asian countries. This reflected a change in thinking at the Fund, strongly propagated from the Brazilian side, that structural conditionality should be limited and streamlined and that this would increase ownership of the program.

It soon became clear that the program had left financial markets unconvinced. Pressure on the real was heavy at times, and the rollover ratio of foreign banks' credits to Brazil hovered around only 60 to 70 per cent, despite a meeting in New York at which major banks promised not to move abruptly to the sidelines. It did not help that the Central Bank prematurely eased the monetary reins. The United States, and other countries that had been supportive, now became more critical of Brazil's policy stance. In the IMF Executive Board, a director remarked that it looked as if "the whole population of Brazil had gone to the beach." A new challenge arose in January 1999, when the acerbic governor of the State of Minas Gerais, Itimar Franco, who had been president before Cardoso, threatened to declare a moratorium on his state's debt. While he was overruled by the sitting president, fears of more widespread moratoria led to more withdrawal of foreign credit to Brazil and stimulated capital flight. As reserves fell further in a futile attempt to maintain the value of the real, and a lack of willingness to increase interest rates became increasingly apparent, Brazil threw in the towel, but not far enough. The decision to abandon the crawling peg and establish a new band for the real, effectively constituting a devaluation of 9 per cent, did not impress markets. No surprise, then, that soon afterward a new exchange rate system was announced. The real was now allowed to float, and quickly depreciated by 20 per cent. But it was surprising that the decision to devalue had been taken in Brasilia without consulting the IMF, despite the existence of an ongoing program with the Fund. Displeasure was expressed, especially by Stanley Fischer, but the incident did not do any permanent damage to the close relationship between IMF management and the Brazilian leadership. It did raise eyebrows elsewhere, strengthening suspicions that Brazil was receiving special treatment.

After an initial period of calm in the markets, new pressures materialized. Within the IMF the radical option of establishing a currency board was now raised by Stanley Fischer, who argued that the Brazilian banks were sounder than those in Indonesia, making a move to a hard currency peg less risky for the real than for the rupiah. But he added that adoption of a currency board could cause political problems in Latin America's biggest economy. Among board members the consensus remained that a floating exchange rate was the only viable option. When the subject of a currency board was raised by Michel Camdessus in talks with the Brazilians, they rejected it outright. At the same time a debate was taking place in Brazil, as had happened in other crisis countries, regarding the extent to which monetary policy should be used to avoid an undershooting of the exchange rate. The new Central Bank President, Francisco Lopes, did not wish to raise interest rates, a position that was not well received in the foreign exchange market. President Cardoso realized the danger and eased out Lopes after a mere nineteen days as head of the Central Bank. His replacement, Arminio Fraga, who combined wide experience in financial markets with sound policy views, was immediately faced with a critical situation. Rollovers of foreign bank credit were down to an alarming 25 per cent, a situation in which currency intervention was of little use and, in fact, could be a convenient vehicle to withdraw from Brazil.

Fraga takes over

With Fraga at the helm of the *Banco Central do Brasil*, the depreciation of the real was contained at about 30 per cent. Interest rates had been raised, as advocated earlier by IMF management, and a decision was made to base future monetary policy on *inflation targeting* (also as advised by Stanley Fischer) instead of on monetary aggregates. After Finance Minister Malan had given his blessing to the combination of a floating exchange rate and an inflation targeting regime, the joke of the day was that Fischer was now the real minister of finance of Brazil and George Soros (the famous financier for whom Fraga had earlier worked) its Central Bank president. In the meantime, discussions were underway between the IMF and the Brazilian team on a revised program. Negotiations generally went smoothly, as recent events had convinced all parties that a number of changes were needed in addition to the reform of the monetary and exchange rate regime. A revised program was announced in early March 1999. The main changes were: fiscal policy was further strengthened by establishing a floor for the primary surplus; a monthly ceiling was set for sales of dollars by the Central Bank (replacing a floor on reserves); and covert intervention by the Central Bank in the forward dollar market was halted. The setting of revised policy, Fraga's appointment and actions, and the new agreement with the IMF combined to restore confidence. This rapid turnaround was aided by the fact that Brazil's crisis had not been unexpected, and, once it was addressed in a forceful manner, markets regained confidence in the country's capacity to deal with its macroeconomic problems (widespread poverty was another matter, but not a concern of the financial markets). Contagion in other parts of Latin America remained limited, as Mexico and (mistakenly) Argentina were seen as following sound policies. The absence of a moratorium on Brazil's debt, in contrast to that of Russia, gave a general boost to confidence with respect to emerging market countries, including those in Eastern Europe.

Michel Camdessus must have considered the return of calm to the world economy to be a good time to step down. In late 1999 he announced that he would be resigning in the spring of the following year. The Frenchman had presided over the IMF for a record thirteen years, during the most turbulent time in its history. Battered and bruised by the many battles he had had to fight – though he had won most of them – Camdessus remained remarkably fit for someone who had taken such punishment. Armed with enormous endurance and a personality that at the same time craved challenge and exuded charm, he became a figure on the world stage as no other managing director had done before him.[8] Camdessus remained very active after his retirement, accepting a variety of part-time positions in his own country and attending high-level meetings abroad. Unfortunately he has not (yet?) written his memoirs. His successor, Horst Köhler, a former State Secretary of Finance in Germany and head of the East European bank in London, seemed to take over at a rather quiet time. But soon the situation in Argentina and Turkey would preoccupy the outspoken first German Managing Director of the IMF.

Learning to love Lula

Unlike other emerging countries that were struck by crisis in the 1990s, Brazil's economy did not shrink, although it experienced very slow growth (only 0.1 per cent in 1998 and 0.8 per cent the following year). At the same time, inflation, after falling to less than 2 per cent in 1998, rebounded to 9 per cent the following year, largely due to the steep depreciation of the real.

The introduction of an inflation target (initially set at 6 per cent within a band of plus or minus 1.5 per cent) subsequently helped to bring down inflation to within a more reasonable range. These favorable developments led to two upgrades of Brazil's credit rating, but, after a year of satisfactory growth (4.4 per cent) in 2000, the economy started to falter again and confidence issues returned to the forefront. The exchange rate continued to fall, including in real terms, and international reserves stayed uncomfortably low at around $35 billion, constituting only a modest fraction of Brazil's short-term external debt. The problem was rooted in another *sudden stop* of capital imports, reflecting worries about Brazil's future economic policies. This uncertainty had a lot to do with the increasingly likely election as the country's president of Luiz Inacio da Silva, better known as Lula, a former left-wing labor union leader. As the October 2002 election drew closer, both foreign investors and wealthy Brazilian residents chose to withdraw their liquid assets from Brazil out of fear that a Lula-led government would follow unorthodox economic policies. Based on Lula's background, there was a widespread expectation that he would aim at improving the lot of the poor by raising taxes on the rich or through inflationary policies. Fears of nationalization, or even expropriation, of privately owned companies added to the anxieties.

Anne Krueger, a former chief economist of the World Bank and professor at Stanford University, who had succeeded Stanley Fischer as the IMF's number two in August 2001,[9] visited Brazil in July 2002. In her report to the IMF Executive Board, Krueger mentioned having advocated to the incumbent policymakers that it would be best to wait for the presidential elections to be over before negotiating a new Fund program (and additional funding) for 2003. However, Finance Minister Malan and Central Bank Governor Fraga were strongly in favor of going ahead before the elections. In their view this was necessary to convince markets that there would be policy continuity and that the presidential candidates would support this action. There was a parallel here with the situation in Korea four years earlier, in that it was necessary to have presidential candidates on board before announcing a new program of support. After a while Lula (to the surprise of many) and the two other candidates declared themselves in favor of such an approach. As could be expected, confusion arose after Lula stated in early August that the government should not accept policies "imposed" by the IMF. During this sensitive period, Paul O'Neill, who had become President George W. Bush's first Secretary of the Treasury, visited a number of South American countries with Brazil as his main destination. After his meeting with President Cardoso, which had almost been canceled after O'Neill had suggested a few days earlier that money in support of South American countries could end up in Swiss bank accounts, an apparently chastised O'Neill stated that the Bush administration supported more assistance to Brazil and Uruguay.

In the meantime, the Fund and Brazilian negotiators were hard at work putting together a new bumper credit for Brazil, and on August 8, 2002 announced that $30 billion would be lent under a fifteen-month agreement. Providing a credit that was larger than expected, in order to make a positive impression on investors, proved to be a strategy that worked. Timothy Geithner, then director of the Fund's policy development department, first proposed this approach. The emphasis was on keeping the fiscal situation on an even keel, with a commitment by Brazil to continue running a surplus on its primary balance of 3.75 per cent. With the real guided by a managed float and monetary policy steered by an inflation target, macroeconomic policy would remain on a steady footing. Little was required of Brazil as regards structural policies, which were much more controversial, especially in the run-up to the elections. Managing Director Köhler declared that he was confident that the terms of the agreement would be supported by the leading presidential candidates. Indeed, Lula had in the meantime considerably toned down his earlier rhetoric, partly because the IMF program would not force Brazil to make highly unpopular budget cuts and was very light on structural conditions. Still, the huge credit – this time without bilateral contributions from creditor countries – bore considerable risk, especially since it depended on foreign investors to maintain their exposure to Brazil. Comfort was taken from the fact that banks again promised to be on their best behavior. But their declarations were no more than statements of intent and the operation was wholly voluntary.

As it turned out, the risks to the Fund program did not materialize. Despite its very high external debt of around $250 billion or 40 per cent of GDP and external debt service of 90 per cent (this includes amortization payments which do not have to be made when the claims are rolled over), Brazil managed to avoid a standstill or any kind of default. This was a surprise to quite a few observers, including the astute former IMF official Morris Goldstein, who in late August 2002 expressed grave concern about Brazil's capacity to service its debts.[10] The key to this turn of events was a rapid restoration of confidence in Brazil on Wall Street and in other international financial centers. What happened was that the markets, the IMF, and the G7 had come to appreciate Lula, as the new president of Brazil succeeded in putting to rest fears that there would be an important change of direction in Brazil's policies. It is quite astonishing, and very interesting from a political economy point of view, to see how Lula and his governing Worker's Party (PT), who had earlier been adamantly opposed to then President Cardoso's "neoliberal" policies, engineered an almost 180-degree turn in their policy stance. This included supporting such delicate areas as reform of the overly generous pension framework, which had been pushed by the previous president. Later these reforms turned out to be very difficult to put into place, but significant progress was made.

Joining the BRICs

Aided by a strong performance of the world economy, a much depreciated exchange rate, and sound macroeconomic policies, Brazil did increasingly well after 2002, especially on the external side. What had seemed unlikely just a few years earlier now proved possible – Brazil's strong export performance led to substantial surpluses on its current account after the seemingly permanent deficits of the past. International reserves increased substantially, with the ratio of reserves to short-term external debt, an important indicator of reserve adequacy, increasing from a paltry 56 per cent in 2001 to a very comfortable 160 per cent in 2007. The high ratio of external debt to GDP, which had understandably worried experts like Goldstein at the time of the crisis, came down spectacularly from 41 per cent of GDP in 2001 to a mere 15 per cent in 2007. Ballooning exports during the commodities boom that preceded the great global recession of 2008–09, and large capital flows, were the main drivers of this remarkable performance.

President Lula's unexpectedly conservative financial policies and his choice of a sound economic team[11] instilled confidence in Brazil's capacity to reduce its vulnerability to future crises. Brazil's external position strengthened sufficiently for it to repay its outstanding debt to the IMF in one shot in 2005; in 2008 its government bonds were rated as investment grade. Brazil also took pride in being included among the BRICs, an informal grouping of rapidly developing emerging countries composed of Brazil, Russia, India, and China. Nevertheless, Brazil's pace of economic growth of 5 per cent on average (only 3.5 per cent per head) in the years before the big recession, while satisfactory by Latin American standards, lagged behind that of the more dynamic Asian countries (China has been growing at over 10 per cent annually in recent years). Structural factors lie at the heart of Brazil's somewhat lagging performance, including high real rates of interest (necessary to contain persistent inflationary pressures), a high level of public expenditure and taxes coupled with rigid budgetary processes, a lack of flexibility in the labor market, and slow or no progress on tax, pension, and social security reforms. With limited progress on much-needed structural reforms during Lula's second term, the old question about Brazil's promise for the future has not completely gone away, despite quite strong growth following the great global recession.

Early warning not heeded

After a false start, the Brazilian crisis was defused successfully. And, while a new crisis threatened in 2002, the main cause was uncertainty generated by possible political developments, rather than poor policies. After the dismal failure of the IMF and its major shareholders to contain the Argentine crisis (described in Chapter 6), the Fund badly needed a success to repair its damaged reputation. An important reason why its intervention in Brazil proved successful in the end was the recognition at an early stage that trouble was brewing in the world's major coffee producer. Unlike in Korea, observers were not taken by surprise when Brazil experienced confidence problems in the course of 1998. The IMF had detected the signs at an early stage, but issued its warnings mainly internally, remaining very reticent about making public any concerns about Brazil's capacity to withstand a currency crisis. The lessons drawn in the Whittome report following the Mexican crisis were, again, hardly heeded. This was partly due to a lack of information provided by Brazil, but a major part reflected unwillingness by IMF management to take a hard line with Brazil. It did not want a confrontation with Cardoso and Malan, with whom Camdessus and Fischer were on friendly terms. Moreover, there was unusually strong resistance from Brazil's policymakers to any warnings from the IMF regarding its policy stance. This was especially true of any hints that the currency might be overvalued. In fact, the IMF staff continually downplayed the degree or even the existence of overvaluation. This was unhelpful in that it prolonged Brazil's problem and the risks it posed for global financial stability. The role played by the United States was also unfortunate, demonstrating that from time to time it gave priority to bilateral political considerations rather than to economic rationale. Within the Fund there were differences of opinion on the exchange rate. These were quite apparent in discussions in the Executive Board, where the Canadian and European members were generally critical of supporting an overvalued exchange rate in view of the lessons from the Mexican, Asian, and Russian crises. They felt that this lesson should have been learned by Fund management.[12] What the Fund should have done is press for floating the real, in a managed fashion, during a window of opportunity. One such window was in early 1997, another during the first half of 1998. But, since a sizable depreciation followed in early 1999 and the Brazilian policymakers quickly reached agreement with the IMF on a revamped economic program, the damage remained limited.

Policy shift

The initial program was well designed, except for the crucial failure to address the exchange rate problem. Fiscal policy objectives were not too lax or too tight. Unlike in Asian countries, relaxation of fiscal performance criteria was not needed under the revamped program of 1999. Doubts were sometimes expressed about formulating fiscal goals in terms of the primary balance (interest payments excluded) rather than the overall balance, which showed a large deficit (3.4 per cent in 1999 against a primary *surplus* of 3.2 per cent). But this was a reasonable approach, which I did not sufficiently appreciate at the time, in view of the large public borrowing requirement and the need to maintain a tight monetary policy. The switch in 1999 to a monetary policy based on targeting inflation, advocated by the IMF, was also appropriate and helped to allay fears of a rekindling of inflation. Several performance criteria were aimed at constraining Brazil's buildup of *external debt*, although in the period between the 1998–99 rescue and the 2002 bailout there was a resurgence of debt. The Fund staff recognized as early as 1996 that the financing of Brazil's current account deficit depended too much on easily reversible capital inflows, but downplayed the problem. Due to lack of information received, Brazil's total short-term debt was continually underestimated by the IMF. Apparently the lessons of Mexico, Thailand, and Korea regarding poor reporting of external debt and the usability of reserves had not been sufficiently taken to heart. Fortunately, these gaps were considerably less important in Brazil than in the case of Korea, so that they did not lead to a seriously flawed diagnosis of Brazil's maladies. Still, the Fund should have insisted on better disclosure of information by Brazil, one of the few major emerging countries that at that time did not subscribe to the IMF's higher standard of data provision. Finally, on the positive side, the Fund staff thoroughly examined the soundness of the banking system in Brazil. As it was found to be generally solid, policy conditions with respect to the *financial sector* were light. Structural conditions were few and far between and were strongly discouraged by the Brazilian policymakers, with the articulate Brazilian IMF Executive Director Murillo Portugal (later to become a deputy managing director at the Fund) repeatedly conveying the message to his colleagues.

The banks get off lightly

The IMF's dealings with foreign banks who had lent large sums to Brazil were timid. An appeal to the banks to maintain their exposures remained fully voluntary at the insistence of Brazil's leadership, which feared that stronger pressure on the banks would damage future access to foreign credit. IMF staff and management seemed to be blowing hot and cold regarding private sector involvement. At the outset the Fund staff, having learned the lessons from previous crises, were in favor of central banks practicing moral suasion regarding their banks' foreign exposure. Fund management, influenced by pressure from the United States, which wanted to be "nice" to Brazil, agreed to limited and voluntary PSI for Brazil. The main action consisted of the Brazilian team conducting a few "road shows" to request foreign banks to maintain their trade and interbank lines. The IMF monitored the rollover rates of the various banks by nationality but refrained from any pressure to ensure high rollover rates. The result was that the voluntary approach did not make much of an impression and rollover rates fell to between 60 and 70 per cent at the time of the first Brazilian crisis. This poor result contributed to the failure of the initial IMF program for Brazil. PSI was again trotted out under the revised program of March 1999. European criticism of the lack of effective PSI under the initial program served to increase pressure on Brazil and other creditor countries to adopt a somewhat less indifferent stance. Meetings took place in a few international financial centers, where high officials delivered mild exhortations to commercial banks to keep credit lines open. Again the IMF's role remained limited to monitoring the process. The Fund's independent evaluation arm (IEO) interpreted Camdessus's public announcement that efforts to obtain voluntary commitments from the banks "would be a key factor in the consideration of the program by the Executive Board" as amounting to some form of pressure.[13] I experienced it the other way around: European directors had made it clear that they wanted substantive PSI to be part of the program. My interpretation is that the Fund's Managing Director was merely relaying that message. Moreover, it has been my impression that during the various emerging market crises of that period both Camdessus and his second-in-command, Fischer, were quite reluctant to push for PSI.

Fortunately, despite the still voluntary nature of PSI under the revised program, confidence in Brazil returned in the course of 1999 and the crisis quickly abated. But this had more to do with the improved policy stance of Brazil and the size of official financial support than with the burden-sharing element in the program. When I later remarked to a senior IMF staffer that PSI had worked well in Brazil, he emphasized that the whole operation was basically "cosmetic," a "show" to appease the Europeans. The role of the private sector came back a third time for Brazil when in mid-2002, before the outside world had developed tender feelings for Lula, a renewed loss of capital forced Malan and Fraga to turn to the IMF once again for a jumbo credit. This time the banks got their act together much better than they had in 1998 and agreed to maintain their exposure to Brazil, helping considerably to defuse the crisis. In combination with the additional $30 billion forthcoming from the Fund – a financial version of the Powell doctrine[14] – the liquidity crisis was overcome. The second wave of the Brazilian crisis was the last such event of the emerging country crises of the 1990s and the early years of this century. PSI as an issue vanished from the radar screen, not to reappear for many years.

Did the double crisis in Brazil foster *moral hazard*? The answer is a qualified yes. The amounts of official financial support were very large, but banks were encouraged to maintain their credit lines to Brazil. In the end they did, and foreign investors subsequently poured huge amounts of money into Brazil in the knowledge that the IMF and its main shareholders considered Brazil "too big to fail." Moreover, the PSI agreement was limited and voluntary, unlike that in the case of Korea. Should the objections of Brazilian policymakers against more formal means of involving private investors have been overruled? In view of the danger of a collapse to the Brazilian economy, it is likely that the men from Brasilia would have stepped back from the brink. But since the United States, unlike Germany, the Netherlands, Switzerland, and the Nordic countries, consistently showed great reluctance to twist the arms of their banks, Finance Minister Malan felt he could succeed in insisting that PSI remained light. In the years between 2002 and the global financial crisis that emerged in the summer of 2007, questions of moral hazard moved to the back burner.

6
The IMF Fails: The Argentine Drama

After Brazil's successful exit from the 1998–99 crisis a period of calm descended on world financial markets, allowing the IMF, ministers of finance, and central bank governors to enjoy a breather after the hectic preceding crisis years. But this restful period was not to last long; clouds began to gather over Argentina. In fact, astute weather watchers had already discerned that all was not well in Latin America's most prosperous country, especially after the hefty depreciation of Brazil's currency. As Argentina operated a currency board based on an immutable peg of the peso to the US dollar at a one to one rate, the drop of the Brazilian *real* in early 1999 resulted in a serious weakening of Argentina's competitiveness. But there were other factors at work in undermining Argentina's apparently healthy economic position, and these bore the stamp "Made in Argentina." Yet early signs of trouble were either overlooked or ignored by overly optimistic investors, lenders, and international organizations. The end result was a disastrous collapse of the Argentine economy, causing severe hardship for a large section of the population. It also marked the biggest failure ever for the IMF in its relationship with a member country.

A brief history

Argentina is blessed with a vast territory with large swaths of fertile soil and the best-educated population in Latin America.[1] An often-quoted fact is that at the beginning of the twentieth century Argentina figured among the richest countries in the world, with an income per head roughly equal to that of France. As an important producer of commodities, especially beef and wheat, Argentina also did very well in the aftermath of the Second World War, but subsequently started sliding backward under the populist policies of dictator Juan Peron. Political instability has continued to plague the country and may well be the most important underlying cause of its underperforming economy.

When Argentina became a democracy again in 1983, following the ouster of a military dictatorship, many felt that a corner had also been turned economically, but, sadly, performance continued to be uneven. The newly elected President, Raul Alfonsin, inherited an economic mess from the military dictatorship. A number of unsuccessful attempts to get the economy back on the right track followed. The first was the *Austral Plan* in 1985, designed as a "shock program," which included the substitution of the austral for the discredited peso, lopping off three zeros in the process. The plan faded away in subsequent years. During this period IMF support was readily forthcoming, but none of Argentina's economic programs with the Fund lasted very long. Nonetheless, hope seemed to spring eternal in Buenos Aires and the *Plan Primavera* was launched six months later. This plan consisted of a package of so-called heterodox measures aimed at breaking the momentum of rapidly mounting inflation. Once again the plan contained too little fiscal adjustment, and this time the IMF refused to resume lending to Argentina. Only six months after its introduction *Primavera* collapsed and the country slipped into hyperinflation. These were the circumstances under which the Peronist Carlos Menem was elected president in May 1989. Again the Fund supported Argentina with a standby credit, but, in line with earlier experience, the arrangement was eclipsed prematurely by political blockades. After experiencing a renewed bout of hyperinflation – prices were increasing by 12,000 per cent at an annual rate – Domingo Cavallo, the charismatic Minister of Finance, engineered a shock effect in April 1991 by introducing a currency board and fixing the value of the dramatically eroded peso at a rate of one per US dollar.

The currency board

The introduction of a currency board was a drastic measure which quickly led to disinflation and a robust turnaround of the economy. On the basis of its initial success, both the author of the convertibility law,[2] Minister of Finance Domingo Cavallo, and the president who had appointed him, Carlos Menem, could look upon their decision with satisfaction. There was also a show of enthusiasm from the international community, especially since Argentina was at the same time embarking on a large-scale privatization program in which foreign investors were very interested. In this almost euphoric atmosphere, more skeptical views of the wisdom of sustaining a currency board in a country that surely did not constitute an optimum currency area with the United States did not hold sway. Moreover, Argentina's economy was one of the most closed in the Western world, while much-needed structural reforms, including the functioning of the labor market, were very difficult to put in place.

Undoubtedly, shock therapy was what was needed in Argentina in 1991, and the introduction of a currency board was probably the most convenient way of administering it. What seems to have fallen by the wayside, however, is the insight that the conditions for a *sustained* maintenance of a currency board – as distinct from administering a temporary anti-inflationary shock – are very stringent. A number of requirements can be listed: the criteria for an optimum currency area need to be satisfied, implying, among other things, that large countries are less likely to qualify; that the bulk of the pegging country's trade should be conducted with the country to which it pegs its currency; that inflation preferences should not diverge much between the pegger and the "main" country; that a flexible labor market is needed to help avoid rising unemployment; and that strong institutions and a consistent application of the law are required. The necessity for conducting a stringent fiscal policy can be added to this list. Keeping up with increases in labor productivity in the country whose currency serves as the anchor is also necessary for the longer-term viability of a currency board. Usually this requires a sustained effort in the area of structural reform. Practically none of these conditions were met by Argentina. That the currency board was maintained for ten years can be attributed to the lack of an exit strategy and the unattractive prospect of having to introduce a different monetary approach fraught with short-term political risk.

One ignored lesson was that there are no instances of sizable countries with closed economies successfully operating a currency board over an extended period of time. After its initial success in bringing down inflation in Argentina, the currency board increasingly constituted a drag on the economy, especially since the authorities allowed it to function more as a suppressor of symptoms than as an engine for fundamental change in the economy. It was especially damaging that insufficient action was taken to bring Argentina's perennial fiscal problems under control. In its programs with Argentina, the IMF concentrated only on the budget of central government, whereas it should have included the \profligate provinces. The currency board was equally undermined by the continuation of large external borrowing, which eventually led to an unsustainable situation. This was recognized too late, not only within Argentina, but also by the international financial institutions and the international capital markets. It is, therefore, too simple to blame the existence of a seriously overvalued exchange rate and the eventual economic collapse entirely on the currency board. The fact that the conditions for a successful operation of the currency board did not exist in the first place, in combination with a persistent lack of fiscal discipline plus a penchant for excessive borrowing, was the true cause of Argentina's slide into a morass of default and depression. This combination of a closed economy, with exports of goods and services amounting to no more than 9 per cent of GDP (the average for Latin America is 19 per cent, and for emerging Asian countries 50 per cent), which remained closed in part because of the overvalued exchange rate, and the high level of external borrowing by the government proved to be unsustainable.

Claims by Argentine officials, made right up to the end, that the government debt position was sound since at 57 per cent of GDP (at end 2001) it was not higher than that of many OECD countries completely missed the point. The fact that Argentina's external debt to export ratio had climbed to the astounding level of around 500 per cent, and that by 1999 it needed to use around 40 per cent of its export proceeds to pay interest on its external debt, was what should have set alarm bells ringing not only on Wall Street and in Washington (as it eventually did), but also in Buenos Aires.

Argentina's serious problems did not come to the fore until late in the day, although signs of trouble were discernable earlier to those willing and able to see them. Argentina got though the "Tequila crisis" of 1995 quite well, but it most probably would have been better off had it had the foresight in the "good" years up to 1998 to abandon its currency board, to float its currency and to introduce an inflation target as an anchor. But politically this was a nonstarter. Since the real (inflation-adjusted) exchange rate of Argentina had already appreciated a fair deal since 1991, and the plunge of Brazil's currency added to this significantly, any exit strategy – had it existed – should have called for abandoning the currency board in Argentina at that time.

Failing that, a second-best solution might well have been to devalue *within* the currency board regime. While this would have been highly unusual, it would probably have been possible with some clever political maneuvering. However, the solution pursued by Cavallo, who returned as Economy Minister in June 2001, was to adjust the parameters of the currency board,[3] to manipulate tariffs, and to introduce export subsidies. This was a serious miscalculation, as was the dismissal of the Central Bank governor under rather unclear circumstances. It served only to undermine confidence and convince the markets that Argentina's currency board was doomed, or that the country would default, or both.

The role of the Fund during Argentina's initial (apparent) success and its subsequent swift decline was later criticized by Michael Mussa, who had been the Director of Research at the IMF until 2001. He rightly concluded that (a) the Fund failed to press Argentina hard enough on its fiscal policy, especially during the period of rapid economic growth from 1995 to 1997,[4] and (b) that it went on too long providing financial support to Argentina. Where I disagree with him is on whether the Fund was right to support Argentina in its decisions to maintain the peg after initial skepticism. Mussa's argument was that the choice of a government as regards the exchange regime it wants to operate should be respected by the IMF, and supported with financial programs if requested. During my tenure on the Executive Board, I took a different view throughout, arguing that, while a country has the freedom to choose or maintain its preferred exchange rate system, the Fund has no obligation to financially support an unviable exchange rate. In fact, it is doing a disservice both to the member country with an unsuitable exchange rate and to itself by lending under such inauspicious conditions. In subsequent years, the Fund became tougher with the diminishing number of emerging countries maintaining an overvalued exchange rate.

The end game

The first clear signs of trouble emerged in 1998, as Argentina slipped into a recession from which it was unable to extricate itself. Declining output led to an increase in the already high rate of unemployment, reaching 18 per cent in 2001. As the recession became more drawn out, fiscal adjustment became increasingly difficult, with tax receipts falling rapidly. Tax evasion – an endemic problem – increased and bouts of capital flight resumed.[5] While initially the financial system was considered to be sound, residents started to convert their pesos into dollars, and later also took out their dollars from the banks in large amounts as they started to doubt the banks' solvency. Argentina's international reserves, which were adequate in relation to the formal requirements of the currency board, declined steeply, after having reached $26 billion in 1999, to a mere $14 billion by the time of the abolition of the currency board in December 2001. In the meantime Argentina continued to borrow from international capital markets, except for an interlude after the Russian crisis of the summer of 1998 when it could not access these markets. It is this combination of inadequate fiscal adjustment and excessive borrowing in foreign currencies which in the end proved so damaging for Argentina's attempt to maintain the currency board and avoid default.

While Argentina's policies were clearly misguided, and the IMF and World Bank were often insufficiently critical of them, its problems were aggravated by unfavorable external developments. The dollar, to which the peso was pegged, kept appreciating, thus further weakening the Argentine competitive position, which had already been dealt a severe blow by the Brazilian devaluation of 1999. But instead of exiting the currency board, in order to avoid a worse outcome, the Argentine policymakers stubbornly continued on the road to disaster. Markets were starting to contemplate the likelihood of an Argentine sovereign debt default, as the economic malaise worsened and the administration of President de la Rua demonstrated a lack of decisiveness.

In early 2001, the IMF once again came to the aid of Argentina with a huge financial package. It provided $14 billion (around 500 per cent of Argentina's quota in the IMF), the World Bank and the Inter-American Development bank contributed $5 billion, and the Spanish government provided $1 billion. The private sector was to provide an additional $20 billion or so, but the details of this part remained vague and seemed to serve mainly to allow announcement of a total package of around $40 billion.

Other possible options in lieu of a large bailout package orchestrated by the IMF would have been a large-scale restructuring of Argentina's sovereign debt or full dollarization. Adopting the dollar as legal tender without a sizeable devaluation would have solved nothing. It would have provided only some short-term solace and locked Argentina for a very long time into a weak competitive position from which it could only have exited by means of prolonged austerity. Adopting an irrevocably fixed exchange rate while suffering from lack of competitiveness condemns a country to long-term high unemployment, especially in the face of low mobility of the labor force.

As matters became worse for Argentina, it fell to Domingo Cavallo in March 2001 to assume the role of *deus ex machina*. Starting off energetically, he introduced a financial transactions tax to generate much-needed government revenue. Less well received was his decision to change the terms of the currency board, as mentioned earlier, and his firing of the Central Bank governor. After all, the rigid application of the rules of the currency board and the independence of the Central Bank had been the main pillars of the success of the board in the early 1990s. Another desperate act aimed at staving off default at all costs was a massive swap of Argentine government bonds for paper with longer maturities so as to lighten the debt service in the immediate years ahead. But in the longer run the operation was very costly. While the operation led to a lowering of the debt service by $12 billion between 2001 and 2005, it added a staggering $66 billion to interest and amortization payments in the years after 2005. Market interpretation generally was that a default was imminent. Still, it took another six months before the final showdown. During this period the Argentine economy went from bad to worse, with output falling rapidly by 4 per cent.

Against this background Cavallo unveiled a 2002 budget deficit plan which envisaged large budget cuts, especially in salaries. But the plan was not realistic in view of falling revenue caused by the recession and widespread tax evasion. Moreover, the assumptions underlying the budget (a positive rate of economic growth) were totally unrealistic. Cavallo, who had an engaging personality, made great efforts to convince skeptical partners that his zero budget approach was feasible. In a meeting with a Dutch delegation in November 2001, he produced a table with matching government expenditures and revenues. Since the calculations were based on positive economic growth, nobody was convinced. The Dutch Finance Minister, Gerrit Zalm – who does not speak Italian – politely took note of Cavallo's numbers and expressed appreciation for hearing the story "from the horse's mouth." Cavallo hesitated for a moment, then burst out laughing, saying, "Yes, I am the Sunday horse." Later I explained to my Argentine colleague that this had been an unintended pun.

When it became increasingly clear during the summer of 2001 that Argentina's efforts were proving futile, as reflected by a rise in interest rate spreads to risk premium levels that indicated a virtually certain default, the IMF once again launched a rescue effort. Opinions were initially divided over the desirability of another bailout for Argentina. In the end it was, as usual, the United States that decided the issue. And, as usual, a considerable dose of politics was involved. Both the secretary of the US Treasury, Paul O'Neill, and his undersecretary for international affairs, John Taylor, had in the early days of their tenure questioned the wisdom of large IMF rescue operations.[6] Moreover, President Bush, on entering the White House, was intent on scaling back the role of the United States in solving international financial crises.[7] Taylor was the point man for the United States in dealing with the IMF and financial crises. Despite starting his job in early 2001 with misgivings about IMF bailouts, he soon became worried about developments in Argentina. In August 2001 Taylor went on a fact-finding tour of Argentina. On his way back he concluded that the large augmentation of the Fund's credit to Argentina in January of that year should probably not have happened, as the debt situation appeared to be unsustainable and Buenos Aires had no *plan B* (debt rescheduling and devaluation were the obvious options). But, faced by a request from the Argentine government for an additional $8 billion from the IMF, and worrying about the consequences for financial markets of a sudden default, Taylor leaned toward giving in to Argentine pleas once again. Memories of the Russian default of 1998 and the risk of *contagion* were his main considerations.

Meanwhile, at the IMF, Managing Director Horst Köhler, who also came to office in May 2001 with a strong dose of skepticism regarding massive bailouts, experienced increasing pressure to support an additional $8 billion credit for Argentina. The Fund staff were internally divided about whether to go ahead with the operation, while in informal briefings of the Executive Board Köhler gave the impression that he was not convinced that extra money was a good idea. But his second in command, Stanley Fischer, who had been intensely involved in dealings with Buenos Aires and who knew Cavallo well, was leaning in the other direction. After an internal debate among policymakers in the United States involving a number of cabinet members, the US Treasury informed its partners in the G7 that it had decided to support the augmentation. With this the deal was done. Yet it was widely recognized that lending more money to Argentina would be very risky, and that political considerations had been the deciding factor.[8] In a follow-up briefing of the Executive Board, Köhler now came out in favor of disbursing the money. I was upset by this state of affairs and informed Köhler in private that I would not support the proposal to increase the Argentine credit if the Dutch Minister of Finance agreed with me. I found out later that Köhler had been convinced by others that world financial markets could not withstand a crisis in both Argentina and Turkey. As it turned out this fear was unfounded, and the $8 billion extra money wasted.

On September7, 2001 the Fund's Board formally agreed to augment its credit to Argentina once again. Having reached the conclusion that this action was the wrong response to Argentina's plight, I stated that I could not support it. My Swiss colleague, Roberto Cippa, did the same. Of course, our protest did not change anything, as the overwhelming majority of votes were cast in favor of the proposal. It did, however, serve to give voice to severe doubts, which were shared with some of our colleagues and outside observers, about giving more money to a country that was following a completely wrong economic course.[9] In support of my position, I argued that most of the assumptions underlying the revamped Argentinean program were unrealistic. I pointed out that the program foresaw an increase in the primary budget balance (the deficit minus interest payments) of 6 per cent, which was surely a leap of faith considering that in the previous ten years the primary surplus had never been higher than 1.5 per cent. Besides, the wisdom of such a severe fiscal contraction in the midst of a deep recession was questionable. There were some other assumptions that were not credible, such as a recovery of exports despite an overvalued peso and a weak world economy as well as the presumed ability to regain access to international capital markets. I argued that it was highly unlikely that more credit would bring about a virtuous economic spiral for Argentina, as matters had been allowed to deteriorate for too long.[10]

By October 2001 it was clear to all and sundry that the additional IMF credit of $8 billion had made no impression on financial markets. Having arrived at this point, Cavallo announced that a rescheduling of Argentina's sovereign debt was needed. He stressed that it would be a voluntary operation and market-friendly. Again the rhetoric proved to be inaccurate. As the downward spiral of Argentina's economy continued, and withdrawals of bank balances became a flood, a bank closure was ordered and a ceiling placed on cash withdrawals. The resignations of Minister Cavallo and President de la Rua followed, amidst widespread unrest and violence. The next step in the drama was a declaration of sovereign default and flotation of the peso by the new President, Eduardo Duhalde, who had taken over on December 30, 2001. Fresh negotiations were started with the IMF, but months elapsed as political differences within Argentina, including a great reluctance by provinces to agree to restrictions on their fiscal autonomy, delayed decisive action. In the meantime, the banking system was in serious trouble and deposit-holders subject to the *corralito* (literally "playpen") – the restriction that had been imposed on cash withdrawals – became more and more upset, adding to the social unrest. In the end Argentina's credibility was badly damaged by its mismanagement of its economy and its dysfunctional political and judicial system.

With the economy in deep recession and the country in turmoil, the challenges facing the new government were of a magnitude seldom seen in modern times. Argentina's woes certainly went far beyond those that other crisis-ridden emerging countries had experienced. With its standard of living falling rapidly, poverty became a problem in what had always been the wealthiest country of Latin America. But the new government did little to improve the situation. It did not help that politicians and public alike, in looking for scapegoats, were bashing the IMF. But, while Argentina's problems were mainly of its own making, the Fund's record in trying to assist Argentina on and off over two decades is not a glorious one. It allowed itself to become embroiled in a power play in which its largest shareholder almost automatically took the side of its Latin American ally. And, since other creditor countries, while often critical, did not want to rock the boat, Argentine politicians banked on being able to obtain credit after credit from the Fund despite subpar economic policies.

The Argentine debacle has not always been interpreted in the same way. Looking back on the Argentine experience, US Treasury Undersecretary John Taylor has defended the decisions taken by the IMF. Instead of seeing a catastrophe, he perceives the episode as one in which contagion was averted, while underplaying the damage that was done to the Argentine economy and its people. In order to convince others of his position, Taylor carried with him laminated graphs showing how much more emerging market credit spreads had risen after the Russian collapse than after the Argentine default.[11] During a golf game with Anne Krueger (the IMF's number two) and myself, Taylor pulled out his laminated cards to illustrate his argument. I doubt that he succeeded in convincing Krueger, as she had shown herself to be a strong critic of Argentine's economic policies. In fact, in dealing with Cavallo's successors after taking over from Stanley Fischer, she became very unpopular in Buenos Aires and was still advised years later to avoid that part of the world.

What Taylor seems to have overlooked in interpreting his graphs was that the reason why spreads did not go up dramatically at the time of Argentina's implosion was that markets had already anticipated a default for quite a while. On a visit to Wall Street in August 2001, I was told quite bluntly by bankers that granting Argentina even more credit was not only a bad idea as such, but would be profitable for them as it would make it easier to pull out their money. Moreover, Taylor's claim of absence of contagion is exaggerated, failing to take into account Brazil's 2002 crisis, which was partly due to uncertainty created by the train wreck experienced by its southern neighbor. But what really is striking is Taylor's assertion that, in the period following the departure of Cavallo and de la Rua, he "from time to time" negotiated with the new Argentine Minister of the Economy, the dour but competent Roberto Lavagna, *on behalf of the IMF*.[12] This, he states, seemed to be appreciated by both Argentina and the Fund. This unusual claim, whether accurate or not, can only help to strengthen the widespread impression among the IMF's critics that the United States has been overwhelmingly running the show at the Fund. It is one thing to work vigorously behind the scenes, but another to state quite publicly that the United States is negotiating on behalf of the IMF and that both parties are content with this. Remarkably, little attention has been paid to Taylor's "revelation," perhaps because it is something many observers think they already know.

Restructuring the debt

The situation worsened in 2002. The economy, which had already shrunk the previous year, continued to head downward. A serious banking crisis developed, no progress was made in restructuring the stupendous external debt, and no attempt was made to negotiate seriously with the IMF. The bleak economic situation, compounded by internal political wrangling, widespread corruption, and a dysfunctional court system, created an atmosphere of great uncertainty and anger among the population. Poverty rose perceptibly and periodic violence erupted. Abandoning the currency board allowed the peso to depreciate from parity with the US dollar to, eventually, a ratio of around three pesos per dollar. A run on the banks ensued. Deposits were frozen, which caused huge resentment. Measures to stabilize the severely undercapitalized banks were taken in a haphazard manner and Central Bank independence was compromised. A quick succession of Central Bank governors, including the respected former IMF staff member Mario Blejer, illustrated the disarray in the management of Argentina's economy. No fewer than twenty-two visits of Fund staffers to Buenos Aires took place in 2002, with the IMF desperately trying to reach agreement with President Duhalde and his aides on the resumption of an economic program. But the Argentine political rulers were not interested in an agreement that would constrain their actions, and blamed the Fund for their country's woes, sometimes in very strong terms. Foreign Minister Carlos Ruckauf declared that "the IMF is a tumor that should be removed."[13] Within the Fund, due to the poor staff performance in dealing with Argentina, a new point man was brought in for Argentina: Anoop Singh, a skilled veteran of the Asian crisis and not in any way beholden to Latin America.

Finally, cooler heads prevailed and a compromise was reached in early 2003 on what was termed a transitional program with the Fund, with limited conditionality and lasting only six months (the presidential elections were due in May). This minimalist program basically served to roll over $3 billion that Argentina had to repay to the IMF and which it had earlier threatened to renege on. Although the Fund's Executive Board went along with the compromise in January, five directors from smaller industrial countries, including my successor Jeroen Kremers, withheld their support. Intensive lobbying had taken place within the G7 in the run-up to the January meeting, with the United States again switching position from firm to soft, to the chagrin of IMF Managing Director Köhler. Allan Beattie commented: "the Argentines dialed 1-800 –BAILOUT and the G7 made the IMF take the call."[14]

Argentina's tactic of issuing threats had paid off, establishing a pattern that was to be continued under the presidency of Nestor Kirchner, who was elected in May 2003. The left-leaning populist Kirchner, feeling strengthened by a recovering economy, was in no mood to bend to the highly unpopular Fund. He gave instructions for Argentina to default deliberately on its debt to the IMF in September, missing a scheduled repayment of around $3 billion. A "solution" was found by providing Argentina with a new Fund credit of almost $13 billion, to be disbursed over a three-year period. This amount exactly matched the repayments Argentina had to make in the coming three years, once again demonstrating the willingness of the Fund's largest shareholders to avoid any out-of-control conflicts with Buenos Aires. Policy conditions were again substandard, with only some slight fiscal adjustment envisaged and a commitment by Argentina to compensate the (mainly foreign-owned) banks for losses incurred following the abolition of the currency board. Clearly Argentina had again successfully applied its brand of brinkmanship. Defending himself in public for accepting the latest deal, Köhler observed that, while "in Germany some may feel I am too much in the camp of the Americans," he was not beholden to any single member of the Fund but owed his duty to his mandate, this being "the Fund and its role in the global economy."[15] At the same time, Argentina's promise that it would soon present a plan for a record comprehensive rescheduling of its foreign debt was greeted positively, although the expected huge discount, or *haircut*, was making private creditors nervous.

Argentina's proposal for restructuring its colossal debt was unveiled at the annual meetings of the IMF and the World Bank held in Dubai in late September 2003. Although it contained no real surprises, its terms were at least as tough as had been anticipated by creditors. The bulk of the record $94 billion of defaulted debt was owed to private creditors (mainly bondholders) with only $5 billion consisting of bilateral official debt, which was to be treated separately. Investors were shocked at the proposed *haircut* of no less than 75 per cent,[16] and it would take another year and a half of wrangling before a deal was finally reached, with an exchange of defaulted bonds against newly issued paper worth around thirty-five cents on the dollar. Eventually 80 per cent of holders of Argentine bonds accepted the offer. The "holdouts" were told in no uncertain terms that they would get nothing. On the way to this outcome, hailed in Argentina as a "triumph," a series of confrontations occurred. Within the IMF, executive directors became increasingly agitated about Argentina's patchy performance under the program agreed in September 2003. On one occasion eight directors, this time also including G7 members Italy, Japan, and the United Kingdom, abstained from supporting a disbursement under the credit. But, since the remainder of the Board had two-thirds of the vote, the payment was made. An interesting development was the turnaround by Italy.

Up until the restructuring proposal Italy had been among the staunchest supporters of Argentina, possibly in view of the large numbers of Argentines with Italian ancestry. But Italian residents, mainly households, held 16 per cent of all Argentine bonds, which meant that individuals would suffer large losses. This led to a different political calculation in Italy, which then became one of the sternest critics of the policymakers in Buenos Aires. President Kirchner responded to this criticism by telling Italian bankers that "you swindled your retirees by selling bonds that were already virtually worthless because [Argentina] was in a state of collapse."[17]

President Kirchner's domestic popularity rose to great heights as the Argentine economy rebounded strongly, reaching growth rates of up to 9 per cent. This remarkable outcome was due only in part to improved macroeconomic policies, owing much to the vast reduction in interest and amortization payments resulting from the jumbo debt restructuring, as well as to an undervalued exchange rate which provided a strong boost to exports. Although inflation was becoming a problem, official figures showed a rate of price increase of only around 9 per cent, the numbers having been kept artificially low by changing the method of calculation. Any criticism of this manipulation was declared taboo. When I visited the likable then Governor of the Argentine Central Bank, Martín Redrado, in June 2008 the word "inflation" never passed his lips. In the meantime, Kirchner continued to denounce the IMF, including the Fund's new Managing Director, the Spaniard Rodrigo de Rato, for critical remarks about Argentina.[18] In a move to rid itself entirely of the Fund's influence, Argentina paid back its debt to the Fund in one shot in January 2006, following Brazil's example. In the following years relations between Argentina and the IMF remained very poor, with policymakers in Buenos Aires even refusing to allow annual examinations of its economy, so-called Article IV consultations, which are obligatory under the Fund's statutes. Argentine intransigence continued under the presidency of Cristina Fernandez de Kirchner, who took over from her husband in October 2007. And an internal squabble led to Central Bank Governor Redrado's resignation from the Central Bank in 2009 when Ms Kirchner laid claim on part of the bank's international reserves. A more conciliatory stance was adopted toward foreign bondholders, since Argentina wanted to regain access to capital markets. In the event it offered the "holdouts" from the mega debt restructuring the same terms as those which had been accepted by the majority of claimants in 2005.

The IMF's poor performance

Over the years IMF surveillance over Argentina's economy did not meet its usual standards, especially with respect to the *exchange rate regime* and *fiscal policy.* This lack of rigor was a contributory factor to Argentina's journey from poster child to basket case. While there were some doubts among the IMF staff about its viability, the currency board introduced in 1991 was understandably given the benefit of the doubt in view of the severe bouts of hyperinflation that had preceded it. Although there was a body of literature[19] arguing that currency boards ought to be temporary regimes and should be exited in favorable times, the appropriateness of a currency board for Argentina was not challenged once it was in place. After Brazil had devalued in 1999 there were strong reasons for the Fund to look closely at the viability of the peso's 1:1 link to the dollar. Three explanations for the IMF's reluctance to highlight (at least internally) the peso's growing real appreciation come to mind. First, the doctrine that a country can choose its own currency regime contributed to a "hands off" approach, enhanced by the Buenos Aires policymakers' refusal even to discuss any alternatives. Second, there was a fear that abandoning the currency board would be a risky operation and could contribute to contagion. And third, political considerations, especially among United States officials, also played a role in giving Argentina the benefit of the doubt time and again. The result was to strengthen Argentina in its resolve to stick to the currency board long after it made economic sense to do so, thus deepening the crisis once the balloon burst.

Surveillance of fiscal policy was also not stringent enough. As monetary policy has no real role to play when operating a currency board, fiscal policy was of particular importance in Argentina. Initially fiscal performance of the central government was more or less satisfactory, although the quality of the data provided was sometimes questionable. Moreover, the often weak finances of the provinces were not scrutinized in depth. Another gap in the Fund's surveillance was a lack of attention to so-called off-budget government operations, which contributed to a rise in Argentina's debt. This debt took off quite spectacularly around 1999 when election politics pushed up the budget deficit to around 5 per cent of GDP and the ratio of external (foreign currency) debt to GDP surpassed 50 per cent. While this was not particularly high for industrial countries, it was quite large for emerging economies like Argentina, whose access to international financial markets was much more uncertain. The Fund staff overlooked this important distinction. Even more serious was the Fund's failure to highlight the very negative development of Argentina's debt service, with its exploding debt and weak export performance producing a ratio of 400 per cent of external interest payments to exports from 1999 to 2001. This was clearly an unsustainable level, but IMF staff described it as just manageable when questioned about it in the Executive Board.

The IMF staff's surveillance of *structural policies* was more satisfactory. Structural issues in the areas of fiscal policy (such as widespread tax evasion), inflexible labor markets, and the social security system were identified early on. Moreover, the financial system was generally sound and supervision strong by emerging country standards (no-one can be blamed for not foreseeing that the financial system would be unable to deal with a mega crisis like that in 2001). The Fund, as well as the World Bank, provided extensive technical assistance in these areas, but the end result was generally disappointing, as the Argentine recipients were apparently not very eager to learn.

As in most IMF programs, surveillance and program design in Argentina were closely connected. The exchange rate regime was off limits, in line with the IMF doctrine that it cannot force a country to adopt a different regime. But the Fund could have made clear to Argentina that granting it fresh credits while its exchange rate was becoming seriously overvalued and its external debt was rising fast was not sustainable. For this reason alone the Fund should have pulled the plug earlier than at the end of 2001. IMF management avoided discussing the issue of contingency planning with its Board, even when asked about it directly, except to say that there was no "plan B."

The importance of fiscal policy was reflected in its prominent role in setting policy conditions for Argentina. If there was one large country where fiscal discipline was very much needed it was Argentina, because of both its inability to use monetary policy and its history of letting government finances get out of hand. The fiscal targets agreed with Argentina mostly lacked ambition in comparison with those for other countries under IMF-financed programs. Despite this lenient approach, Argentina failed to meet its agreed fiscal targets every year from 1994 to 2002. Moreover, the Fund frequently granted waivers for missed performance criteria, adjusting targets to "ease the pain," or negotiated a new program with relaxed targets. Similarly, targets for public debt were insufficiently stringent.

This leniency was also very much on display as regards structural measures. Reforms such as more flexible labor markets were, like fiscal discipline, very important for the successful functioning of the currency board. While the Fund staff were diligent in discussing those structural reforms essential for good macroeconomic performance with their Argentine counterparts, the actual programs contained only a smattering of structural conditions. Despite staff's persistent concerns about the lack of structural elements in the credit agreements, they were time and again overruled by IMF management, with the Executive Board following like sheep. Here again is an example of how lack of decisiveness and fears of upsetting the apple cart prolonged Argentina's problems and should have led to an earlier end to IMF involvement.

Argentine's creditors suffered a severe blow after having banked on receiving a bailout if the worst came to the worst. And Argentina banked on being saved by the IMF, as had happened in Korea and Brazil. As such, Argentina provides a case study of double moral hazard ending in tears. The IMF's soft approach in dealing with Argentina, giving it the benefit of the doubt virtually every time it failed to meet some of the conditions agreed on, generated a heavy dose of *debtor* moral hazard. Usually this does not occur when the Fund provides credit to its members, since it almost always responds to repeated failures to meet policy targets by cutting off its financing. Political leaders in Buenos Aires, who had become used to the depiction of their country as a poster child for economic policymaking, grew confident that the IMF would not enforce policy conditions as it had done in Asia. The discovery that it could get away with frequently breaching targets, and could escape from politically difficult structural measures, greatly contributed to the eventual collapse.

Creditor moral hazard was widespread. Investors, both private entities and individuals (among them small savers), were eager to buy government bonds issued by star performer Argentina. And, since recognition of a deteriorating economic performance was delayed and financial support from the IMF continued to the very end, investors continued to pour money into Argentina beyond the point of normal prudence. Professional investors started to withdraw their money from the late 1990s onwards, but households were still buying Argentine bonds, which provided attractive yields, even once warnings of default became louder. While overly aggressive bond salesmen can certainly be faulted for their actions, the incentive structure in the banking system promoted such behavior. Bond salesmen and loan officers are not rewarded for risk aversion, but, on the contrary, are expected to generate as many sales and loans as possible. It is supposedly up to the risk managers at banks to avoid excessive exposure to certain borrowers. In the case of providing loans to potentially weak debtors, limits are, as a rule, adopted to avoid excessive exposure. At the same time, during boom periods and whenever competitive pressure is strong, limits are often surpassed and risk managers frequently overruled. Bond sales are free of credit risk for the banks, who act as underwriters and secondary dealers, and handsome fees can be earned through this activity. Credit risk is transferred to the buyers of bonds, who in the case of Argentina (and some other emerging countries) are often individuals with little or no understanding of the risk they are taking on.

The combination of debtor and creditor moral hazard, for which the Argentine leaders, the IMF, and international bankers share the blame, produced a catastrophe. The worst financial crisis since the Second World War led to the largest sovereign default and debt restructuring ever. The Argentine population suffered severely, but a combination of improved policies and luck (a drastically lowered debt service and a commodity boom) produced strong economic growth from 2004 onwards. Among investors, small savers were badly hurt, whereas many large investors had withdrawn their money on time or had already written off their losses before the giant restructuring of 2005. For the IMF, the experience was a painful one with considerable damage to its reputation. In addition, the full repayment by Argentina of its outstanding debt to the Fund, following Brazil and later followed by other countries, reduced the IMF's income position to such an extent that it decided to sell some of its gold and invest the proceeds.

7
Turkey Stumbles

After the First World War, which heralded the end of the already much-weakened Ottoman Empire, Turkey attempted modernization under Kemal Atatürk. While some limited successes were achieved, Turkey remained a very poor country. Turkey was widely seen as the sick man of Europe for a very long time, being its least developed country and showing little dynamism. Corruption and military coups were distinguishing features. But things started to improve as North Atlantic Treaty Organization (NATO) membership transformed Turkey into an important strategic partner of the West, from which it benefited in its dealings with institutions like the IMF and the World Bank. The IMF extended its first credit to Turkey in 1961, and seventeen others were to follow. The World Bank and the OECD were also actively involved, but results were generally modest. This began to change around 1980 when Turkey's proactive Prime Minister, Turgut Özal, ushered in some important reforms. Still, the country's economic structure remained weak and its macroeconomic policies tended to veer off track regularly. Moreover, political instability discouraged foreign investment. By the time the crisis in Mexico broke out, Turkey was in a vulnerable position.

Two earthquakes

With its national income comparable to that of Indonesia, Turkey could hardly be considered a systemically important country. But, in a situation in which several emerging countries faced payments problems at the same time, the addition of Turkey to the ranks of potential defaulters constituted a real risk. Turkey entered the emerging country fray in late 1999 after a devastating earthquake struck the country. Already vulnerable on account of serious weaknesses in its economy, Turkey turned to the IMF first for natural disaster credit, followed by a regular standby of $4 billion (300 per cent of quota). Chronic high inflation (70 per cent in 1999) and huge budget deficits (more than 10 per cent in 1999) had contributed to slow growth and high unemployment, and poorly regulated domestic banks were used as a channel for large-scale funding by the government. Connected lending (lending by banks to companies with which they have close ownership relationships) was rampant, and badly run state enterprises gobbled up resources from the state budget. But a deep recession and renewed hopes for joining the European Union helped to create an atmosphere in which the coalition government in power at the time was willing to attempt a new stabilization program. The pillars of the Fund program were to achieve stabilization by using the exchange rate as an anchor, fiscal tightening and some structural reforms. The program contributed to lower inflation and interest rates at first, but the rigid exchange rate regime (a quasi-currency board) soon caused trouble. With inflation in Turkey remaining much higher than that of its main trading partners, the Turkish lira became seriously overvalued.

At the end of 2000 the economy was in serious trouble, triggered by a liquidity crisis within the weak banking system. Interest rates shot up, prompting the Central Bank to inject large amounts of money into the system, which resulted in Turkey breaching its monetary target under the Fund program. International reserves fell rapidly as the excess liquidity spilled over into capital outflows. A patch-up operation was put in place in December 2000 and additional IMF money provided, bringing total credit to $10 billion. Some executive directors, myself included, were unhappy that additional money was going to be provided despite the continuing overvaluation of the lira. IMF management had seemingly not yet fully absorbed the lesson that fixed exchange rates did not work for large emerging countries in a world with highly mobile capital. Moreover, the decision-making process, as experienced by members of the Executive Board, was not very transparent. In a highly restricted meeting (I usually objected to those, not only because of lack of transparency, but also because I had to write my own reports on such meetings), the Managing Director of the Fund briefed the board members on those parts of the revised agreement with Turkey that would not appear in the staff report (which itself was also not to be published). The (then) secret elements dealt with the process of closing insolvent banks, the excessive open foreign exchange positions of banks, and an attempt to limit public sector wages as a contribution to bringing down inflation. In addition, there was a so-called stop loss rule for supporting the lira exchange rate so as to avoid an excessive depletion of already meager reserves. When we asked what the maximum amount of foreign exchange sales was, the answer was that the Turkish side considered this information too sensitive to be provided to the Board. Some of us conveyed the message that this was not a satisfactory situation.

Not long after the program with the IMF had been tweaked, things went very wrong, resulting in a financial earthquake. The main culprit was the exchange rate, which had remained fixed at the insistence of the Turks despite a serious overvaluation of the lira. In a jittery atmosphere on the foreign exchange market, a bizarre political incident at the highest level[1] triggered a major sell-off of the lira. With rapidly falling reserves and extremely high interest rates to defend the pegged currency, the government threw in the towel in late February 2001 and let the lira float. It soon dropped by around 30 per cent against the dollar. Horst Köhler, who as the Fund's new Managing Director had inherited the Turkish problem, immediately welcomed the lira flotation. He helpfully added that continued involvement of private creditors was critical to the success of Turkey's adjustment program. Many foreign –mostly European – banks had not done their homework and had lent generously to Turkey without adequate risk analysis, and, as usual, now wanted to find the exit as soon as possible. While the devaluation solved the competitiveness problem, there remained enough to be concerned about. The new Finance Minister, Kemal Derviş, an astute former high official at the World Bank, was immediately faced with the near-collapse of the dysfunctional Turkish financial system. Many banks had to be rescued and insolvent ones closed, adding to the already huge budget deficit, which reached a staggering 20 per cent of GDP at one point, although it was much lower when the huge interest payments were not included (the so-called operational balance, which was the figure usually quoted).

Four major challenges had to be dealt with. The first was to ensure the rollover of the vastly increased government debt (gross external debt shot up from 59 per cent in 2000 to 93 per cent the next year, in part due to depreciation of the lira). Second, high real interest rates needed to come down. The third challenge was to replace the exchange rate with another anchor for monetary policy. Failing that, a vicious spiral of inflation and depreciation could take hold. Fourth, the banking system needed to be drastically restructured. Without a properly functioning banking system, any reform program stood no chance of success. As it turned out, the cost of cleaning up the banking system was extremely high, amounting to around one-third of Turkey's GDP. Although Derviş and his team did better than his predecessor in complying with the Fund program, they could not avoid a very deep recession: GDP fell by almost 10 per cent in 2001 while inflation shot up to previous high levels (almost 70 per cent in 2001). It did not help that real interest rates came down more slowly than expected. The only positive development was a turnaround in the balance of payments, with the current account showing a surplus. However, much of the improvement was caused by the collapse of domestic demand, with the result that deficits returned the following year as consumption and investment recovered. The lira plunged by 60 per cent against the dollar after it was freed to float, correcting a serious overshooting of the currency. A new monetary anchor was introduced in the form of a ceiling on the creation of base money (banknotes and banks' balances held with the Central Bank). Restructuring of the banking system proved to be an extremely tough assignment as many special interests were at stake. But the IMF countered this resistance by sending a highly skilled team to Ankara and to the financial center, Istanbul. Stefan Ingves, a dour Swede who often answered questions from Fund Board members with a simple "yes" or "no," was in charge of restoring confidence in the Turkish banking system. Ingves had wide experience with bank restructuring, including in his own country, which had gone through a severe domestic financial crisis in the early 1990s. The Fund team tackled the problems head-on. After many difficult negotiations a major overhaul of the Turkish financial system was launched. (In 2006 Ingves, whose success in Turkey had enhanced his reputation internationally, was appointed Governor of the Swedish Central Bank.)

In the meantime it became clear that additional financing for Turkey was needed to avoid a free fall of the exchange rate and a worsening of the overall economic situation. There was also concern that a Turkish collapse would lead to significant financial contagion, which, together with the troubles in Argentina, would pose a systemic threat to the global financial system. Moreover, the strategic location of Turkey and its role as an important NATO member contributed to strong support for aiding Turkey. Managing Director Köhler and his deputy, Stanley Fischer, were therefore determined not to let Turkey go under. In fact, in April 2001 when the IMF and World Bank spring meetings were underway, Köhler told several country delegations that came to see him (one of which was from the Netherlands; hence my participation) that he was optimistic that, after the recent injection of $10 billion, the revamped Turkish IMF program would be a success. At the same time, and to the surprise of his interlocutors, he added that if the program were to fail he would resign. In the event such a bold step was not necessary, although in the course of 2001 things got worse before they got better. Attempts to secure high rates of rollovers of foreign bank credits were disappointing, the external rollover rate reaching only 50 per cent in 2001. When these voluntary agreements with the banks expired at the end of 2001, they were not renewed.[2] Once again voluntary private sector involvement in an emerging country crisis had turned out to be a failure.

During the crisis year 2001 it was regularly suggested that Turkey would be better off by restructuring its government debt. Those in favor pointed to the Fund's indicators of external vulnerability, which provided an ugly picture. Turkey had become the second largest emerging country borrower, and its huge government debt required it to pay an astonishing 23 per cent of GDP in interest per year. While international reserves on a gross basis stood at $20 billion at the end of 2001, not all of which was usable, the net usable position (that is, subtracting Turkey's IMF borrowing) had turned negative by that time. Together with a number of fellow executive directors, I felt that an orderly restructuring was preferable to further large injections of IMF money. This would ease the dire government budgetary situation without the need for further punishing belt-tightening by the population. But resistance against restructuring was strong, on the side of Turkey as well as from IMF management. They preferred the option of providing more official lending to Turkey. Taylor[3] relates how, soon after he arrived at the US Treasury in mid-2001, Köhler asked the United States directly for a bilateral loan of as much as $10 billion for Turkey. There was enough money in the Exchange Stabilization Fund, which had been used in the Mexican rescue in 1995. But, in view of the political difficulties that could be expected and the United States' preference for letting the IMF take on the burden, Köhler and Derviş were told that no such loan would be provided. This is precisely what happened, despite attempts by other G7 countries to press for bilateral loans instead of ever-larger IMF support. Taylor[4] writes that this episode was a good lesson in how the Fund could be maneuvered into a position in which it would increase its lending when programs threatened to fail. And, since borrowers from the IMF could figure this out too, moral hazard was clearly present.

After the attacks on New York and Washington on September 11, 2001, the issue of more money for Turkey surfaced again. Derviş repeated a request for topping up IMF credit. Strong doubts existed in Europe about providing more money to a country whose performance was not very satisfactory. But, with the strong backing of the United States, IMF management was able to announce an increase of the Fund's credit of $5 billion in November 2001 as part of a new three-year program. Altogether $24 billion had been committed by the IMF, one of the largest support operations it had ever mounted. This was not the end of Turkey's requests for additional funds. After the AK Islamic Party won the elections in November 2002, its new Finance Minister, Ali Babacan, tried to extract huge bilateral loans from the United States. Taylor,[5] who was intimately involved in the negotiations, mentions that the initial demand was an astonishing $92 billion. But Turkey had a fair deal of leverage, given its proximity to Iraq and the United States' imminent invasion of that country. The United States was particularly keen on having military access to Northern Iraq through Turkey in order to open a second front while attacking from the South. In the end a package of US grants and loans was agreed with the Turkish government, but, to both governments' surprise, the Turkish Parliament narrowly opposed allowing American soldiers to enter Iraq via Turkey. All that remained was a small US loan to Turkey agreed in late 2003. In the meantime, the United States had also exerted pressure on the European Union to speed up the process of Turkey's accession to the Union. President Bush even called some European leaders to that effect, an action that was seen by many as meddling in Europe's internal affairs. One unofficial reaction was that the EU would be prepared to make Turkey a member as soon as the United States opened its borders to all Mexicans.

The 2002 IMF standby arrangement with Turkey was clearly an improvement over the 1999 program, which had centered on the exchange rate as a stabilizing anchor. This time base money ceilings were applied to perform the role of anchor, with the aim of bringing down inflation to 35 per cent by the end of 2002 and reaching 12 per cent by the end of 2004 when the program came to its end. The target was credible, especially since full operational independence of the Central Bank had been granted in May 2001. Moreover, the Turkish side committed itself to maintain a floating exchange rate and to a floor for net international reserves in order to avoid large-scale intervention. In addition, sales of foreign exchange to the market would be limited to preannounced auctions, thereby precluding haphazard intervention. Since the debt situation was so precarious – and debt restructuring was rejected as an option – Turkey was again prepared to accept severe fiscal restraint. The primary budget surplus was targeted at a level of no less than 6.5 per cent, much more than had been agreed with Argentina. The program also contained a host of structural reforms, leading to as many as thirty-four structural conditions. Most of these related to much-needed fiscal and banking sector reforms. The most important fiscal measures were setting goals for improving the efficiency of public expenditure, reform of the tax system, making state enterprises perform better, and reforming the notoriously inefficient civil service. As for reforming the banking sector, the aim was to increase banks' capital base and improve their loan risk evaluation. In addition, insolvent banks had to be closed down. Finally, regulation and supervision had to be further strengthened. All these actions were aimed at completing the restructuring of the banking system, which had been set in motion by Ingves and his team. The results turned out to be very positive.

Turnaround

Toward the end of 2002 the Turkish economy was improving rapidly: economic growth reached an impressive 8 per cent for that year, while inflation dropped to 30 per cent. While political uncertainty had increased with the change in government, there were no apparent effects on the economy. The Turkish economy continued to grow very fast in subsequent years (7.5 per cent on average from 2003 to 2006, before returning to a somewhat slower pace). Also spectacular was the fall in inflation to below 10 per cent after 2003. At the same time, the growth of imports outstripped that of exports, contributing to current account deficits in the order of 7 per cent of GDP after a number of years. But, since capital inflows grew very strongly from 2005 on, as Turkey looked increasingly attractive to foreign investors, official reserves soared to $77 billion (gross) in 2007. The IMF continued to be closely involved with Turkey after the successful completion of the 2002 program and agreed to a new standby credit of $10 billion in 2005. This program was geared toward consolidating good monetary and fiscal policies, also in the light of Turkey's EU ambitions. The primary fiscal surplus remained at 6.5 per cent of GDP in order to further bring down the public debt ratio. This was a success, and in 2007 the debt to GDP ratio had fallen to 50 per cent. Another reason for providing Turkey with fresh credit was that it had been making repayments to the Fund while the new arrangement allowed it to smooth its debt service. By the time the 2005 program expired in May 2008, much had been achieved. The Turkish economy had been significantly transformed, thanks also to the World Bank's efforts, but remained somewhat fragile and vulnerable to sudden changes in market sentiment. This was apparent in the difficulty the Central Bank had in bringing down inflation to below 10 per cent. Inflation targeting was introduced in 2006, but this turned out to be too soon. Targets for the first years were overly ambitious, therefore lacking credibility, and were missed three years in a row. And inflation returned to double digits in 2008. Since then Turkey has wavered between concluding another standby with the Fund and relying on its strengthened external position to ride out medium-sized storms. Although Turkey's economic problems have not all been resolved, its intensive engagement with the IMF has, all in all, been successful and has helped to improve its financial reputation significantly. Beyond that, its membership of the G20 has allowed it to directly voice its opinions in this important forum.

Tough love works

As the IMF had a long-standing close relationship with Turkey, thanks to the many programs that were concluded with Ankara, surveillance was generally of high quality. The major flaw in the staff's assessments was the assumption that a fixed exchange rate could be maintained despite an excessive appreciation of the Turkish lira in real terms. But the IMF staff may well have taken this position at the insistence of their management, who wanted to avoid a confrontation with the Turkish government. As a result, the 1999 program mistakenly accepted the Turkish desire to continue using the exchange rate as an anchor, with serious consequences. Had the exchange rate been allowed to float at that time, the severe recession of 2001 would most likely have been avoided. To be sure, there would still have been serious challenges, such as cleaning up the banking system, but the lethal attack on the lira would not have occurred. Once the peg had been given up and competitiveness restored, conditions for a viable program were in place. The success of the 2002 standby arrangement reflects this.

The Fund staff had also spotted the unsustainable budget and debt problem in a timely fashion. The 1999 program was quite tough with respect to *fiscal consolidation*, requiring an adjustment of around 6 per cent of GDP in the primary balance with the aim of stabilizing the public debt ratio. In Turkey's 2002 program with the IMF the main objective was to ensure debt sustainability. This was to be achieved by setting the primary fiscal surplus as high as 6.5 per cent of GDP and requiring new deficit-reducing measures of 2 per cent of GDP. In comparison to most other countries that had programs with the Fund, Turkey made a huge fiscal effort. It was prepared to swallow such bitter medicine since it was determined to structurally improve its government finances and to avoid defaulting on its debts. At the time there was a feeling among some (myself included) that the fiscal adjustment was so harsh that a default would have caused less hardship to the population. But, in retrospect, it can be concluded that Turkey succeeded in bringing about a remarkable turnaround of its economy through a combination of a floating exchange rate, a huge fiscal adjustment, and a major overhaul of the banking system. Another important plank of the reform effort was to make Turkey's Central Bank fully independent, a necessary condition for bringing down inflation permanently. *Inflation targeting*, in itself a good strategy, was introduced too early and the target was missed repeatedly in its first years. The lesson here is that inflation targeting requires careful preparation, which can take several years, especially in a country such as Turkey with a long history of high inflation.

The extent to which the *banking system* was rotten at its core was initially not fully clear, partly because of a lack of transparency. Nonetheless, the 1999 Fund program contained several conditions affecting the banking system. There was strong emphasis on strengthening supervision of the banking system and on cleaning up problem banks. Recapitalization of weak banks and closure of insolvent ones followed. Oversight of the notoriously inefficient state banks was strengthened, preparing for eventual privatization. This effort was in the domain of the World Bank, which provided a Financial Sector Adjustment Loan to Turkey for this purpose. Under the 2002 program with the IMF, banking sector reform was to lead to a full restructuring of the banking system. This included strengthening the capital base of private banks, improving their credit risk management, and closing down unviable banks. The state banks were to be further restructured and banking supervision improved further. All this took time, however, and by 2005, when a new program was agreed with the IMF, more needed to be done. Reforming the state banks proved to be an especially difficult task, but an IMF financial sector adjustment program (FSAP) conducted a few years later passed a positive verdict on reform of the Turkish banking system.

The negative attitude of foreign investors toward Turkey gradually diminished as its close involvement with the Fund was maintained and political stability increased. But for a long time foreign banks remained reluctant to roll over their claims on Turkey, and attempts to involve them in sharing the burden on a voluntary basis were initially not successful. Turkey regained access to international capital markets only after the IMF drastically increased the size of its financial support.

The overall judgment on the rescue operation for Turkey has to be positive. After an initial false start, and an unnecessarily deep recession, the Turkish economy turned around swiftly, despite very strong fiscal adjustment. As the bitter budgetary medicine succeeded in stabilizing and reducing the public debt ratio, confidence returned. In addition, Central Bank independence and a responsible monetary policy, a major cleanup of the banking system and stronger financial supervision, greatly transformed the Turkish economy. The sick man of Europe had thrown away his walking stick with the support of the IMF and was striding confidently forward, but had to remain careful not to stumble badly again. At the same time, Turkey's long-standing effort to join the European Union did not make much headway, as the existing reservations of Union members became stronger following increased concern about human rights issues and creeping Islamization.

8
Lessons Learned, Not Learned or Ignored

The Mexican crisis of 1995 spawned a debate on such issues as moral hazard caused by large bailouts, a lack of candor in IMF analyses, and a lack of transparency and poor data provision by debtor countries, as described in Chapter 1. Ways to reach a comprehensive debt structuring when most of the outstanding debt consisted of bonds rather than bank loans were also discussed. Some improvements were made in candor and transparency, but the really big issues such as moral hazard remained unsolved. Moreover, the Asian crisis erupted not long after things had calmed down in Mexico. And, following the shock of the Russian default in 1998, a wide-ranging debate on the international monetary and financial system developed. The Brazilian rescue of 1999 added to the urgency of the debate. This time a number of lessons were learned, but others were either not learned or ignored because they were too complex to solve or too politically contentious. The G7, still under *de facto* American leadership, continued to take the main initiatives, but emerging countries gradually raised the level of their voices in the discussions. On the European side, divisions between the main players remained a source of weakness. Common positions were seldom reached, strengthening the position of the United States despite the fact that its voting share in the IMF (17 per cent) was considerably smaller than that of the European Union members together (36 per cent). At the same time, the position of Japan showed a marked shift from habitually falling in line with the US stance to a much more critical tone regarding the IMF. This was mainly due to its judgment that the Fund had treated the Asian countries embroiled in the crisis of 1997–98 too harshly.

Anatomy of the main crises

To recapitulate the main features of the most serious emerging country crises, their main causes, the domestic and international responses, and the aftermath

in Mexico, Korea, Russia, Brazil, Argentina, and Turkey are presented here in
condensed form.

Six major crises

Mexico (1995)
Main causes: overvalued exchange rate, large external debt, weak banking system.
Domestic response: floating exchange rate, balanced macroeconomic policies,
reform of the banking system.
International response: large rescue operation: US loan and record IMF credit.
Aftermath: stabilization, no default, permanent improvement in economic per-
formance, but structural reform lagging.

Korea (1997–98)
Main causes: pegged exchange rate while externally vulnerable, highly lever-
aged corporate sector, contagion.
Domestic response: floating exchange rate, tighter monetary policy, structural
reforms.
International response: Unprecedented rescue package: IMF credit plus second
line of defense, foreign bank loans restructured.
Aftermath: quick turnaround, highly successful recovery.

Russia (1998)
Main causes: overvalued fixed exchange rate, persistent capital flight, weak fis-
cal policy, incomplete transition to market economy.
Domestic response: floating exchange rate plus inflation targeting, default on
domestic bonds.
International response: large IMF credits, after default cut off from capital markets.
Aftermath: no further IMF programs, recovery led by oil boom; private sector
learns a lesson, but it is soon forgotten.

Brazil (1998–99)
Main causes: overvalued exchange rate, large external debt, wrong macro policy
mix, contagion.
Domestic response: floating exchange rate plus inflation targeting, tight monetary policy, improved fiscal performance, very little structural adjustment.
International response: IMF packages plus voluntary rollover agreement with
foreign banks.
Aftermath: gradual improvement, better mix of macro policies, structural
reform lagging, new crisis in 2002 narrowly avoided with huge IMF package
followed by significant improvement.

Argentina (2000–02)
Main causes: overvalued exchange rate (currency board), unsustainable external debt, inadequate fiscal policy, weak financial system, weak institutions,
dysfunctional domestic politics.

Domestic response: initially austerity measures, clinging to currency board too long, giving up dollar peg in chaotic fashion, record debt default.

International response: succession of failed IMF programs, IMF and World Bank *de facto* rollover their claims on Argentina.

Aftermath: capital controls, deposit freeze, decimated banking system, depression, debt restructuring with huge haircut, poor relationship with IMF. Subsequently a strong recovery aided by undervalued exchange rate and commodity boom, return of inflation.

Turkey (1999–2001)

Main causes: overvalued exchange rate, public debt overhang, chronic high inflation, unsustainable fiscal position, dysfunctional financial system, weak institutions, contagion.

Domestic response: floating exchange rate, fiscal tightening, granting of Central Bank independence, drastic cleanup of banking system, structural reforms.

International response: IMF package, augmented several times, unsuccessful PSI.

Aftermath: initial deep recession followed by sharp turnaround, default avoided, major transformation of economy followed by strong growth.

If we compare these six cases, the Korean crisis represents a clear example of acute *liquidity* problems allowing the situation to be turned around quickly once Korea's leaders fully cooperated with the IMF. By contrast, the Argentine experience reflects a state of deep-seated *insolvency* which could not be solved by large injections of liquidity. The four other crises described here contained elements of both liquidity shortages and questions about debt sustainability. Besides these differences, a number of common features can be identified in these six major crises.

- In all cases, a fixed exchange rate was involved, which in five out of six cases was overvalued (Korea being the exception).
- In five cases excessive borrowing was an important cause, whereas in Korea the composition of the debt (mainly short-term) caused problems.
- In five cases a large share of external debt was denominated in foreign currency or indexed.
- International reserves were inadequate in five cases, and some were not usable. Brazil's reserves were initially adequate, but were bled in futile attempts to prop up its currency.
- All six countries had significant structural problems, with weaknesses in the banking sector the most egregious.
- Weak institutions and serious governance problems, especially in Argentina and Russia but also in Turkey, greatly complicated matters.

Lessons from the emerging country crises

The lessons to be drawn from the financial crises that hit emerging market countries between 1995 and 2002 are manifold.

- In several cases the state of the *domestic financial system* represented an accident waiting to happen. Due to poor supervision and lack of transparency, especially serious in Indonesia and Thailand, problems only surfaced at an advanced stage of the disease. Only in Brazil was the banking system in relatively good shape. The obvious remedy was to weed out insolvent and corrupt financial institutions and greatly improve transparency and supervision. This lesson, strongly communicated by the IMF, was taken to heart in most cases.
- It is dangerous to maintain a *fixed exchange rate* in a world with increasingly mobile capital, especially in emerging countries whose foreign exchange markets are generally thin. *Managed floating*, coupled with an *inflation target*, has become the preferred regime for large emerging countries. Currency boards are only viable under very special circumstances, such as those prevailing in Hong Kong, or for a limited duration, for instance as shock therapy to eradicate hyperinflation. This lesson was initially not consistently drawn by the IMF.
- Heavy reliance on *foreign borrowing* by governments, especially when trade openness is limited, as is the case in most of Latin America, is equally dangerous. The situation improved vastly after the crises, as countries either took this lesson to heart (Brazil) or received large inflows of foreign exchange through trade surpluses or capital inflows (Russia, enjoying an oil boom). Unfortunately, the lesson on excessive borrowing was missed by many countries in Eastern Europe in the 2000s and subsequently in the Euro Area (as described in Chapter 10).
- Orderly workouts of unsustainable debts need to be promoted to avoid Argentine-type disasters. Various schemes have been proposed and some adopted, but the matter has not been fully resolved.
- An adequate stock of *international reserves*, fully usable, is an essential first line of defense for emerging countries. Transparent information on reserve losses, provided with little delay, is an essential tool for providing early warnings of trouble. The quality of reporting of reserves has vastly improved in recent years, while emerging countries' holdings of foreign exchange reserves have ballooned, often far beyond what would normally be required as a first line of defense (Asia).
- *Capital account liberalization*, while in itself welfare-enhancing, should be introduced gradually and properly sequenced. Liberalizing short-term capital flows first instead of long-term transactions (Korea) can have serious

repercussions. Capital controls on inflows, if properly designed and not maintained too long, can help avoid future capital outflow problems.

- Financial crises, whether of a systemic nature or not (sometimes difficult to establish), should not be resolved through the provision of official finance alone, as this would generate unwanted *creditor* moral hazard. A degree of *domestic demand contraction* cannot be avoided in combating a serious financial crisis, unless such huge amounts of financing are available that a surge in inflation is likely to occur. Moreover, financing without adjustment will foster *debtor* moral hazard.

- *Involvement of private creditors* in resolving financial crises is highly desirable in order to limit moral hazard and to share the burden of solving the problem with the public sector. While the approach is still *ad hoc*, this lesson seems to have been learned.

- In a confidence crisis in which the national currency threatens to go into free fall, *foreign exchange intervention* has only a limited role to play. Monetary tightening will generally be more effective in stopping the bleeding. If executed skillfully, high interest rates need to be maintained only for a limited period in order to turn market sentiment around. The use of tight *monetary policy* in a crisis remains controversial, especially in academic circles, but is in practice acknowledged as an important ultimate remedy.

- *Fiscal policy* has a more limited role to play during a financial crisis, unless – as in the case of Russia and Turkey – a continuous lack of fiscal discipline stimulates capital flight.

- *Sound institutions* and good governance are essential elements in a successful longer-term strategy to achieve high economic growth. Countries enjoying both are less crisis-prone than others. While there is general agreement on this issue, carrying out structural adjustment remains one of the greatest challenges for underperforming countries.

Besides these lessons in the area of public policy, the major lesson to be drawn by the *private sector* was to improve the risk management of banks and the assessment by institutional investors of risk embedded in foreign bonds.[1] To the extent that these lessons were learned, this probably happened only after the Argentine collapse. More recently, imprudent risk-taking by financial institutions came back with a vengeance (as described in Chapter 9).

While the debate on modifications to the international financial system following the Mexican crisis was inconclusive and short-lived, the dual shock of the Asian and Russian crises triggered a much deeper discussion of possible reforms. An influential conference on reforms of the international financial and monetary system, organized in May 1999 by the IMF,[2] brought together prominent academics, policymakers, bankers, IMF senior staff members and a few Fund directors. The topics discussed included exchange rate regimes, the role of capital controls, and involvement of the private sector in crisis prevention and resolution, as well as financial assistance and the role of the IMF. While, as was to be expected, no full agreement was reached, Stanley Fischer, the IMF's First Deputy Managing Director and a highly respected former academic, drew a number of tentative conclusions in his closing remarks. He cited six areas of progress. The first was the introduction of official credit lines, which had great potential for crisis prevention, despite the criticism which had been leveled at it. The second area of progress was involvement of the private sector in financial rescue operations, although he admitted that PSI was more difficult to achieve than in the 1980s (the days of concerted action put into practice by De Larosière).[3] A third positive development was the establishment of the Financial Stability Forum (more about this in the next section), which was off to a good start. Fourth and fifth were greater transparency of the IMF and the setting up of international standards, such as for statistics. Fischer's final point was that changes in exchange rate systems, especially the movement toward floating rates in many emerging countries, alongside countries like Argentina which would continue to "peg very hard," was strengthening the international system. While Fischer was proved right about Argentina's intentions, the consequences would turn out to be catastrophic (Chapter 6).

The reform effort

The upheavals caused by the Asian and Russian financial crises not only triggered an intensive debate about their causes and the lessons to be learned, but also led to a number of important policy initiatives in the late 1990s. While this did not result in a major overhaul of the international architecture, as the building was considered to be sturdy enough to withstand more bad weather, a serious attempt was made to renew the wiring and plumbing. This effort was partially successful, bringing about some important modifications to the global system. There are two main reasons why no more was achieved. First, important differences of opinion remained on how to deal with the various problems. Not only was there no full agreement on the lessons to be learned – between advanced and emerging and developing countries, but sometimes also within the G7 – but political considerations also made full agreement difficult. Second, as the world financial markets stabilized after the series of crises and the global economy embarked upon a remarkably strong performance in the early 2000s, the sense of an urgent need to make deep-seated changes disappeared. "No reform without a crisis" has remained an uncomfortable truth throughout modern economic history.

Four major reforms were initiated in the aftermath of the various emerging country crises: improving the monitoring of the international financial system; establishing an IMF contingent credit line; creating a mechanism for orderly debt workouts; and streamlining collective action clauses in bond contracts. The first and last mentioned succeeded, but the contingent credit line was not a success and the workout scheme failed to materialize. A number of other initiatives that were taken showed mixed results. The first major initiative was inspired by a perceived need to get a better grip on the global financial system, following the Russian and LTCM scare of 1998. The G7 decided that a thorough examination of financial stability issues and recommendations for improvement were needed. Hans Tietmeyer, who led the German *Bundesbank* with a firm hand during the 1990s, was asked to do the job. His main recommendation was to erect a *Financial Stability Forum* (FSF), which would provide an international platform for discussing stability matters. Tietmeyer's proposal was swiftly adopted and the FSF started its work in April 1999. Membership was not limited to G7 countries, but also included others whose financial system was of a size and connectedness that could cause disruption globally. The non-G7 members were: Australia, Hong Kong, the Netherlands, Saudi Arabia, Singapore, and Switzerland. During its first four years the FSF was chaired by Andrew Crockett, the outstanding Scottish General Manager of the Bank for International Settlements (BIS). Working with a small secretariat of BIS staffers, Crockett burnished the FSF's reputation. Unfortunately, as the fear of crises disappeared, the FSF's role diminished, contributing to a lack of preparedness of those supervising the national and international financial system when the crisis of 2007 struck. In reaction to this situation, the FSF was upgraded to become the Financial Stability Board (FSB) ten years after its establishment. Its membership was extended to include all G20 countries. The IMF, the ECB and some other international organizations are also represented. The FSB has been heavily involved in finding common ground in the effort to reform the damaged international financial system in the wake of the global crisis which erupted in the summer of 2007.

At roughly the same time as the FSF framework was developed, the Clinton Administration launched a proposal to create a new IMF facility that could provide quick financial support to countries that were "innocent bystanders," hit by a crisis that had emerged elsewhere. The *Contingent Credit Line* (CCL) was intended for countries that were facing a sudden large outflow of capital as a result of contagion. A sudden stop of capital inflows, or a bout of capital flight, could wipe out a country's international reserves swiftly if it was not prepared to defend its exchange rate mainly through raising interest rates. The idea that countries following "sound" policies would be able to tap the IMF for large amounts at short notice and without policy conditions had a strong appeal for emerging countries. After Germany's reluctance had been overcome, the CCL proposal was put before the IMF's Executive Board.

Normally speaking, once there is agreement in the G7 on a proposal which also is broadly supported by emerging countries, its adoption by the Fund's Executive Board is a done deal. However, a number of especially important proposals, such as an increase in quotas or sales of gold, or the introduction of a new lending facility, require a majority of 85 per cent of the voting power in the IMF instead of the normally applicable simple majority. This special majority rule has worked very much to the advantage of the United States, which has a voting share of 17 per cent. It can, therefore, always veto any proposal requiring the Fund's "super majority." No other country or constituency (a group of countries pooling their votes) enjoys a similar position. But, by working together, countries and constituencies which together surpass 15 per cent of the total votes can also exercise veto power. This is seldom the case, but once in a while such a "coordinated" veto threat is used effectively as a bargaining chip. The CCL was such a case, and four non-G7 European constituencies, represented at the Fund Board by the Netherlands, Belgium, the Nordic countries, and Switzerland, who together could muster 16 per cent of the votes, used their potential veto power to bring about adjustments in the original proposal. Like Germany, these smaller European countries were concerned that access to the CCL would be too easy and thus contribute to moral hazard. They also shared Germany's preference to conclude precautionary standby arrangements, which would include policy conditions, for well-performing but vulnerable countries. Since Germany had already gone along – with mixed feelings – with the CCL proposal in the G7, the European "little Germanies," as a high US official once dubbed them, took it upon themselves to make the CCL a stronger facility, but without wanting to block it. Together with my colleagues from these countries, which included the long-serving Belgian Director Willy Kiekens, we caucused regularly to decide how best to achieve our aim. There was also regular but informal contact with the German side, who sympathized with our cause. We focused on making the CCL less automatic and on tightening its eligibility criteria. An example of the latter was to insist that countries who had not subscribed to the IMF's high standard for statistics, known as the Special Data Dissemination Standard (SDDS), would not be eligible to tap the CCL. This effectively prevented Brazil, which at the time was not applying a sound policy mix, from using the CCL. Since Camdessus as the chairman of the Executive Board was fully aware of the not so dwarfish "Group of 4" veto power, he soon conceded on this point. The CCL also did not become open-ended, as potential clients hoped, but was set to expire in 2003 under a sunset provision.

After the CCL's inception it was expected that the first candidate to tap it would be Mexico, which had indeed been following responsible policies, but remained vulnerable to contagion. While the United States and the IMF were clearly in favor of a Mexican request for a CCL, the Mexicans declined the offer. Most likely they considered that, while a CCL could provide Mexico with some comfort that it could deal with a sudden stop of foreign capital, an exit from the facility could erode confidence in its policies. This would be especially damaging if the Fund judged that Mexico was no longer eligible to use the CCL. It was this lack of a convincing exit strategy, as well as the possible fear of a "market stigma" attached to a CCL ("maybe the authorities know something we don't") that explains why the facility was never used. IMF management, eager to activate the new facility, but with Brazil ineligible to do so, also went looking for customers in Eastern Europe, but found no takers. Although the CCL lapsed, the idea of having a facility available at short notice to deal with capital account crises resurfaced, and in 2009 an improved version of the CCL, designated the *Flexible Credit Line* (FCL), was established.

The next major reform initiatives were related to *sovereign debt restructuring*. Recent experience had highlighted the disorderly process which followed many emerging country debt crises. There was a widespread feeling that a well-designed procedure for orderly workouts was needed. This idea had already surfaced shortly after the Mexican crisis, with proposals ranging from imposing a standstill or moratorium on debt service to an international bankruptcy mechanism akin to the United States chapter 11 procedure. At the time, none of these ideas garnered enough support to be placed on the policy agenda. But after the traumatic Argentine crisis of 2000–02, which resulted in the largest sovereign default in history, the notion of debt workouts surfaced again. Two proposals were rolled out more or less simultaneously. One was a plan for a comprehensive mechanism for restructuring the debt of governments that could no longer make regular interest and amortization payments. The other was narrower in scope, aiming at including collective action clauses in sovereign bond contracts that would make it easier to conclude debt workouts. Both proposals were discussed intensively within and outside the IMF. The management of the Fund supported both initiatives and pushed for a two-track approach, as the plans were complementary.

Soon after taking over from Stanley Fischer as the number two at the IMF in the late summer of 2001, Anne Krueger put forward a proposal for a *Sovereign Debt Restructuring Mechanism* (SDRM). Krueger's strong analytical yet practical approach to economic issues was reflected in the design of the restructuring mechanism. After concluding that there was a gaping hole in the plans for reform of the international monetary and financial system, she described the aim of the SDRM as being to promote the orderly and rapid resolution of unsustainable sovereign debt situations.[4] Pointing out that debtor countries usually waited too long to turn to their creditors to discuss a workout, Krueger suggested a number of incentives for governments to address their problems promptly. This would be the best way to return to a sustainable situation and for the problem country to return to economic growth. Most creditors would also benefit if the debtor acted quickly and before it had depleted its reserves.

Comparing sovereign debt restructuring with domestic workouts under US law, Krueger noted that, while there are similarities, there was one particularly important difference. Under chapter 11 of the US bankruptcy code, often considered a model for sovereign debt workouts, corporations can be liquidated if all else fails. But, as liquidation is not possible for sovereign states, chapter 9 of the code, dealing with municipalities, is a better example. As municipalities carry out government functions, there are important differences from the procedure for corporate bankruptcy, the most relevant being that there can be no liquidation.

Building on these considerations, the SDRM would have as its main features majority restructuring, a stay on creditor enforcement, protection of creditor interests, and priority financing. As to guiding the process, the IMF would play a central role. Working with a qualified majority (75 per cent was often mentioned during the discussions) would avoid the problem of holdouts who could act as free riders and demand full payment after agreement had been reached on a workout. Collective action among the whole range of creditors would provide an incentive for the debtor to reach an early agreement. A temporary stay on litigation by creditors in case of a default would avoid the disruptive effects of a race among creditors to seize assets. And, to protect creditor interests, the sovereign debtor would not be allowed to pay nonpriority creditors. There would also need to be an IMF-supported economic program to ensure that the country would follow policies that would help protect asset values, especially the depletion of its foreign reserves. The provision of new money, besides credit from the Fund, would also be part of the SDRM. With private creditors providing fresh money during a stay, a serious deterioration of the debtor country's economy could be prevented. This would help to bring about a quicker resumption of debt service payments. With the aim of making the SDRM as effective as possible, Krueger proposed that the IMF would play a central role, for instance by letting the Fund determine whether a country needed debt restructuring and by how much.

The Krueger plan, which became a formal proposal from the Fund's management, was ambitious. Although it initially had the blessing of the then Secretary of the US Treasury, Paul O'Neill, it soon ran into serious opposition, including from his Undersecretary, John Taylor. The main concern was that the Fund would become an international bankruptcy court with wide-ranging powers. The resulting loss of some sovereignty for member countries would be anathema to the United States Congress, and O'Neill later silently withdrew his support. Taylor was not silent on the subject, but made it clear that he did not support the SDRM. Since Krueger had been effectively appointed by the US Treasury to the number two position in the IMF, the first signs of disagreement within the US administration on the Krueger plan caused some confusion.

Executive directors informally sought clarification from Krueger, but were told that Taylor would come around. During discussions on the SDRM in the Fund Board explicit support came mainly from Europe, which was insufficient to proceed. Attempting to salvage its project, IMF management watered it down, but sufficient support remained elusive and the SDRM rode quietly into the sunset. Still, this was not quite the end of the story, as proposals were put forward for developing a voluntary scheme. The then Governor of the Banque de France, Jean-Claude Trichet, was the first to suggest establishing a *Code of Conduct* regarding sovereign debt rescheduling. Such a code was eventually adopted with the blessing of the private financial community and the G20. The code, officially known as the *Principles for Stable Capital Flows and Fair Debt Restructuring in Emerging Markets*,[5] is a useful initiative and can help to speed up debt restructuring. But, since it is fully voluntary in nature, it is far from certain that in a serious case of sovereign debt problems the code would be adhered to. So far this piece of "soft law" has not been put to the test with respect to systemically important countries, although it has been applied in the restructuring of debt in some small countries such as Belize, Cote d'Ivoire, and Liberia.

Without the SDRM, there was no longer a two-track approach to debt restructuring within the IMF. The focus shifted entirely to the introduction of *collective action clauses* (CACs) in sovereign bond contracts, which was pushed hard by the United States in the person of John Taylor. To help overcome the often serious complications in past attempts at debt restructuring because no agreement could be reached between bondholders, a number of clauses would be introduced into sovereign bond contracts. The main clause would allow binding majority decisions, making it impossible for a small minority of bondholders to torpedo an orderly debt rescheduling. Another clause would describe the manner in which debtors would engage with their creditors, such as government officials negotiating with representatives of a bondholder committee. The third clause would explain how the debtor would initiate the restructuring process and whether there would be a stay while the process was underway. This market approach, which was less ambitious than the SDRM, would, however, require each sovereign bond issue to be restructured individually. Moreover, it would take time for a critical mass of bonds with collective action clauses to materialize. (The terms of bonds already issued could not be changed.) At the same time, there was increasing recognition that CACs would over time be helpful in defusing dangerous and disorderly debt disputes.

It took some time to convince all interested parties to accept the introduction of CACs. Creditors worried about an increase in cost due to changes in contracts, while emerging countries expected that their borrowing costs would go up. To get the process moving, the G7 countries adopted an action plan that included a strong endorsement of CACs in April 2002. The G7 then followed up with a pledge to include CACs in their issues of sovereign bonds outside their own countries. The practical importance of this promise was limited, as none of the G7 countries, with the possible exception of Italy, could be envisaged as ever needing a debt rescheduling. Its significance lay in demonstrating to emerging countries that the rich countries were not discriminating against them. The United States had once again taken the lead in introducing a new element into the international monetary system. Along with Taylor, Randy Quarles, a former American executive director at the IMF who had moved to the US Treasury, was intensely involved in promoting CACs. On the side of the emerging countries, Agostín Carstens, then the Mexican Vice-Minister of Finance and also a former IMF executive director, played a leading role in getting CACs accepted. Mexico indicated in early 2003 that it was ready to issue a government bond that included CACs. But it wanted something in return, and successfully asked the US Treasury to clearly express its opposition to the SDRM, which had not yet been fully buried. Subsequently Mexico floated the first government bond containing CACs in February 2003. To the surprise of many, there was no extra cost involved and the loan was oversubscribed. A raft of other countries followed. But, as was not discovered by many observers until 2010, a number of smaller European countries, such as Ireland, had not adopted the collective action clauses approach, complicating matters within the Euro Area (treated in Chapter 10).

While the reform effort launched after the string of emerging country crises brought about some important changes in the international monetary and financial system, these were upgrades of the plumbing and wiring of the international financial architecture instead of a complete overhaul. The main improvements were better international cooperation by means of erecting the FSF and the widespread adoption of collective action clauses in bond contracts. Other, less important, changes, which included limiting the size of exceptional access to Fund credit, were swept away when the next big crisis hit in 2007. Streamlining policy conditionality, introduced in 2002, was a positive step, but initially did not help much to improve the IMF's image as a strict and intrusive taskmaster. And the failure to agree on a comprehensive framework for sovereign debt rescheduling after the US sank the project left a bitter taste with many European policymakers, who had not forgotten that the United States had also shot down the proposal to give the IMF jurisdiction over capital transactions.

In the meantime, the strong performance of the world economy, which on average grew by an impressive 4.1 per cent between 2000 and 2007 against an average of 2.9 per cent in the 1990s, created a climate of optimism in which neither global imbalances nor financial sector fragility were a major preoc-cupation. Against this background of steady and high global growth, increas-ingly fueled by emerging countries, low unemployment, and some creeping but not soaring inflation, the financial firestorm that broke out in the summer of 2007 came totally unexpected for all but an unhappy few.

9
A Global Firestorm

The global financial community had been lulled into complacency. The world economy was humming along at a fast clip, financial markets remained generally calm, and private financial institutions were making impressive profits. The International Monetary Fund was running out of clients and suffering from an identity crisis. Suggestions that the Fund was no longer needed, or was at best useful as a provider of analyses and statistics, were becoming commonplace. And the IMF itself failed in detecting signs that the global financial system was becoming dangerously vulnerable. It was certainly not alone in missing the onset of a new and truly frightening crisis that threatened to bring down some of the world's largest banks and in its wake burn to ashes large swaths of other parts of the economy. But there were a few voices that had issued well-argued warnings of a possible financial cataclysm. William White, the perceptive Canadian-born Chief Economist of the Bank for International Settlements (BIS), was on record as highlighting the dangerous course the global system was taking. As an experienced central banker, he was sensitive to the fuel that excessive liquidity creation was providing to asset markets. Moreover, he issued repeated warnings about the increasingly obscure securitization practices and the dubious role of rating agencies.[1] But White's admonitions mostly fell on deaf ears. At the IMF, apparently following the line taken by the Federal Reserve, rapid growth of monetary aggregates and credit was largely ignored. And it was this easy availability of cheap money that allowed the housing boom in the United States to get out of hand, leading to widespread foreclosures and securitized mortgages becoming toxic. Nouriel Roubini, an original thinker from the Stern School of Business at New York University, at an early stage predicted that a dangerous housing bubble had developed in the United States and that it was going to burst. His repeated warnings earned him the sobriquet Dr Doom. At a talk Roubini gave at the IMF in 2006 he warned of an impending collapse of house prices, foreclosures, and other misfortunes. I was impressed by his predictions, but got the impression that most of the audience thought Roubini a *Cassandra*. Intriguingly, a year earlier Raghurum Rajan, then Chief Economist at the IMF, had warned against the buildup of excessive risk in the financial system in an address to a gathering of the world's foremost central bankers.[2] This was apparently a completely private view, as it is not to be found in a single official Fund publication. To be sure, the IMF had for a long time warned about global imbalances (the combination of very large current account deficits in the United States and excessive surpluses in China and oil exporting countries), but it never sounded a critical note on developments in the American financial system, from which the catastrophe originated. It can be argued that, even if the IMF had joined the few dissenting voices, a crisis would still have occurred, but its depth and spillovers would likely have been more limited. And, without a doubt, if the Federal Reserve and other American financial supervisors plus their European counterparts had taken timely preventive action, the course of events could have been quite different. But it has to be kept in mind that going against the conventional wisdom, which strongly supported a lightly regulated system, especially in the United States and the United Kingdom, requires not only courage but also very impressive powers of persuasion.

An unquiet day in August

As the vast majority of the world's financial activities are conducted in the Northern hemisphere, the month of August is usually a boring one for financial markets. Masses of people head for the beaches and mountains. Financial executives, traders and policymakers take a break from the hectic activities that occupy them for much of the rest of the year. But once in a while a financial fire breaks out in the middle of summer that has suntanned CEOs, ministers of finance, central bank governors and IMF officials rushing back to their workplaces. And when, in August 2007, the first signs of a widespread liquidity crisis appeared in the United States and the advanced countries of Europe, shock waves reverberated around the world.

August 2007 began quietly. While there had been some worries earlier in the summer about the state of the housing market in the United States, the general opinion remained that, except for some short-term blips, house prices in the US could only go up. Some eyebrows had also been raised because of the extension of easy mortgage financing, especially to individuals with questionable creditworthiness. In addition, some smaller banks and mortgage financiers in the United States had gone bankrupt. Whereas this would have rung alarm bells in other countries, such events were viewed without panic in the United States, where large numbers of small financial institutions go under every year. Other signs of impending disaster – such as the ballooning of credit derivates and banks' massive evasion of capital requirements through off balance sheet transactions, as well as increasing risks of contagion and recession – were down-played or ignored by market participants. Things had been going smoothly for so long that the optimistic and risk-taking personalities operating in Wall Street and other financial centers seemed incapable of envisaging a meltdown scenario.

All this changed dramatically in the (European) morning of August 9, 2007. Suddenly money markets started to seize up, first in Europe and then in the United States, the actual epicenter of the crisis. What triggered the severe market reaction was the discovery that a number of European investment funds and banks had exceptionally large exposures to US *subprime mortgages*. These mortgages, extended to low-income or even no-income homeowners, had been packaged with other mortgages and sold off to investors worldwide. Amazingly, the senior tranches of securitized mortgages had been declared to be of AAA quality by the major credit rating agencies. A herd of American and European investors took the favorable ratings at face value while looking for higher-yielding investments than low-interest bonds. Other categories of assets were also massively securitized, such as credit card debt, auto loans and student loans. All in all, such *asset backed securities* (ABS) had become an important source of profits for banks, as selling them allowed the banks to free up room for extending more credit. This process of *overleveraging* led to unhealthy ratios of loans to capital. As often happens in markets, a process that has gone on too long can abruptly come to a halt when a certain threshold of fear is surpassed. Financial markets operate in a climate of uncertainty in which – as is well known – greed and fear battle for the upper hand.

By August 9, fear had started to dominate. As a result, banks became distrustful of each other, withdrawing interbank lines and freezing credit to other clients. Interbank lending rates shot up, reflecting the wholesale drying-up of liquidity on money markets. Many banks in Europe had difficulty covering their financing need in US dollars, which sharply pushed up interest rates in the US money market. The European Central Bank (ECB) was the first public institution to react to the unfolding liquidity crisis, soon followed by the Federal Reserve and the Bank of England. On August 9, when the affable and experienced head of the Market Operations Department of the ECB, Francesco Papadia, got wind of the dramatically changing situation, he realized that swift action was needed to avoid "an infarct of the payments system."[3] Once alerted to the dangerous development, Jean-Claude Trichet, who had taken over from Wim Duisenberg as president of the ECB in November 2003, immediately sprang into action. He contacted the national central banks that are part of the European System of Central Banks (ESCB) and whose heads, together with the six executive directors of the ECB, make up the decision-making *Council* of that body. It was quickly decided to drastically increase the amount of liquidity that the ESCB routinely provides to banks through its open market operations.

Four huge operations were conducted in the early days of the liquidity crisis. Still the pressure continued, reaching an initial peak on August 16, when widespread aversion to taking risks triggered sharp declines in the prices of a wide array of assets, such as stocks and bonds, and caused convulsions in foreign exchange markets. The Fed and the Bank of England likewise stepped up their liquidity support to the markets in spectacular fashion. This helped to ease market jitters, but the situation remained tense for a long time, as banks were very reluctant to lend to each other given the uncertainty about the extent to which their usual counterparties were carrying large amounts of subprime assets on their books.

The first phase of the global firestorm of 2007–09, an acute *liquidity crisis*, lasted until early 2009. Interbank spreads (the difference between the London interbank rate and the benchmark government short-term interest rate), a good indicator of money market tensions, which had reached more than 4 per cent for the dollar and somewhat less for the euro (against a fraction of a per cent under normal conditions), did not fall steeply until 2009. During this period major central banks had taken exceptional measures to combat the extreme drought in money markets. Besides providing banks with unprecedented amounts of credit, they drastically lowered their lending rates – in spectacular coordinated fashion on one occasion – to close to zero and introduced a host of new lending facilities. The Fed, under the guidance of the softspoken former academic Ben Bernanke, was especially creative in developing new instruments. Central banks tend to provide the banking system with short-term money, often only on an overnight basis. But, in view of the persistence of the liquidity problems, the Fed started to provide loans for longer periods, first for around a month and later for even longer (the so-called Term Auction Facility), while the ECB did the same under its policy of Long-Term Repro Operations, which eventually included the provision of liquidity for up to a year.[4] Another important step taken by the major central banks was to relax their collateral requirements, making it easier for banks to borrow very large sums. The Fed established a Term Securities Lending Facility (TSLF), from which it supplied highly liquid Treasury securities to primary dealers (market makers) against collateral which included mortgage backed securities of "high" quality. The American Central Bank also provided dollar swap lines to the ECB, the Bank of England and the central banks of Canada and Switzerland, so that they could lend on dollars to their dollar-starved banks. These actions constituted a coordinated response by central banks to renewed tensions in money markets, agreed at a secret meeting at the margins of a G20 gathering held in Cape Town in November 2007. Continued close cooperation between major central banks proved to be crucial in defusing the dangerous liquidity crisis which had swept across the globe since the ostensibly quiet beginning of August 2007.

Solvency at stake

Liquidity crises are dangerous, not only because they cause credit to dry up, but also because they can rapidly morph into a *solvency crisis*. This is clearly demonstrated by the experience of two mortgage lenders on both sides of the Atlantic Ocean in late 2007. First, the largest American mortgage lender, Country Wide Financial, went bankrupt in tumultuous circumstances. Soon after, a sizable British mortgage lender, Northern Rock, experienced a bank run. Northern Rock was initially saved from a quick demise through a $50 billion loan by the BoE and an even larger guarantee extended to depositors. After much debate and recrimination, the mortgage lender was nationalized. Both Country Wide and Northern Rock had relied heavily on funding themselves in the interbank market, which meant that, if doubts about their solidity were to arise, they would quickly have to find other sources of finance. Since their short-term funding needed to be renewed constantly and their mortgage loans had maturities of decades rather than years, they were operating on the basis of a very risky business model, one that should not have been acceptable to bank supervisors. Other, sometimes much larger, vulnerable banks and shadow banks (nonbank financial institutions behaving like banks) on both sides of the Atlantic were to get into trouble in large numbers during the course of 2008.

Thus, the second phase of the global firestorm consisted of a series of *solvency crises* that rocked the financial system to its foundations. The first severe crisis of confidence involving a Wall Street firm surfaced in March 2008 with the near-demise of the investment bank Bear Stearns, whose excessive risk-taking led to a sudden stop of its access to money market financing. Since it was judged to be too *interconnected* to fail, if not too big to fail, a rescue operation was arranged with the help of the Fed. The Central Bank stepped in by taking on $29 billion of Bear's dubious assets as collateral. It also acted as intermediary in making banking giant JPMorgan the "proud" owner of the troubled, relatively small, investment bank at a bargain price. While most stakeholders sighed with relief, some observers felt that saving Bear Stearns (and Northern Rock) generated serious moral hazard and should not have occurred. One of the most outspoken critics of the rescue turned out to be former Fed chairman Paul Volcker, who described the Central Bank's intervention as taking actions "that extended to the very edge of its lawful and implied power, transcending certain long embedded central banking principles and practices."[5] But the majority view among policymakers and academics (market participants were delighted by the swift action of the Central Bank) was that, in a very serious crisis, moral hazard considerations had to be trumped by stability considerations. The point is made clearly by the person most closely involved in deciding the fate of Bear Stearns, Henry Paulson, who was US Treasury Secretary at the time. His judgment call was "that the risks to the system were too great" to let the investment bank go under.[6]

It is easy to criticize policymakers for some of their decisions taken in response to the burgeoning crisis. A fair evaluation should take into account that in fighting financial fires, especially when the danger of market panic looms, decisions have to be taken quickly (often during a weekend) in the face of uncertainty and a lack of clarity. In the film documentary *The Fog of War* (2003) the protagonist, Robert McNamara, who served as the US Secretary of Defense during part of the Vietnam War (and later became president of the World Bank), explains how difficult it is in a combat situation to ascertain all the facts necessary to take the right decision. The "fog of war" is a military term used to describe the level of ambiguity in situational awareness by participants in military operations.[7] Likewise, a "financial crisis fog" exists in which the decision-makers are not in possession of all relevant information and do not know the extent of spillover effects of their actions. In such situations decision-making often becomes a matter of hasty discussion and quick judgments. (Fortunately, the actions taken by governments and central banks during the global firestorm were much more successful than those that characterized the war in Vietnam.) Following the Bear Stearns scare of March 2008, the fog seemed to thicken as one financial institution after another in the United States threatened to go under. The so-called monoline insurers (companies who specialize in bond insurance) were the first who had to be supported to avoid disruption of the bond market, followed by a host of large Wall Street firms which were teetering on the brink of insolvency.[8]

From bad to worse

While the news coming out of Wall Street, and increasingly from European financial centers, continued to worsen, trouble was brewing in Washington DC. The American capital is not renowned for its private financial institutions, but it is the home of two *government sponsored entities* (GSEs) which in the summer of 2008 were on everybody's lips. Popularly known as Fannie Mae and Freddie Mac, they are enormously important in buying and guaranteeing household mortgages, which they finance by issuing securities. Together they have more than $5 trillion in loans outstanding, some 40 per cent of the US GDP. Although privatized, they have retained some of the characteristics of public enterprises and have enjoyed an *implicit* government guarantee. And, since investors were convinced that in the event of losses the government would step in to bail them out, they bought huge amounts of Fannie and Freddie's securities, known in the market as *agency paper*. Since this paper offered a somewhat higher yield than US Treasury securities (typically 50 to 80 basis points) and were seen as secure investments, they were popular with investors at home and abroad looking for a safe way to remain liquid. Among these investors were foreign central banks, which had amassed hundreds of billions of dollars in agency paper as an alternative to lower-yielding Treasury notes. As the poor quality of mortgage backed securities, despite their AAA ratings, was increasingly recognized, questions about Fannie's and Freddie's creditworthiness became acute. Heavy losses by GSEs would not only erode their domestic funding, but would also scare away foreign investors, including such institutions as the Chinese Central Bank and other official holders of large amounts of agency paper, which their American banking advisors had been strongly promoting up to the end. If foreigners were to actually dump their holdings of GSE paper and switch out of the dollar, the international monetary system could be in serious trouble. Secretary Paulson was acutely aware of this possibility, and was taken aback to learn that Russian officials had suggested to their Chinese counterparts that they should force the US government to bail out the GSEs by selling large amounts of agency paper.[9] No doubt this knowledge hastened the decision to put together a massive rescue package for the troubled Washington lenders, who had earlier been racked by accounting scandals. While receiving a staggering $200 billion credit line from the US Treasury, they were at the same time placed in receivership, their management dismissed and shareholders wiped out. Here, finally, was a blow of some sort against moral hazard. But Fannie and Freddie were left intact as the difficult decision on how to reshape them was pushed forward.

Next in line were some of the world's largest banks and the largest insurance company in the world. One after the other American banks reported huge losses, stemming from large holdings of what came to be known as *toxic assets* (mainly related to mortgage loans). Washington Mutual, the largest savings bank in the United States, Wachovia, and finally financial behemoths Bank of America and Citicorp hovered on the brink of bankruptcy. All were saved either by takeovers or by extensive government support. A major initiative was launched to help troubled banks, including many smaller ones, to clear toxic assets from their books. A $700 billion Troubled Asset Relief Program (TARP) was launched, which made an impression on markets, and was later modified to provide direct loans to vulnerable banks. In the meantime the insurance giant American International Group (AIG) landed in serious trouble. A London-based financial arm of AIG had aggressively sold trillions of dollars of *credit default swaps* (CDS), normally a kind of insurance against default of a debtor but bought by many investors as a side bet. This casino business threatened to blow up as the collateral posted by AIG lost value at an alarming rate and margin calls forced it to pledge additional assets. While AIG's problem was initially a shortage of liquidity, it soon found itself facing a solvency crisis. Large investment banks such as Goldman Sachs and Morgan Stanley were also experiencing increasing skepticism about their soundness, while Merrill

Lynch was saved through a takeover by Bank of America. In addition, mid-sized investment bank Lehman Brothers was eyed with suspicion by investors and its stock pushed down by aggressive short selling.

Lehman goes under

Support for unprecedented bailouts was eroding. On the one hand the need for avoiding a complete collapse of the financial system was recognized, but on the other hand the staggering amounts involved, and what was seen by the public as an arrogant attitude of "fat cat" bankers, raised deep concern and anger. Against this background, the failure of Lehman Brothers on September 15, 2008 unleashed a panicky reaction not only on Wall Street, but across a large part of the globe. Stock prices plunged, interbank markets dried up again, the commercial paper market came to a standstill and even money market funds experienced serious problems. Because of the severe reaction by markets in already deteriorating economic conditions, governments and central banks were plunged into a desperate mode of saving the system. The decision by the United States' top policymakers to let Lehman go under was heavily criticized. Many Europeans felt that, while taking a stand against moral hazard was in itself a good thing, doing so in such a volatile situation was unwise and was putting the global financial system at risk. But was Lehman's collapse a conscious decision to strike a blow against moral hazard? According to the main "decider," US Treasury Secretary Henry Paulson, neither the government nor the Fed had the powers to save Lehman. He has related in detail how, in close cooperation with Tim Geithner, then President of the New York Federal Reserve Bank, the various possibilities for saving Lehman were examined, as "a Lehman collapse would be a disaster," the firm being "bigger and even more interconnected than Bear Stearns."[10] Attempts were made to organize a takeover of Lehman, with the argument that the Fed did not have the powers to lend to Lehman, an unsupervised investment bank. Paulson has emphatically denied that he was "drawing a strict line in the sand about moral hazard" and has made a distinction between Bear Stearns, for which there was a buyer, and Lehman, for which after much effort no buyer could be found.[11] And Fed Chairman Bernanke, testifying before the *Financial Crisis Inquiry Commission*, apologized later for not being "more straightforward" with Congress in 2008, as this had created the impression that the Fed would somehow be able to bail out Lehman.[12]

Had it been possible, should Lehman have been saved? The answer is not obvious. In the short run the Lehman bankruptcy created immense turmoil and most likely deepened the recession in the United States and Europe. At the same time, in a medium to long-term perspective, the fact that a strongly interconnected, although not huge, investment bank[13] was allowed to go under did *de facto* draw a line in the sand as regards moral hazard. But the bailouts that soon followed undermined this effect. The most spectacular of these was the rescue of insurance giant AIG, which was considered so interconnected in the financial system that it had to be saved one way or the other. AIG's management had been a shambles and had vastly underestimated the liquidity risks it was running.[14] While this caused aversion, and although insurance companies were not part of the banking system, a decision was reached to have the Federal Reserve lend the gigantic amount of $85 billion to the wayward company, though at a punishing interest rate of 11.5 per cent. In the end the government poured a staggering $182 billion into AIG and became the owner of 80 per cent of its equity.

Why could the Fed save a company selling insurance, an activity completely outside its sphere of competence, but not an investment bank (Lehman), which, though not normally enjoying access to liquidity support by the Fed, was part of the regular financial system? Paulson has provided a number of explanations. First, he argues that "[t]here had been no legal basis to bail out Lehman."[15] In addition, he explains that the Fed's position was that it could help out AIG, since the insurer suffered from a liquidity problem and not a solvency problem, whereas Lehman was experiencing both. Further on in his book,[16] Paulson relates how Fed Chairman Ben Bernanke explained to Senator Christopher Dodd that an obscure section of the Federal Reserve Act enabled the Fed to support an insurance company under "unusual and exigent circumstances." In lending to Bear Stearns the same case had been made by the Central Bank. The narrative raises some questions. As is well known among market participants, central bankers, and supervisors, it can be quite difficult to ascertain when a crisis is "only" a liquidity issue. Moreover, as explained earlier, liquidity crises can easily slip into solvency dramas. In the case of AIG it remains unclear why it was necessary for the government to take over the ailing company almost completely if a solvency problem was not lurking around the corner. And, finally, if the provision giving special bailout powers to the Central Bank could be applied in rescuing Bear Stearns, which surely had a solvency problem, why was it not applied in the case of Lehman Brothers? It has been suggested that Lehman was allowed to go under because the mood in the US Congress had become highly critical of large-scale bailouts. But the political calculation had apparently changed when, soon after Lehman's demise, the systemically important insurer AIG found itself in serious trouble. This is not to say that Lehman should have been saved at all costs. The debate on whether it would have been preferable for the Central Bank to lend to the deeply troubled investment bank under its special emergency powers, and possibly have the government temporarily take over Lehman, is bound to continue for many years. One way of looking at it is that letting the medium-sized but highly interconnected investment bank go under caused serious disruption in the short run and was therefore experienced by many as unwise, whereas from a longer-term perspective it could be argued that a much-needed blow was struck against moral hazard. It may well be that over time the second argument will gain the upper hand.[17]

As the fires raged on, the Fed provided support to the commercial paper market, which is a crucial financial vehicle for short-term funding by corporations, while the United States government guaranteed the money market industry. For this purpose it used the Exchange Stabilization Fund (ESF) as a backstop, the first time that it had been used since the Mexican crisis in 1995. And, in a move that signaled the end of the existence of investment banks as separate entities, Goldman Sachs and Morgan Stanley were granted bank holding company status, enabling them to call on the Fed for liquidity support in the future. The price was that they would from then on be regulated as banks. But all these measures could not quell the unrest in markets, and equity prices kept falling. The Dow Jones industrial index, which had reached a high of 14,100 before the crisis, kept sliding until it hit bottom at around 6,500 in March 2009. With the situation in the United States in continuous turmoil throughout September 2008, negative news coming from Europe added to investor fears. Losses were piling up at banks in Britain, Germany, Switzerland, the Benelux, Ireland, and other countries. And, since the European banks were slower than their American counterparts in recognizing their bad assets, uncertainty about their actual losses made things worse. This was the backdrop against which finance ministers and central bank governors met during the annual meetings of the IMF and the World Bank in early October 2008. A special meeting of the G20 was also announced, with a cameo appearance by President Bush, who had earlier received the G7 representatives at the White House.

The tide finally turns

The atmosphere at the meetings was extremely somber and tense, with fears of a collapse of the global financial system and a depression akin to that of the 1930s constantly lurking below the surface. This was worse than the unusually jittery mood at the October 1998 IMF gathering shortly after the Russian default. The huddling policymakers were totally preoccupied by the contagion from the American firestorm in Europe and – to a lesser extent – in emerging countries. On Saturday October 4, 2008 the government heads of France, Germany, the United Kingdom, and Italy had met in Paris to develop confidence-building measures. The meeting produced only a vague communiqué about coordination. Market reaction was unfavorable, as the opposite of coordination was taking place, with Ireland unilaterally deciding to give a blanket guarantee on bank deposits. There was little choice for Britain but to follow this controversial example. It also decided to take large equity stakes in major British banks so as to avoid chaos in the all-important London financial markets. Other countries, including the Benelux and Switzerland, also proceeded to bail out their banks. Germany initially resisted similar measures for fear of creating moral hazard, but suddenly reversed its position (as it would again during the euro crisis of 2010) and announced that it was providing a large guarantee to save middle-sized Hypo Real Estate, in addition giving a blanket guarantee for bank deposits. What had become glaringly clear was that European banks had more or less blindly followed their American peers in gorging on subprime asset backed securities issued in the United States, all in a mad rush for yield.

These far-reaching measures taken by Britain and other European countries did not calm markets, but added to the already pervasive unrest and outright fear. The contrast between the somber mood of the delegates convening in Washington and the glorious fall weather could not have been greater. And an unusual coordinated interest rate cut of 0.5 per cent by the Fed, the ECB, the BoE and the Swiss National Bank did little to calm markets, demonstrating that the role of monetary policy in combating a severe banking crisis is limited. After its meeting on October 10, the G7 produced a communiqué in which it promised that its members would take all possible action to support systemically important financial institutions and prevent their failure, but did not specify how this would be accomplished. At this stage markets were focusing squarely on Europe, with ECB President, Jean-Claude Trichet, playing a central role in the deliberations among the harried European top policymakers. When he was not attending meetings, Trichet was working the phones in the ECB's modest office rented from the IMF, trying to broker stronger coordination. In the end Trichet and the national central bank governors from the Euro Area decided that the ECB should lower the requirements for the collateral it accepts against its loans, and support the covered bond market with purchases. But they felt that any further action had to be taken by governments, who bore the ultimate responsibility for financial stability.[18] Throughout the weekend of October 11–12 frenzied discussions took place, with the IMF Ministerial Committee emphasizing the need for coordinated action. On Sunday European policymakers left *en masse* for Paris to attend a meeting of state and government leaders called by French President Nicolas Sarkózy, in a desperate attempt to avoid a total collapse of the financial system. As the British Prime Minister, Gordon Brown, did not represent a Euro Area country he had not been invited, but he nevertheless showed up in Paris to tout the British approach to quelling the crisis.[19] Leaders recognized that the British plan, with its focus on injecting capital into troubled banks by taking preferred shares and providing interbank guarantees, was probably the best option. The Paris meeting proved to be a turning point in the global financial crisis. A host of measures were announced, the most important being guarantees on interbank positions and various financial support measures for Euro Area financial institutions. The total sum of government support announced was 2 trillion euros, much larger than – though not fully comparable to – the $700 billion allotted by the United States to TARP. The real breakthrough came when Germany agreed to granting interbank guarantees and taking shares in private banks, which was an unprecedented step for Berlin. Coming on top of the spectacular European measures, the United States government announced that it was providing loans to nine large banks, whether they wanted them or not. The result was that on Monday October 13, 2008 markets rallied first in Asia, then in Europe, and finally on Wall Street. Interbank spreads started to come down, though only modestly at first.

While October 2008 proved to be a turning point in the global financial crisis, it was not until the spring of 2009 that markets truly reached calmer waters, after the United States had engineered a massive bailout of the bank–insurance giant Citigroup and the newly appointed Secretary of the Treasury, Tim Geithner, had ordered *stress tests* to be conducted for the twenty largest American banks. These tests allowed the Fed to judge whether in the event of serious setbacks these banks would have enough capital. Those who turned out to lack sufficient capital had to add to their present levels. Despite some skepticism, expressed, for instance, by the then German Minister of Finance,[20] publication of the test results proved to be very successful in reducing fears that several large American banks were too poorly capitalized to withstand adverse economic conditions. On a global level, the G20, in its meeting of November 15, 2008, pledged greater policy coordination and followed this up at its London gathering of April 2, 2009 by announcing a $1 trillion package of financial resources to support countries seriously affected by the worldwide crisis.[21]

Why the system failed

While there is widespread consensus on the main causes of the crisis triggered in August 2007, this is not the case regarding their relative importance. An all-encompassing explanation often put forward is that greed dominated the banks' behavior. While greed is certainly a powerful driving force, it is not unique to the financial sector. Herd instinct is another general behavioral flaw which is widely mentioned as a major factor in causing the firestorm. Herd behavior has also played a significant role in previous important crises. Banks and other financial entities have demonstrated a tendency to follow each other in and out of particular countries. Their group panic has been compared to lemmings collectively running off a cliff. As well as these very general explanations, more specific causes can be identified, ten of which are described here, roughly based on what can be seen as their respective weights.[22]

The dismal *failure of risk management* should rank as the number one cause. Banks and also other financial institutions, both in the United States and in Europe, threw caution to the winds in their short-term pursuit of profits. Excessive reliance was placed on "sophisticated" models whose underlying assumptions were often much too optimistic, including vastly underestimating "tail risks."[23] A failure to properly incorporate liquidity risk into decision-making led to disastrous results in some cases, AIG being the prime example. Not only were risk management systems defective, but risk managers were frequently overruled or ignored when they issued warnings. In their defense, banks have claimed that they had to look for riskier opportunities as easy monetary policy led to a flood of deposits and low-interest rates, making it difficult to make attractive profits on low-risk assets. It is hard to be impressed by this short-term reasoning. Banks should properly weigh risks and returns and not gorge on such risky investments as subprime mortgages. A good example of responsible behavior, encouraged by sound supervision, has been that of Canadian banks, whose more conservative approach to risk-taking has paid off in the longer run.[24]

Closely related to poor risk management were *skewed incentives* in the financial system. A rapid growth of assets, encouraged by risk-rewarding compensation policies, contributed to enormous *leveraging*. Such leveraging implies that when assets drop in value a financial institution will much more quickly get into trouble than if it maintained a more conservative ratio of total assets to capital. Leverage ratios of over 20 became commonplace among banks, with Bear Stearns going as high as 33. Loans were pushed onto naïve or reckless borrowers and then sold to various investors, freeing up banks' balance sheets to provide additional loans. And the bonus culture on Wall Street, copied more and more in Europe, rewarded bankers for focusing on short-term profits.

Securitization was the instrument of choice to increase leverage. While securitization has brought benefits, such as deeper and more liquid markets, the process got out of hand as it contributed to more risky behavior and opaqueness. The most common form of securitization has been the origination and selling on of mortgage loans (originate and distribute model). These were then packaged as asset backed securities ("slicing and dicing"). The process allowed banks to generate much more business than if they had simply kept such loans on their books until maturity. Another pervasive financial practice, in which underlying financial variables such as interest rates served as vehicles, often referred to as *derivatives*, became very complex and were often imperfectly understood by those who invested in them. Collateralized debt obligations and credit default swaps were initially hailed as great boons to the functioning of financial markets, but turned out to have a poisonous sting. Even more pernicious were the *special purpose vehicles* (SPV), basically shadow banks through which regular banks diverted certain risky activities from their balance sheets.

The aim was to circumvent capital requirements laid down by bank supervisors. In retrospect, it is quite astonishing that no action was taken by supervisors to close this lucrative and dangerous loophole.

Another link in the chain of unhealthy practices was the role of *rating agencies*. These private institutions, the three largest of which enjoy a Securities and Exchange Commission (SEC) 'seal of approval', displayed a remarkable willingness to provide – often toxic – mortgage backed securities with the highest achievable rating. These "triple A factories" operated on the basis of a flawed business model, whereby they are paid for their services by their debt-issuing clients. Not only does this make the agencies reluctant to downgrade their clients' paper, but it also encourages "rating shopping" by issuers of debt. Buyers of asset backed securities usually depended blindly on their impressive ratings, not bothering to carry out their own due diligence.

Without a widespread and comprehensive *failure of regulatory and supervisory systems* the crisis would have been considerably less onerous and could possibly have been prevented. Not only did existing regulations in the United States, and often elsewhere, fall short of what was needed, but even more damning is the fact that they were poorly implemented. Fed chairman Greenspan's philosophy of "the market knows best" enjoyed widespread support, despite warnings from the late low-profile Fed Governor Edward Gramlich, which surfaced after the debacle. As to bank supervisors, they failed to identify many of the risks. There are several explanations for this. First, it is difficult to get a good grasp of complex new products and the risks they carry. Second, supervisors are reluctant to cry wolf without being very sure of their case. In the international context, supervisors outside the United States were also reluctant to question the judgment of their American counterparts regarding US-issued asset backed securities. Third, a range of institutions (investment banks, special purpose vehicles, hedge funds, and private equity funds, as well as the financial arms of insurance companies), often referred to as the *shadow banking system*, were largely or wholly devoid of supervision. Fourth, supervisors were also not paying (enough) attention to systemic risks and spillovers from problems experienced outside their jurisdictions. Bodies like the Financial Stability Forum and the IMF could have done more to remedy this situation. Moreover, the IMF proved to be insufficiently critical of the United States' economic policies in general and the functioning of its financial system in particular.[25]

As regulation and supervision did not perform up to standard, and in a climate where the "magic of the market" was revered, banks and other financial institutions were able to grow spectacularly. In many advanced countries, including the United States, the United Kingdom, Switzerland, and the Benelux countries, the share of the financial sector in the economy reached impressive proportions. Individual banks sometimes became *too big to fail*, as not rescuing them was seen as too dangerous for the financial system as a whole, which in turn could have serious repercussions for the real economy.

Moral hazard was ingrained in the system, as banks that believed they were too big or too interconnected to fail displayed more risky behavior then they would have done otherwise. The rescue of the large hedge fund LTCM in 1998, in which creditors were "made whole," as well as some of the support operations of the various emerging country crises described in Chapters 1 to 7, convinced large banks that, when they got into serious trouble, the Central Bank or the government was likely to step in to save their hides. Moreover, there was a widespread belief, known as the "Greenspan Put," that whenever important financial institutions found themselves in a pickle the Fed would lower interest rates as well as providing generous lender-of-last-resort support. Actual events confirmed the banks in this expectation.

Easy monetary policy maintained for too long is also often cited as a major cause of the global crisis of recent years. Here the main "culprit" identified is the American Central Bank. The Fed is criticized for providing easy money for too long in the first part of the 2000s, allowing banks and shadow banks to pour the masses of new money deposited with them into risky assets. Major US policymakers have different views of the role monetary policy has played in causing the crisis. Fed Chairman Bernanke has blamed regulatory failure rather than monetary policy for the catastrophe.[26] Still, there is little doubt that the Fed kept interest rates too low for a number of years during which it was overly fearful of deflation, helping to fuel the unsustainable housing boom. It is interesting to see that some of the present-day critics of the Fed's easy money policy up to 2004 were supportive of this stance during those years and applauded its stimulus effects. Overall, there was little recognition of the role of an overly relaxed American monetary policy on asset price inflation, the Central Bank claiming that it could not predict booms but could only clean up after a mishap.

Hedge funds (a more appropriate name would be speculative funds) are frequently blamed for their role in the crisis. Speculation can be stabilizing or destabilizing. No doubt hedge fund activities played a predominantly destabilizing role in the events of 2007 and 2008, especially when selling short bank stock under crisis conditions. Some of this activity took the form of naked short selling, whereby assets which the seller does not own, or borrows, are sold at a date in the future. At the height of the troubles of the large American and European banks, short selling was prohibited for a while in view of the extreme drop in financial stocks. But, in terms of their overall impact on the crisis, hedge funds played a secondary role, being considerably smaller than the banking system, as well as less leveraged (by a factor of four rather than twenty). This is not to say that hedge funds operations should not be monitored and regulated as has been the case in the past, since these speculative funds could be an important destabilizing factor in future crises.

Finally, the *global imbalances* in the world economy are often identified as a major cause of the great financial crisis. These imbalances are certainly a serious problem, as is discussed in Chapter 11, but their existence was not a prime cause of the global firestorm. Large and persistent American balance of payments deficits on current account, mirrored by surpluses in China, other Asian countries, and oil exporters, have led to an enormous growth of international reserves, mostly held in US dollars. The willingness of China and other surplus countries to continue financing the United States' external deficits in its own currency helped to provide liquidity to the American economy, and in this indirect way made it easier for its financial system to provide cheap and often risky credits. But without such imbalances the crisis of 2007–09 would have still occurred, given the importance and structural characteristics of the other causes described here.

Lessons ignored

The great crisis that hit advanced economies in 2007, and continued for almost two years, led to a deep recession, with output in advanced economies declining in 2009 by 3.2 per cent and globally by 2 per cent (calculated at market exchange rates). The big surprise to most observers was not so much that a new crisis occurred but that it emerged in the United States, spread swiftly to Europe and other advanced countries, and had only a limited effect on most emerging countries. In describing the causes of the great crisis we can detect some important differences from the crises of 1995 to 2002, such as the role of rating agencies, banks that are too big to fail, and runaway financial innovation. But other causes are in principle no different from those that underlay the crises in Latin America, Asia, and Russia. However, many of the lessons that could have been learned from the crises treated in Chapters 1 to 7, as well as earlier crises,[27] were ignored, as they were not considered applicable to advanced economies. But the financial systems of many advanced countries, while more sophisticated, did not prove any less vulnerable than those of less advanced economies. A particularly nasty surprise for many "experts" was that the financial system of the United States, often held up as an example to others, proved to be seriously flawed.

Had more of the lessons that could have been drawn from previous crises been heeded, the world economy would have suffered less. But a lack of imagination with respect to the possibility of serious weaknesses in the financial systems of the large Western countries led to a form of professional blindness among market participants, governments, central banks, financial supervisors and regulators, as well as international organizations. It is especially disappointing that an otherwise highly competent institution such as the IMF failed to grasp the serious risks that underlay the globalized and highly intricate financial system that had evolved over the years. This failure applies in particular to the degree to which the IMF underestimated the fault lines in the United States' financial system (it did better with respect to European countries, and issued timely warnings about weaknesses in the financial systems of countries like Germany and Switzerland). In fairness, it has to be recognized that for official organizations issuing dire warnings about risks can be challenging. Governments of large countries can exercise their influence to suppress messages they do not like. No doubt this is part of the explanation. But, as William White from the BIS has shown, timely warnings can enhance reputations even if they are dismissed at first. This is a lesson the IMF and other official bodies should take to heart.

Once again, as in the series of emerging crises, risk management practices of Western banks during most of the 2000s were a shambles. Assessing the riskiness of credits in advanced economies is in some aspects different from assessing those in emerging market countries, but the general principles are the same. Such seemingly sophisticated approaches as calculations of *value at risk* (VAR) turned out to be flawed or applied incorrectly. Especially egregious was the failure by banks to take into account certain "tail risks" such as the possibility that house prices in the United States could actually fall. Moreover, risk managers were often overruled due to competitive considerations, as had happened in previous crises.

As in the emerging country experience, banking supervision in many advanced countries turned out to be inadequate. The lesson for advanced countries from earlier crises was to closely examine their own regulation and supervision and, especially, their implementation. Again, the feeling that their own systems were up to standard, as well as the philosophy espoused by "gurus" like Chairman Greenspan that regulation should be implemented (very) lightly, proved to be a dangerous misapprehension. During the Mexican and Asian crises, decisive government intervention in the financial system, including the closing of insolvent banks, was crucial to restoring confidence in the system. The insistence of the IMF on taking drastic measures to clean up banking systems played an important role at the time. In the advanced countries, the reaction to the developing solvency problem was hesitant at first and the IMF largely silent on what needed to be done.

The relaxed attitude toward moral hazard in advanced countries with respect to their own financial institutions could have been mitigated if the lessons of the negative effects of moral hazard in previous crises had been taken to heart. The tendency to bail out countries with large financing packages without insisting on a substantial contribution by private sector lenders encouraged them to take unwarranted risks. Banks and shadow banks in advanced countries should have been warned that in the case of solvency problems they could not rely on being saved every time. Beginning with the hedge fund LTCM, some entities, not only small fry, should have been allowed to go under. A more difficult question is whether already large banks in the United States and Europe should have been allowed to merge with or take over other banks or insurance companies, creating institutions that became too big to fail.

Finally, continuing too long with easy monetary policy can stimulate poor lending decisions by the private sector, as was amply demonstrated by the Asian crisis and in Latin America. Contrary to the practice in many other countries, monetary policy in the United States has a dual mandate: to keep inflation in check as well as to strive for full employment. The difficult balancing act that this involves probably contributed to the Fed's reluctance to raise interest rates in the years of the accelerating housing boom. Publishing an inflation target and taking into account asset price developments could reduce this problem.

Reform of the financial system

The firestorm that almost brought down the global financial system and threatened to lead the world economy into a severe depression was contained only by extraordinary measures taken by governments, central banks, and supervisors. In a climate of "never again," discussions on deep-seated reform of the financial system were launched. These took place at the national level but also in such international forums as the Financial Stability Board and the Basel Committee of Supervisors. At the level of heads of governments, the G20 strongly supported reform and emphasized the need for international coordination so as to create a level playing field among banks. Intense deliberations and much horse trading among politicians produced comprehensive new legislation in the United States and a raft of reform proposals in Europe. Not surprisingly, international coordination has proved to be quite challenging.

The *Dodd–Frank bill*, or Wall Street Reform and Consumer Protection Act, signed into law by President Obama on July 21, 2010, addresses many of the causes of the serious flaws that almost brought down Wall Street. Many of the changes to the system included in the reform act are formulated in general terms and will need to be made specific by the various agencies dealing with them. Any evaluation is therefore subject to the actual manner in which many of the provisions will be applied in practice.

Potentially the most far-reaching provisions are the resolution authority firmly established in the law and the possibility of breaking up banks when they pose a "grave threat" to financial stability. The *resolution* provision allows orderly liquidation of failed or failing *large, interconnected* financial firms when stability of the system is threatened. The Federal Deposit Insurance Corporation (FDIC), with the concurrence of the US Treasury, will be the agency responsible

for the unwinding procedure. The explicit introduction of wide-ranging resolution powers is a direct answer to Lehman-type crises. If implemented strictly,
the new resolution regime should ensure that no future bailouts take place. A
most useful innovation is the requirement for large banks to draw up *living
wills*, plans for how to deal with an orderly closing down of the firm when
insolvency becomes unavoidable.

A closely related provision deals with the authority to require *large, complex* financial companies to *divest* some of their holdings if they pose a *grave
threat* to financial stability. This new approach is intended to prevent banks
from becoming too big to fail. A *Financial Stability Oversight Council*, under
the chairmanship of the Secretary of the US Treasury, which includes representatives of nine financial agencies, has been given the power to approve
a decision by the Fed requiring a bank to sell off some of its business. The
Council is also charged with identifying emerging stability risks and desig-
nating financial firms as systemically significant. This requires setting up an
early warning system.

Other important features of Dodd–Frank are imposing higher *capital requirements* for banks (in accordance with the international agreement known as
Basel III), leading to deleveraging, and subjecting *derivative trading* to closer
scrutiny. Central clearing and exchange trading will be required, allowing regulators and clearing houses to determine which contracts should be cleared.
The aim is to prevent AIG-type meltdowns. In a similar attempt to clamp down
on harmful speculation, traditional banking will be separated from banks'
trading for their own account. Such *proprietary trading* will be phased out – with
some exceptions – in accordance with the "Volcker rule," which aims to protect
taxpayers and depositors from reckless activities by banks.[28]

The establishment of a *Consumer Financial Protection Bureau* is of great political significance, but less important from the perspective of battling financial
crises. The task of this independent watchdog is to ensure that clear and accurate information is provided to consumers on mortgages, credit cards, and
other financial products. The aim is to root out hidden fees, abusive terms,
and deceptive practices. Another reform in the area of mortgages is an element
of *risk retention* by sellers of mortgage backed securities. To ensure "skin in the
game," a minimum of 5 per cent credit risk is to be borne by the originator.

Contrary to earlier proposals by Treasury Secretary Timothy Geithner,
a comprehensive merging of federal financial agencies is not part of Dodd–
Frank. Only the *Office of Thrift Supervision* has been abolished and its activities
transferred to the *Comptroller of the Currency*. In an unimpressive attempt to
increase shareholders' influence on *compensation and benefits*, they are granted
a "say on pay" with a right to a nonbinding vote on executive pay and golden
parachutes. Finally, the new law also deals with hedge funds. Advisors to hedge
funds and large private equity funds need to register with the SEC and provide

information on the amount of assets managed by these funds, their leverage, risk exposure, and other information necessary to assess the systemic risk of the fund. This information is shared with the Financial Stability Oversight Council.

Evaluating Dodd–Frank

Reactions to the reform bill have ranged from the enthusiastic to the highly critical, as befits a politically sensitive initiative. Where you sit is where you stand, except for those experts who do not have a particular agenda. Michael Foot, a former high official at the Bank of England, the IMF and the British Financial Services Authority, is such an unbiased expert. Foot sees a number of positive elements in the US reform bill, but gives it only "one and a half cheers" in view of several watered-down provisions and the lack of some elements.[29]

Dodd–Frank being the outcome of political horse trading, it falls short of what would be needed to significantly reduce the frequency and depth of financial crises. Of the act's most crucial elements, the provision on resolution is the most likely to be implemented, especially the "living will" part. But, as Foot points out, governments may still resort to bailouts when a severe crisis hits. Moreover, a tougher attitude toward holders of bank-issued bonds would have been useful to make them more prudent in their investment decisions. The possibility of breaking up banks is potentially game-changing, but the chances of implementation are limited because of the politically highly charged nature of decision-making in this area. The American political process, with its excessive reliance on campaign financing by lobby groups, has proven to be an obstacle in achieving sufficiently far-reaching reforms and is likely to stymie forceful implementation of powers to break up banks. It appears that fully adequate financial reform would only be possible after deep-seated reform of the campaign financing rules in the United States.

A serious omission in the new structure is the continuation of the patchwork of agencies involved in fostering financial stability. Coordination between these agencies is likely to prove very challenging, notwithstanding the establishment of the Oversight Council. Allowing rating agencies to operate largely as before is another missed opportunity. This can also be said of the weak provision on bankers' compensation. A change in the Wall Street bonus culture is, therefore, unlikely. And the proposal for a levy on banks' profits fell by the wayside, as the threat of a filibuster (a practice to endlessly occupy the Senate floor, which can only be broken by a vote of sixty persons or sheer fatigue) by the Republican Party led to a withdrawal of the plan. The Dodd–Frank Act does not deal with the government-sponsored agencies Fannie Mae and Freddie Mac. Their future will be decided in a separate decision, which is also likely to be greatly influenced by the political process.

While it took more than a year to adopt a (revised) financial reform bill put on the table by the Obama Administration, the United States succeeded in having comprehensive legislation in place before the European Union. This conferred a certain advantage on the US in the attempt at international coordination of financial reform. In the words of US Treasury Secretary Timothy Geithner and the then Director of the National Economic Council, Larry Summers, in June 2009: "We will lead the effort to improve regulation and improve supervision around the world."[30] Once again the United States took the lead in a crucial reform effort, but it did so in close cooperation with European countries through the G20, the FSB and the Basel Committee of Supervisors.

In a union comprising twenty-seven countries, decision-making is difficult, especially when it comes to matters touching on members' sovereignty. The European Union, although lagging behind the United States in reaching agreement on financial reform, did work swiftly toward adopting new rules. It has also actively participated in discussions in the international forums tasked with coordinating approaches to financial reform. Coordination does not have to lead to uniform rules, but does require harmonization. In areas such as supervision of rating agencies and hedge funds, as well as executive pay in banks, the EU has taken the lead. It has also developed measures in these areas going beyond what is taking shape in the United States.

Following recommendations made by a committee chaired by former IMF Managing Director Jacques de Larosière, the EU adopted a new *supervisory architecture*. The main elements are the creation of a *European Systemic Risk Board*, which is tasked with early detection of macroprudential and macroeconomic risks, and three *European Supervisory Authorities*, responsible for banking, insurance, and securities markets, aimed at reinforcing supervision and improving coordination among national supervisors. Useful as these measures are, they fall short of creating a fully integrated system of supervision in the EU, which will be needed to provide a smoothly working defense mechanism for dealing with future crises. But striving for such a far-reaching supranational structure will require a greater degree of political cohesion than presently exists in the EU. And, since London's interests, as by far the largest international financial center in the EU, do not always run parallel with those of financial centers on the European continent, reaching compromises is hard to achieve. Here, too, harmonization in certain areas is the best that can be aimed for in the foreseeable future.[31]

Measures in areas such as *short selling*, especially of the naked kind, and *credit default swaps* have received special attention in the EU. Harmonizing *deposit guarantee schemes* in order to better protect depositors is also a priority area. And, as in the United States, capital and liquidity requirements are to be strengthened, subject to international agreement on the extent of such reforms. The Basel Committee of Supervisors agreed in late 2010 on increases in the size of capital and liquidity that banks should hold as a minimum. These rules, known as *Basel III* (after the city in which central bankers meet periodically at the premises of the BIS; earlier, less demanding, requirements were known as Basel I and II), although nonbinding, constitute a standard from which regulators and banks are reluctant to deviate. The main features are a minimum capital ratio (capital as a percentage of assets) of 4.5 per cent, plus an additional 2.5 per cent capital conservation buffer and the introduction of standards for maintaining sufficient liquidity by banks, which were lacking under earlier agreements. The definition of high-quality (tier 1) capital has been drastically adjusted so that the average risk-weighted capital ratio under Basel II of 11.1 per cent would only be 5.7 per cent for the largest banks under Basel III. The implication is that these banks will have to raise almost $600 billion in capital in coming years. Although this is a big number, bankers were somewhat relieved by the agreement. They had bemoaned earlier, tougher, proposals, claiming that their implementation could reduce global economic growth by as much as 3 per cent in the US, the Euro Area, and Japan combined.[32] These numbers were challenged by the Financial Stability Board, chaired by the Italian Central Bank Governor Mario Draghi, and by the Basel Committee of Bank Supervisors (BCSB) led by the head of the Dutch Central Bank, Nout Wellink. According to their calculations, global growth would be reduced by no more than 0.2 per cent for every percentage point increase in capital requirements during a four-year phase-in period of the new rules.[33] The calculated increase in capital required by 5.4 percentage points would therefore reduce total output by only 1.1 per cent compared with what it would be otherwise.[34] Moreover, and at least as importantly, greater stability of the international financial system through the introduction of Basel III will be favorable for economic growth in the long run. But, without proper implementation, beneficial effects will be limited. It is therefore essential that the G20, the FSB and the IMF monitor the process closely and flag any slippage.

Another important feature of Basel III is to establish a simple maximum leverage ratio in the future. An innovative part of Basel III is the introduction of a *countercyclical capital buffer* – an increase of capital required by up to 2.5 per cent – that should be imposed whenever a bubble is detected by a participating supervisor. Supervisors in other countries whose banks have claims on the "bubble" country should then also require a buffer in proportion to the size of their banks' exposure. For instance, if country A sees a bubble coming and imposes an additional buffer of 2 per cent, country B, whose banks do 10 per cent of their business in country A, should ask its banks to hold 0.2 per cent more capital. The economic effect would be to raise the cost of credit. If the extra buffer rule is properly implemented, an important macroprudential tool will have been created. But, as Michael Foot points out, the new tool will only be effective if supervisors have the political courage to declare a credit bubble.[35] And having others follow suit will be quite a stretch.

As to developments on a national scale, an important change in the structure of the *British supervisory system* was put in place. The Financial Services Authority (FSA) as the agency responsible for prudential supervision was abolished and its powers transferred to the Bank of England. This reversed the decision by the then new Chancellor, Gordon Brown, in 1997 to remove the supervisory responsibility of the Bank of England and transfer it to the newly created FSA. The bad experience with the rescue of Northern Rock is often cited as having induced the incoming Cameron government to undo the earlier reform. Whether to grant a central bank responsibility in supervisory matters, in addition to its traditional task of maintaining monetary stability, remains a much-debated question, which is touched upon in Chapter 11.

Finally, a fundamental discussion of the size of countries' financial institutions relative to their overall economy is taking place. Politicians, policymakers, and academics have raised the question of whether what they see as bloated financial institutions have not become so big that they are doing more bad than good on balance. For instance, Adair Turner, the last head of the FSA, went as far as suggesting a reduction in the size of the British financial sector, which he considers to be a net liability to his country.[36] A similarly outspoken position has been taken by the Governor of the Bank of England, Mervyn King, who is in favor of breaking up large banks.[37] But, while the question of size is very important, determining whether a country's financial system is too big is complicated and controversial. At the same time, it could become a fertile area for researchers. In the case of Iceland and Ireland the answer is clear, but what about Switzerland and, indeed, the United Kingdom?

Looking ahead

The policy reaction to the financial firestorm of 2007–08 was swift and mostly decisive. Central banks and governments were fully aware of the dangers of a wait-and-see stance, thereby preventing a global depression. Crisis management was followed in timely fashion by proposals for crisis prevention in the future, with the G20 playing a central role. The IMF was initially largely a bystander, but became heavily involved when secondary effects from the crisis, as described in Chapters 10 and 11, posed new and serious challenges. Not unexpectedly, time was needed for agreeing on new rules and regulations to strengthen financial stability. This is inherent in the political process. Regrettably, this process also led to a significant watering-down of initial proposals. Also, some of the new measures, such as attempts to set up early warning systems and improving risk management, are little more than old wine in new bottles. The effectiveness of the Dodd–Frank Act and EU financial directives will depend critically on how they are implemented. Here prospects may be somewhat better for the EU than for the United States, in light of the tendency of the US Congress to play politics whenever there is an opportunity. It is positive that the Fed, with its wide experience and highly qualified staff, has been granted more powers, but some doubts exist about how independent the American Central Bank will turn out to be at the end of the day.

10
Europe's Turn

While the global financial crisis of 2007–09 was concentrated in the United States and Europe, it also affected other advanced countries, as well as emerging markets. But the effects were mostly due to contagion through the trade channel, the financial systems of Asian and Latin American countries, as well as those of most of the smaller advanced countries and South Africa, withstanding the crisis much better than those hosting large financial centers. The emerging countries of *Central and Eastern Europe* (CEE) were not so fortunate. Most of them fell into a serious financial swoon that brought some of them to the brink of sovereign default and steep economic decline. In several instances large official support operations, involving both the IMF and the EU, were needed. On top of that, in early 2010 *Greece*, a member of the Euro Area, got into serious trouble following a sudden stop of capital inflows. Other Euro Area countries were affected as well, leading to an attack on the common currency itself.

A new victim: emerging Europe

CEE countries emerged from Communism around 1990 with weak and antiquated economies. As related in the Prologue, the IMF and Western countries made a strong effort to help them create market economies, in the process fostering strong growth. These efforts were so successful that a number of CEE countries became serious competitors to their Western neighbors in such activities as automobile and steel production. Economic growth in the CEE countries averaged 5 per cent during 2002–07 and was even higher in Ukraine, the largest of the former Soviet republics (besides Russia). But the global financial crisis starkly revealed the CEE countries' vulnerabilities, causing their collective economies to shrink by 6 per cent in 2009. Exports took a nosedive, while private capital inflows, much of them in the form of borrowing from banks, which had reached an astounding $186 billion in 2007, plunged to a mere

$23 billion in 2009. The domestic credit boom that most CEE countries had experienced, and which had fueled domestic demand, came to an abrupt halt as local banks (mostly subsidiaries of Western European banks) were cut off from their main source of funding. While the crisis that hit emerging Europe was primarily the result of the global financial crisis, it was also to a significant extent homemade. Policymakers had allowed rapid domestic credit growth to go on for too long, had often turned a blind eye to foreign exchange risks, and had not taken adequate action to slow down their overheating economies with budgetary measures.[1]

While the region's vulnerability was underestimated by many policymakers and observers, it was fully recognized by some experts. At the IMF, staffer Bas Bakker had already issued warnings several years earlier based on comparisons between the Asian countries that had lapsed into crisis in the 1990s and emerging countries in Europe.[2] Although such admonitions were usually considered too dire, the Fund, in its annual examinations of CEE countries, had regularly criticized their reliance on short- term capital flows, the practice of denominating loans in foreign currencies with low interest rates (euro, yen and Swiss franc), exposing corporations and mortgage borrowers to foreign exchange risks, and the need to cool down their overheating economies. As the CEE countries and Ukraine at that juncture did not need the IMF to finance their large current account deficits, they felt no pressure to heed these warnings. But, when cross-border lending dried up as a result of the global crisis, a raft of Eastern European countries got into serious financing difficulties and had to turn to the IMF and the European Union hat in hand. This was in the best interest not only of the countries facing problems servicing their debts but also of their creditors, many of which had become overextended in emerging Europe. German, Austrian, and Swedish banks in particular had gone on a lending rampage in Eastern Europe and were in danger of suffering large capital losses.

Distress in Hungary, Romania and Ukraine

Twenty-two countries, ranging from Albania to Ukraine, make up the CEE area. Among these, nine countries received credits with strict policy conditions from the IMF following the crisis in advanced economies, whereas another five narrowly avoided the same fate. Poland, which had followed prudent policies and was the only European country to maintain positive growth in 2009, received a $20 billion Fund credit under its new *Flexible Credit Line* facility (FCL). No policy conditions are demanded under this facility, which serves as a safety net for countries following sound policies. Less careful borrowers such as Hungary, Romania, and Ukraine did not qualify for FCL credits.

Hungary, with a reputation as an early reformer among former Communist countries, proved to be an underperformer as time went by. A combination of

fiscal indiscipline, an inappropriate exchange rate policy, excessive foreign borrowing, and political instability hampered the country's forward movement.
In earlier years Hungary had already suffered from bouts of contagion when
other emerging markets got into trouble, but was able to ward off attacks on its
currency. When it took a hard hit from the global crisis, from 2008 onwards,
its exports (mainly directed toward Europe) suffered and foreign lending
(mainly through foreign-owned Hungarian banks) dried up. To fill the gap a
$25 billion credit was extended to Hungary jointly by the IMF ($16 billion) and
the European Union ($8 billion), with the World Bank adding another billion.
In an innovative cooperative effort, the Fund and the EU negotiated in coordinated fashion with Budapest on the policy conditions. The main measures
demanded were a substantial reduction of the budget deficit and an immediate
recapitalization of the weakened banking system. The credit package was large
by Eastern European standards, as it was intended not only to substitute for the
sudden stop of capital inflows but also to strengthen Hungary's international
reserves.

To ensure that banks would not all head for the exit (a rollover rate of 80
per cent was assumed), a crucial agreement was reached with the major banks
involved with Hungary to maintain their exposure. The IMF and the East
European Bank (EBRD) played a central role as brokers in what came to be
known as the *Vienna initiative*,[3] so named after the initial meetings held in
the Joint Vienna Institute, a training center for officials from transition economies sponsored by international organizations. This initiative, supported
by international organizations, bank supervisors, and private banks, constitutes a major innovation in dealing with the old problem of foreign banks
withdrawing their credits when they sense trouble ahead. Despite being in
their immediate self-interest, such action is self-defeating in the end as a collective flight can lead to default and big losses for the banks. In the case of
Hungary the agreement with the banks included the acknowledgment "that
it is in our collective interest...to reconfirm, in a coordinated way, our commitment to maintain our overall exposure to Hungary."[4] The Vienna initiative is an excellent example of successful involvement of the private sector as
promoted – mostly without the desired result – in the past. Actively brokering
this kind of burden-sharing demonstrated that the IMF had taken to heart an
important lesson from previous crises. Following Hungary, the initiative was
also applied with respect to Romania, Serbia, and, somewhat less successfully,
Latvia. It has also been introduced in a forward-looking way in countries
without a standby credit from the IMF, such as Poland, to avoid a sudden
pullout of foreign banks.

Also urgently needing official assistance was *Romania*, which had been a lag-
gard in the transition process from Communism to a market economy. Despite
being a member of the IMF since 1972, Romania's totally centrally planned

economy remained in place until the 1990s. During the middle of the 1980s Romania conducted a standby agreement with the Fund, which led to naught as the higher interest rates and devaluation demanded had no impact in such a command economy. After the overthrow of its dictatorship in late 1989, Romania embarked on a process of reform. Although the IMF and the World Bank became deeply involved, the going was slow. Five Fund credit agreements with Romania went off track, until in the early 2000s an IMF program was finally completed. Mugur Isarescu, the long-serving Governor of the National Bank of Romania, who also did a stint as prime minister at a crucial time, was often the only voice of reason against bad economic policy proposals concocted by a dysfunctional political class. The Central Bank's close cooperation with the IMF, later joined by various cabinets, proved to be fruitful in the end, as economic growth soared to 6.4 per cent on average annually between 2002 and 2007 and inflation came down significantly with the aid of an inflation target serving as an anchor.

In 2008 a sudden stop of capital inflows, which had fueled a very rapid expansion of domestic credit (close to 30 per cent annually on average between 2003 and 2007) and a sharp drop-off in exports, created a severe financing gap. With the economy shrinking at a rate of 7 per cent, Romania once again turned to the Fund, as well as to the EU. A support package of $26 billion was put together, the Fund providing $16 billion (no less than 1,110 per cent of Romania's quota), the EU euro 5 billion ($6.5 billion) and the remainder contributed by other international organizations. Bringing down the high fiscal deficit and strengthening the banking system constituted the core of the program. Again the joint effort by the IMF and the EU proved to be fruitful. Had the credit been granted solely by the EU (Romania had become a member in 2007), doubts could have arisen about the stringency and implementation of the conditions, damaging the much-needed return of confidence. Completing the rescue operation, foreign banks pledged to keep their exposures to Romania intact in the spirit of the Vienna initiative.

Even more challenging were the events unfolding in *Ukraine* as a result of the global financial crisis. Among the former Soviet republics, Ukraine had been the last to regain former output levels after independence. To be sure, it faced an exceptionally difficult situation in the early years of its existence as a separate state. It had no international reserves, its budget deficit was outlandish (around 35 per cent of GDP at the outset) and the skills of its leaders and bureaucracy were particularly ill-matched with the demands of a market economy.[5] The IMF and the World Bank were very active in Ukraine from the start. In late 1994 the Fund granted the country a credit under the Systemic Transition Facility (described in the Prologue), followed by more credits up to 2000. Recovery was initially slow, but, in part thanks to good cooperation between the Fund and the National Bank of Ukraine under the governorship of reform-minded Viktor Yuschenko (who later became prime minister and president in 2004 following the Orange revolution), the economy took off. Growth peaked at 12 per cent in 2004, aided by a surge in world steel prices, but also by largely sensible economic policies. But political game-playing and hardcore corruption kept direct foreign investment lower than in neighboring countries.[6] Instead heavy foreign borrowing, much of it to finance domestic consumption, made the country very vulnerable to sudden shocks.

Following several more years of high growth, but accelerating inflation (25 per cent at its peak), aided by the booming world economy, Ukraine was hit especially hard from 2008 on as its exports plunged and capital inflows dried up abruptly. Economic growth slowed to a trickle and in 2009 turned negative to the tune of 15 per cent, one of the steepest declines in the world. While this disaster led to a severe compression of imports which brought down the trade deficit, a huge financing gap opened up as foreign investors headed for the exit. Close to default, the Ukrainian government obtained a $16 billion credit from the IMF in November 2008. Despite much talk at the time about lighter Fund conditionality in general, the Ukrainian program included harsh but necessary measures in order to maintain its solvency. Conditions included lowering its budget deficit, raising gas tariffs closer to reflecting the actual cost, and restructuring the weak banking system. The IMF had earlier pressured Ukraine into letting go of its overvalued fixed exchange rate to restore competitiveness. After two disbursements under the Fund standby policy, slippages caused a third disbursement, scheduled for November 2009, to be placed on hold. Due to particularly vicious political infighting with a presidential election campaign underway, as well as the anachronistic mindset of some politicians and policymakers, the government's pledge to increase gas tariffs was not implemented, the budget deficit exceeded the target, the exchange rate continued to be heavily managed, and monetary policy yielded to political pressure. The government narrowly escaped defaulting on a eurobond as it was able to use a windfall of $2 billion on account of its share in an SDR allocation that had been agreed by the G20 as part of a huge package to combat the global financial crisis.

Discussions with the Fund were resumed, but did not lead to results until considerably later. In the meantime, advice was offered to Ukraine from various sides, including Russia, with which its relations were mostly complicated. In a different vein, a commission of high-level independent international and Ukrainian experts, of which I was a member, published a report with comprehensive recommendations on reform around the time of the presidential election in early 2010.[7] The main recommendations were to carry out reforms of the poorly managed gas sector, to make the National Bank of Ukraine independent, to direct monetary policy through inflation targeting in combination with a flexible exchange rate, to cut government expenditure, and to get privatization going again. This was very much in line with what the IMF was advocating, but could only be brought about through financial leverage. With its financial position remaining dire and capital markets closed to Ukraine, the new government, under President Yanukovich, decided after a while to resume negotiations with the Fund. These culminated in a new credit agreement in July 2010, allowing Ukraine to receive up to $15 billion, to be disbursed in tranches as usual. The main policy conditions related to the budget and the banking system, but also the need to move toward inflation targeting in tandem with more exchange rate flexibility. It was also agreed that the pension system would be reformed in view of its unsustainable size – no less than 18 per cent of GDP. But details of this politically hot potato were left to a later date.

The IMF moved swiftly to contain the crisis in Central and Eastern Europe, in close cooperation with the European Commission and the European Central Bank. In all, $108 billion was made available in conditional support packages for these countries, $70 billion of which was from the Fund. On top of that, Poland was granted an FCL credit of $20 billion, which was augmented in late 2010. The amounts were very large in proportion to earlier rescue operations to countries of similar size. This was made possible by an adjusted high-access policy, allowing the Fund to provide larger credits than before. All in all, the hands-on approach pursued by the IMF, in close cooperation with European institutions and others, did not only avoid a long period of deep recession in emerging Europe, but also prevented a domestic banking crisis in the most vulnerable of these countries.

Grecian Formula

American television frequently carries a commercial for a hair dye for men by the name of Grecian Formula. It enables its users to hide unwanted gray streaks in their hair, thereby looking younger and fitter. In the real Greece, which became a member of the Euro Area in 2001, the formula of hiding unwelcome budget numbers had been elevated to an art.[8] Why did Greece take this route? To qualify for the sought-after membership of the group of countries using the euro as their currency, certain conditions have to be met (known as the *Maastricht criteria*, named after the Dutch city where these conditions were agreed in 1992), the most important of which is a budget deficit of no more than 3 per cent of GDP. Once in the Euro Area, the new member has to comply with the rules of the *Stability and Growth Pact* (SGP), which was adopted to ensure that countries continued to stick to the Maastricht criteria. This was a tall order for Greece, where fiscal discipline did not come naturally. Apparently the temptation to cook the budgetary books outweighed concerns over eventual embarrassing disclosures. While some such disclosures had taken place before, the announcement by a new government in late 2009 that the situation was much worse than presented previously came at a particularly bad time, with financial markets still dealing with the aftershock of the global crisis. Not only was the Greek budget deficit for 2008 revised upward by 2.7 per cent of GDP to 7 per cent, but "misreporting" of the projected deficit for 2009 led to the number almost doubling to a shocking 13.6 per cent. External debt as a percentage of GDP, already 115 per cent, would climb much higher unless drastic measures were taken. On top of that, Greece's competitiveness had been eroded, as reflected by a current account deficit of 11 per cent of GDP. The IMF estimated that Greece's exports had become too expensive and imports too cheap by a combined 20 to 30 per cent. As was to be expected, the news coming out of Athens caused a new bout of jitters. It did not help that Prime Minister George Papandreou claimed that Greece could solve its economic problems on its own.

After six months of trying to calm markets by announcing a number of austerity measures which did not convince investors, Greece threw in the towel and accepted outside help. In the fear that a Greek sovereign debt default could spread to other overborrowed European countries such as Ireland and Portugal, a consensus emerged among Euro Area policymakers that a very large rescue operation was needed for Greece. While the Greek economy as such is quite small, representing only 3 per cent of Euro Area GDP, Athens' external borrowing had been so massive that holders of its sovereign bonds, many of which were Western European banks, would suffer big losses if a default were to occur. Within the Euro Area opinions were initially divided over whether to bail out Greece and for how much. And it also had to be decided whether to involve the IMF. In Germany, the traditional paymaster in the EU, public sentiment was negative. German taxpayers, suspecting that Greece would not pay back its loans in full, found it hard to stomach that they were asked to pay for Greek pensioners in their fifties sipping coffee in the sun. German policymakers, on the other hand, were also concerned about contagion and its ultimate effects on the euro. After much political wrangling, Euro Area representatives announced on April 11, 2010 that they were willing "in principle" to provide Greece with a large loan and that the IMF would add its support. While this calmed the markets for a while, the ponderous European decision-making process contributed to fresh market nervousness. As a result, Greece had to pay much high interest rates on its borrowing. The spread over German government bonds (the European benchmark) shot up from a modest fraction of a per cent before the Greek bubble burst to about 3 per cent in early April and as much as 9 per cent later in the year. Such pricing indicated that market participants considered the chances of default to be very high.

Financial markets can swing wildly when sentiment changes. Greece presents an excellent example of this phenomenon. With the adoption of the euro, Greece's long-term interest rate came down spectacularly, as it had done earlier in other high interest rate countries such as Italy. Markets apparently reckoned that Euro Area countries running large fiscal deficits and with high debts would either adjust their policies over time or be bailed out. Although the EU Treaty forbids countries to bail out another member, interpretations of what exactly constitutes a bailout differ. Markets also drew comfort from the fact that banks could borrow from the ECB against collateral which included securities from countries with less than stellar credit ratings. While these factors help to explain the long period of modest spreads on euro government bonds, it is surprising that it took investors so long to demand (much) higher yields on bonds issued by weaker countries using the euro. But when the sentiment finally changed it abruptly fueled a major firestorm.

Euro Area members initially indicated that they were willing to lend euro 30 billion ($40 billion) to tide Greece over until its adjustment measures were sufficient to avoid a default. But, as the dithering in European capitals continued, it became clear that larger amounts would be needed to get the job done. In the meantime, bond yields in "peripheral" Euro Area countries moved up alarmingly. While the need for swift action became more and more urgent, German internal politics caused a nerve-racking delay. Chancellor Merkel, who was facing an important midterm election, was reluctant to push too hard, but was willing to enlist outside help. On April 28, 2010, two Frenchmen, Jean-Claude Trichet, President of the ECB, and Dominique Strauss-Kahn, Managing Director of the IMF, met with Merkel and her outspoken Minister of Finance, Wolfgang Schäuble, emphasizing the extreme importance of taking immediate action. In a press statement following the meeting, the German Chancellor responded that a Greek rescue was "a matter of stability of the Eurozone as a whole" and that negotiations between Greece and the IMF plus the European Commission (EC) needed to be accelerated. Taking a shot at earlier, politically inspired, decisions, she added that the question of Greece's admission to the Eurozone had "not been examined thoroughly enough" in 2000.[9]

After the German Parliament had reluctantly gone along, a gigantic credit package for Greece of euro 110 billion ($146 billion) was approved by the IMF (euro 30 billion, representing a record 3,200 per cent of Greece's quota) and the Euro Area countries (euro 80 billion). The Euro Area credit, provided on a bilateral basis by Greece's fifteen partner countries, is based on a floating short-term euro interest rate plus 3 per cent (around 5.5 per cent at that time). It is considerably more expensive than IMF credit, but the higher rate was necessary to reach agreement within the Euro Area. And, to justify the unprecedented size of the financial support, unusually stringent policy conditions were demanded. The program with Greece focused on bringing down the much too large fiscal deficits, excessive foreign borrowing, and untenably high spending on pensions and health, as well as weak competitiveness and a number of structural deficiencies. The approach followed is known as an *internal devaluation*, reflecting that, as a user of the euro, Greece could not devalue its currency. Internal devaluation can require severe austerity which a "normal" devaluation can blunt, but it provides better prospects for achieving permanently higher growth in the medium term. Moreover, a Greek devaluation would be economically (debt default, high interest rates, high inflation) and politically (loss of Euro Area membership and a seat on the ECB's Governing Council) very costly.

There were many doubts about the chances of Greece achieving the required major adjustments, which were estimated to cause the economy to shrink by 8 per cent in the next three years. Fiscal adjustment of 11 per cent over a three-year period is a tall order, and pension reform politically difficult. At the same time, the Greek government showed a strong commitment to the reform program and took immediate action. More optimistic observers noted that huge adjustments had been achieved in the past in Europe, such as in Sweden in the early 1990s. A comparison with Latvia's internal devaluation, launched in 2008, and Turkey's achievement of very strong adjustment and avoidance of default or debt rescheduling (described in Chapter 7) seems more appropriate. Greece is not Sweden, which benefited from its strong institutions and stable political situation. But the scale of fiscal adjustment required in Greece is not that different from what Turkey faced some ten years ago, and is projected to take place more slowly. Structural weaknesses are also quite similar. The main difference between the Greek and Turkish cases is that the latter gave up its pegged exchange rate in 2001, while Greece is opting for internal devaluation. But an important advantage for Greece was that its banking system was in good shape when it got into serious trouble, whereas Turkey's financial system was a disaster before it was thoroughly reformed.

Relative optimism gave way to fresh concerns as the spread on Greek sovereign bonds shot up again in early 2011. In reaction, Euro Area political leaders agreed in March to lower the interest rate charged on their bailout loan by one percentage point, easing Greece's annual debt service by more than $1 billion. In addition, Greece was granted an extension of the maturity of the loan, from 4.5 years (which was too short) to 7.5 years. The price demanded of Greece is mass privatization of state-owned enterprises, estimated to bring in $50 billion. At this juncture (June 2011) it remains to be seen to what extent it will be a success.

The Celtic Tiger comes a cropper

Greece's rescue calmed the markets for a while, but unease about the financial situation in Ireland, Portugal, and Spain returned in the course of 2010 like a fire doused initially but flaring up again. In the case of Ireland, objective observers started to realize that it was only a matter of time before the Celtic republic would have to seek aid from the EU and the IMF. The Irish government resisted such notions with force, claiming that it could solve its problems on its own, echoing Greece's initial position. And, as in Greece, the unnecessary delay in accepting the inevitable by the Irish politicians only made matters worse, causing the eventual rescue to be larger than would otherwise have been needed. Governments tend to resist turning to the IMF for as long as possible, in the process sacrificing the best outcome for their country for their own political survival.

Few countries can match Ireland's roller-coaster experience from the 1980s onward. Once one of the poorest countries in Western Europe, it produced a winning combination of sound macroeconomic policies, a shrewd business model to attract foreign investment, and good use of EU funds. High economic growth (6.5 per cent on average annually from 1990 to 2007) contributed to a spectacular reduction in the debt to GDP ratio (to a mere 25 per cent in 2007), inspiring confidence in what came to be known as the Celtic Tiger. Ireland succeeded in becoming one of the richest European countries on a per head basis and was held up as a model for a host of struggling countries. Its success in job creation was such that, after a century or so of large-scale emigration, Ireland began to benefit from significant immigration, including skilled workers from Eastern Europe.

In the meantime, success bred potentially dangerous side effects, in particular a real estate boom and an associated credit boom largely financed by short-term borrowing on international financial markets. Irish banks, in a state of hubris, threw caution to the winds and lent indiscriminately in a fashion similar to American banks' foray into high-risk activities. In effect the Irish banks "went crazy," as an insider described it, and totally ignored sound risk management practices. Adding to the eventual collapse was the failure of the Irish bank supervisors to put a halt to this behavior. As in some other small European countries – Switzerland and Iceland come to mind – the Irish banking system expanded to the point where it became (almost) *too big to save*.[10] Irish banks' assets reached a staggering level of over 500 per cent of GDP. The first big mistake by the Irish government was to provide a blanket guarantee to the banks in 2008. In addition, it provided gargantuan support to its failing banks after they had been cut off from international markets. By November 2010 the Irish government had spent around one-third of GDP in bailouts. The Irish banks were also able to stave off bankruptcy by borrowing heavily (euro 130 billion) and cheaply from the ECB, which was willing to extend unlimited loans to Euro Area banks pledging acceptable collateral (the requirements for collateral had been eased during the financial crisis). It is no surprise, therefore, that the ECB pushed hard for Ireland to tap the new European Financial Stability Facility (EFSF) and to apply for an IMF credit. A number of Euro Area governments, especially those whose private banks held large claims on Ireland, were also prodding Dublin to take the money, even if it made their taxpayers unhappy. Of course, in the case of an Irish default, bailouts of other countries' banks might be needed, affecting their taxpayers by another route.

After prolonged hard bargaining among European leaders about how to address financial crises in the Euro Area in general, combined with unwillingness by the Irish government to face facts in a timely fashion, Irish Prime Minister Brian Cowen announced on November 21, 2010 that his government had requested financial emergency support from the Euro Area and the IMF. After agreeing to a tough program, Ireland was granted euro 85 billion ($112 billion), with the European Commission contributing euro 45 billion, the IMF euro 22 billion and Ireland itself using euro 17.5 billion from its National Pension Fund and its cash reserve. In addition, three countries from outside the Euro Area (the United Kingdom, Sweden, and Denmark) pledged around euro 5 billion in bilateral loans. So as to give Ireland more time for repayment than under a normal IMF standby, the Fund credit was granted under its Extended Facility, which has to be fully amortized in ten years. The bulk of the funds (euro 50 billion) was intended as budget support, while the remainder would be used to aid the Irish banks. On average, the interest rate charged on the support package was expected to be around 5.8 per cent, depending on the rate at which the EFSF could borrow. While on the high side, it was considerably lower than the rates at which Ireland could borrow in the market. At the same time, it implied that, in order to stabilize the debt to GDP ratio, the Irish economy would have to grow by around 4 per cent, assuming an inflation rate of 2 per cent. Tough policy conditions to be met by Ireland included reducing the budget deficit from over 30 per cent of GDP to a sustainable level of 3 per cent in 2015. It was made clear from the Irish side that the size of its banks would shrink very substantially. No action was taken on private sector involvement, except that junior bonds (subordinated debt) underwent haircuts. The fact that senior bondholders were not subjected to any type of haircut did not sit well with the public – in either Ireland or Germany – most of whom resented having to undergo austerity while senior bondholders escaped scot free. Not surprisingly, the political fallout of the Irish debacle was considerable, and the governing coalition lost the elections in early 2011. The same fate was in store for Portugal, where Prime Minister José Sócrates stepped down in March 2011 after a futile attempt to regain market confidence. In May an IMF/EC package of $116 billion was agreed with Portugal.

There are important differences between the Greek and Irish crises. Greece allowed its public finances to get out of hand and covered the extent of its excesses, whereas the Irish problem did not originate in its public sector but in a private financial system gone wild. This has led to some suggestions that, unlike the Hellenic crisis, the Gaelic crisis should not be addressed by fiscal austerity. But, since a combination of massive bailouts of its banks and an absence of economic growth caused Ireland's fiscal deficit to balloon and its debt to GDP ratio to reach over 100 per cent, there would be no escape from drastic spending cuts and tax increases unless Dublin allowed its banks to go under. Another difference between the case of Greece and that of Ireland is the role played by IMF surveillance. The Fund was more alert to the risks developing in Athens than the worsening underlying situation in Dublin. But, while surveillance of the Irish economy did raise concerns about a number of risks, there were some serious shortcomings as well. The IMF's 2007 annual examination of the Irish economy, although mentioning a number of concerns, painted a picture of continued prosperity.

The euro under attack

Impressive though it was, the Greek rescue of May 2010 did not bring a return of confidence. Fear spread that Ireland, where the banking system needed to be bailed out at huge cost to the government, and Spain, where a collapse of the real estate market caused serious ripple effects, as well as Portugal, whose overall debt levels appeared to be unsustainable, were in danger of following Greece's example. If these countries were to default, it was argued, the cohesion within the Euro Area would be severely put to the test. The result was intense pressure on the euro. The common currency had been valued at a rate of near 1.50 to the dollar in late 2009, near to its peak of 1.60 in early 2008. While these levels were generally seen as too high to compete successfully in world markets, the euro's rapid decline in the spring of 2010 – after gradually declining to 1.33 on May 3, it plunged to around 1.20 – was considered dangerous for the stability of world foreign exchange markets. Excessive movements in the world's major currencies can cause serious economic disruption and lead to trade protectionism. This is especially dangerous in times of economic downturn, as the 1930s so clearly demonstrated. In the United States policymakers became concerned that the dollar was appreciating too much, hurting America's exports and delaying its slow recovery from the recession.

Following heated discussions lasting into the early morning, the ministers of finance of the sixteen Euro Area member countries surprised the world – and possibly themselves – by announcing on May 9, 2010 that they stood ready to rescue the weaker members of their bloc by up to $1 trillion. Expressed in euros, the Euro Area share was 500 billion, to be supported when necessary by up to euro 250 billion from the IMF. To invoke a military analogy, here was the equivalent of the application of the Powell doctrine (overwhelm the enemy with disproportionate numbers) intended to create a "shock and awe" effect. Market reaction was immediately positive, but suffered from some erosion, with the euro sliding to 1.19 on June 8. The main concern was that the countries saddled with too much debt and unsustainable budget deficits would take insufficient action to return to a viable situation. While Ireland and Portugal quickly announced austerity packages, Spain's Prime Minister, José Luis Zapatero, had to be prodded into action, as he feared that his country's shockingly high unemployment rate of 20 per cent would climb further if he implemented belt- tightening policies. He also worried about losing the support of his labor union allies if he were to engineer much-needed labor market reforms. In an unusual gesture, President Obama added his voice to those of European leaders by calling Zapatero to convince him of the need for bold action. Realizing that there was no other way out, Spain soon announced an impressive package of budgetary and structural measures. Italy, although not directly in the danger zone, but with external debt too high at over 100 per cent of GDP, followed with a more modest austerity package. France, which had already initiated a number of reforms, pushed for further measures. In the realization that pensions had become too generous in the ageing societies of Europe, the retirement age was raised in several countries, despite widespread protests. Once again the maxim "no reform without a crisis" proved to be true for democratic societies.

The European Central Bank did its part by announcing that it stood ready to *purchase bonds* issued by Euro Area governments directly from the market. This took markets by surprise; such extraordinary actions had not been expected from the ECB, generally considered to be among the more conservative central banks. At the same time, the ECB, wanting to avoid the impression that it was now creating money by buying bonds, explained that it was offsetting the monetary effects of the purchases through its money market operations. Still, the step was highly unusual, as it included buying Greek government bonds as well as those issued by other weaker members of the common currency area. Earlier, commercial banks in the Euro Area had been able to borrow heavily from the ECB against collateral consisting of government bonds issued by high debt countries, which would have caused raised eyebrows before the global crisis erupted. But direct large-scale purchases by the ECB of bonds with a low rating would have been unthinkable in normal times. This flexibility was generally appreciated by others, but did not enjoy unanimity within the ECB's Governing Council, with the President of the German *Bundesbank*, Axel Weber, revealing that he had opposed the move. Bond purchases by the ECB rapidly reached euro 60 billion (about $80 billion) and continued at a variable pace (Weber resigned soon afterward).

And still the unrest did not fully subside. Worries remained about the solidity of various European banks that had been slower in revealing their losses than most banks elsewhere. Some bad surprises had occurred earlier, for instance with respect to Dutch and Belgian banks. Many of them had had to be bailed out by their governments, resulting in a number of nationalizations. Foremost among those deemed still vulnerable were some of the German banks, which for many years had shown low profitability. A particular problem existed with respect to the so-called *Landesbanken*, banks owned by German States but stripped of their subsidized status as a result of EU rules. In order to elevate their profits, Landesbanken had invested heavily in higher-yielding, more exotic, and often toxic assets, such as American asset backed securities. And, as a consequence of receiving substantial government support, the European Commission instructed the Dutch bank and insurance group Internationale Nederlanden Groep (ING), on grounds of fair competition, to split its banking and insurance business into two separate entities. In another development, many voices suggested that stress test results of the largest European banks should be published to bolster confidence. It took time to sway the German government to follow the successful American example in releasing stress test results. Finally, in July 2010, the EU followed, having conducted stress tests on a quite large scale, with ninety-one European-based banks, covering 65 per cent of the total banking market, participating as against nineteen in the American exercise. Only seven banks failed the test (one already government-owned German bank, one from Greece and five Spanish medium-sized savings banks).[11] Critics were quick to argue that the examiners did not calculate what losses could be incurred in case of a default by the weak Euro Area countries. But regulators parried by providing details of banks' holdings of sovereign bonds by nationality, indicating "you do the math." In the end the exercise turned out to have a calming effect on markets. But, as the Irish banks soon after went on life support, it became clear that the stress tests had indeed not been rigorous enough and that tougher new ones had to be conducted in 2011.

Had the stress tests taken place earlier and been more convincing, and the Greek rescue decided earlier, the euro crisis could have been mitigated. While the Irish crisis produced renewed market unrest, this was due more to the likelihood that senior bondholders would undergo a haircut than to pressure on the euro, whose rate stayed mostly stable at that point. With renewed uncertainty about the soundness of the finances of Portugal and Spain, the euro lost some ground, but the correction was not as sharp as in May. While capital was flowing out of Lisbon and Madrid, the money mostly stayed within the Euro Area, since the main creditors of Iberia were banks in Germany, France, and other Euro Area countries. It is often overlooked that, to the extent that capital does not leave the Euro Area, there is no effect on the euro exchange rate. Nevertheless, in a panicky market investors could abandon the euro, and short selling could well amplify the effect. Against this background, European policymakers scrambled at the end of 2010 and in early 2011 to develop a toolbox of measures that would be sufficient either to prevent crises from spreading or to contain fires that were burning out of control in some of the weaker Euro Area countries. In the meantime, the euro strengthened more than expected, reaching 1.40 against the dollar in March 2011, not a level that would indicate a lack of confidence in the common currency. As a corollary, markets and policymakers increasingly saw the crisis as one of unsustainable sovereign debt in parts of the Euro Area and of undercapitalized European banks.

The superfund and the bailout mechanism

A major result of the crises in the Euro Area was the establishment of the EFSF and the agreement to develop a European sovereign debt rescheduling mechanism, the *European Stability Mechanism* (ESM), which is to replace the EFSF in 2013. Once again a major crisis was needed to bring about drastic change. While the EFSF was hastily put together following the Greek crisis, agreement on developing a debt rescheduling instrument was announced at the same time as the Irish bailout in November 2010. In both instances intense political maneuvering, involving the leaders of France and Germany as well as the President of the ECB and the Chairman of the Eurogroup,[12] preceded the agreement on both initiatives. Such momentous decisions cannot be taken by finance ministers and heads of central banks on their own, but need the stamp of approval of government leaders, who bear the ultimate responsibility. The main players were, as usual, French President Sarkózy and German Chancellor Merkel, mainly supported by Southern and Northern Europe, respectively. This is not to say that other countries using the euro simply accept any compromise reached by the two largest countries of the Euro Area, but generally their contribution is mainly one of a technical nature, as well as, from time to time, in facilitating agreement. Other important players are Herman van Rompuy, the former Belgian Prime Minister, who became the first president of the European Council (composed of heads of government), and Jean-Claude Trichet, who, since becoming president of the ECB in 2003, has significantly raised his profile and the reputation of his institution.[13]

The EFSF was established to provide the Euro Area with an impressive pool of money to support members in dire financial straits. The facility had to be sufficiently large to deal with simultaneous debt crises in a number of (smaller) Euro Area countries and to convince markets of the resolve of the Euro Area to head off sovereign defaults. Member countries pledged euro 440 billion for this purpose. Together with funds available under an already existing EU financing mechanism (the European Stability Fund) and an IMF announcement that it could contribute another euro 250 billion, a total package of euro 750 billion (around $1 trillion) was announced to the world on May 9, 2010. But detractors soon pointed out that the effective capacity of the superfund was only euro 250 billion, since guarantees from potential borrowers could not be taken into account.

Arriving at a suitable legal framework for the EFSF proved to be very hard. During a long nocturnal session of European finance ministers, the impasse was broken when Maarten Verwey, a member of the Dutch delegation, suggested that the EFSF should be a *special purpose vehicle*. This vehicle has the authority to borrow on capital markets supported by guarantees from Euro Area governments (up to 120 per cent of their *pro rata* shares), enabling it to obtain a triple A rating. Troubled countries can therefore tap the EFSF at (much) lower interest rates than they would have to pay on sovereign bonds issued by them. IMF involvement is mandatory to provide extra funds and to promote well-designed programs. To sell the EFSF to the German Parliament and the skeptical German public, Chancellor Merkel issued several dire warnings about the future of the euro if the proposal was not approved. (In the event her threats had the desired result.) While such pronouncements are often necessary for domestic political purposes, they can spook investors. But, since Ms Merkel also on various occasions forcefully expressed German support for the euro, the damage was limited. Doubts still remained whether the EFSF was large enough to deal with financial crises in a larger number of countries, including Spain. This led to a decision on March 24, 2011 to increase the effective lending capacity of the superfund to euro 500 billion (this includes the resources of an older fund of euro 60 billion). It was also agreed that the enhanced EFSF could buy bonds directly from distressed sovereign debtors, but that purchases of such bonds in the market (at a discount) were not to be undertaken by the facility. This is unsatisfactory, as it leaves the ECB as the only institution that can intervene in bond markets for the purpose of lowering spreads on, for instance, Irish government debt. It represents a failure by Euro Area governments to place the responsibility for possible losses where they belong, that is, with the governments themselves. The task of central banks is to supply short-term liquidity support where needed, not to provide bailout facilities indefinitely.

In the meantime, Euro Area leaders were looking for additional ways of preventing sovereign defaults, and of appeasing taxpayers who were unhappy with bailouts, of countries in trouble because of their own policy failures. This led to proposals for some type of *sovereign debt rescheduling mechanism*, akin to the idea that had been launched in the early 2000s and discussed at length in the IMF, but not adopted (see Chapter 8). A scheme of this kind would under certain circumstances impose losses on private creditors, easing the potential burden for taxpayers in the countries providing the bailout funds, as well as serving as a warning to imprudent lenders. Many observers felt that not only would financial bailouts without private sector involvement (PSI) foster moral hazard, but also that there was a considerable chance that countries tapping the EFSF would still in the end default on their sovereign debt. At the same time, other stakeholders expressed concern that an automatic rescheduling mechanism would tempt countries with large budget deficits and high debts to use the mechanism as a way out of their predicament. Among those opposing the German initiative for a full-fledged debt rescheduling mechanism, the ECB spelled out its opposition on various occasions. For instance, Lorenzo Bini Smaghi, an ECB executive director, argued that an automatic debt rescheduling mechanism would not be compatible with euro participation.[14] In his view, substantial haircuts imposed on bondholders would "hammer" the domestic financial system and damage the economy. Access to capital markets would be impaired for a long time, while a failure to repay official support funds would have "major political consequences." In other words, for Euro Area countries in trouble there was no good alternative to going the route of internal devaluation while borrowing from the EFSF (and the IMF).

Discussions on whether the Euro Area needed a debt rescheduling mechanism continued for several months, with German Finance Minister Schäuble publicly touting his proposal for an automatic system for "misbehaving" countries. The timing of this communication, no doubt mainly intended for internal consumption, was unfortunate as it worried investors in bonds issued by Ireland, Portugal, and Spain, driving up the spreads they had to pay on their international borrowing. Politics and markets do not always mix well, and often a choice has to be made between obtaining political support for certain actions (in this case a big bailout for Ireland following on the heels of the Greek rescue) and avoiding negative market reaction.

In a meeting between Sarkózy and Merkel in the French coastal resort of Deauville a compromise was reached. It was further worked out and agreed by the Euro Area ministers of finance.[15] The ESM, which is to replace the EFSF in mid-2013, is to develop an appropriate mix of financing and adjustment for Euro Area countries having trouble servicing their debt. Unlike the EFSF, the ESM will require a (limited) change of the Treaty of the European Union (the Lisbon Treaty). National legislatures will have to give their approval, including the critical German Parliament. Moreover, the red-robed members of the German Constitutional Court will also have to be satisfied that the new mechanism is in conformity with the EU Treaty. But, given the high stakes, it is likely that these obstacles will be overcome. The newly established body will incorporate a degree of private sector involvement (PSI), which has been absent in the EFSF, with the dual objective of protecting taxpayers and reducing moral hazard.

The main rule of the ESM will be that Euro Area countries in financial distress can receive a financial bailout under strict economic and fiscal conditions and that private creditors will share the burden when solvency is at stake. Debt sustainability analyses, to be conducted jointly by the IMF, the EC, and the ECB, will determine whether the country in trouble is going through a liquidity crisis or whether the problem is one of solvency. If the issue is one of liquidity, PSI will be limited to "encouraging" private creditors to maintain their exposure "in line with the current EU and IMF practices." In this regard the model would be the Vienna initiative (described in the section on Eastern

Europe). Compulsory PSI only comes into play when the problem is diagnosed as one of insolvency. The miscreant will not only have to undertake strong adjustment measures, but will also have to negotiate a debt restructuring deal with its private sector creditors. If the country's debt can be made manageable again through this route, financial support will be given. Otherwise it will have to go it alone and face a messy default.

The most important element of the ESM approach is that, instead of an automatic (or *ex ante*) debt rescheduling mechanism, *collective action clauses* (CACs) will be included in all new Euro Area government bond contracts, starting in June 2013. This will bring Euro Area practices in line with those under UK and US laws.[16] The Eurogroup Ministers also spelled out that qualified majority decisions on debt relief for governments could take various forms: standstills, extension of maturities, interest rate cuts, and haircuts. To protect it from losses, the EMS will be granted preferred creditor status, "junior only to IMF loans." And, to help prevent refinancing crises in the future, Euro Area governments will strive to lengthen the maturities of new bonds they issue "in the medium term." An exhortation to do this straightaway would have made more sense.

As was to be expected, reactions to the plans for an ESM were mixed. Banks and other investors were positive and relieved that there was no immediate threat of haircuts. But some outside observers were highly critical, arguing that Greece and Ireland would be better off defaulting in the short run, as their debt burden was unsustainable. Why did the European policymakers not take the route of introducing private sector burden-sharing (except for junior bond-holders) before 2013? A major consideration was that announcing an immediate involvement of private investors would be pouring oil on the fire, inducing markets to run for the exit faster than before. Delaying PSI until 2013 was, therefore, seen by European policymakers as taking the sting out of market fears, while sticking to the burden sharing-principle. Giving banks more time to strengthen their balance sheets was another consideration.

Choosing to go the route of CACs rather than an automatic rescheduling mechanism in cases of insolvency should reduce debtor moral hazard, but only if policy conditions are strong enough to discourage troubled countries from applying for a loan from the ESM. At the same time, since CACs will be required only from June 2013 onward, it will take considerable time for new bond issuance to provide a "critical mass" to allow meaningful debt workouts. In cases of "mere" liquidity crises, voluntary pledges along the lines of the Vienna initiative can be seen as PSI "lite." But banks and other investors should realize that collective dumping of a country's government bonds could easily lead to liquidity problems morphing into a solvency crisis. They would then end up having to negotiate a debt rescheduling anyway.

Political leaders have been slow to take sufficiently confidence-inspiring measures to combat the crisis in the Euro Area. While new actions have generally led to initial positive reactions by markets, renewed pressures have usually emerged after a while. The ECB's Jean-Claude Trichet and European Commission officials have pressed for more decisive action, advocating a "quantum jump" in the euro bloc's decision-making. The political agreement reached in March 2011 to strengthen the Stability and Growth Pact goes in the right direction. Not only is the budget deficit rule of no more than 3 per cent of GDP to be interpreted more strictly, but the rule of debt ratios of no more than 60 per cent – broached by most members of the club – is to be enforced by sanctions. And, in a far-reaching agreement, governments have committed to bring down their debt ratios by one-twentieth a year until they reach the 60 per cent level. Noncompliance will result in fines. Finally, a Pact for the Euro, aimed at improving competitiveness in underperforming member states, has also been agreed.

These initiatives have been demanded by Germany, and supported by the Netherlands, Austria and Finland, as the price for providing more resources to the superfund and the future European Stability Mechanism. While they represent real progress, successful enforcement is not guaranteed. No doubt countries having problems adhering to the strengthened SGP rules will look for exemptions. Therefore, establishing a separate independent body monitoring fiscal policy should help to keep Euro Area members' feet to the fire. Collecting fines from countries breaching the rules could prove challenging. Telling Italy, for instance, that it has to send a check will not go down well. As an alternative to slapping pecuniary fines on countries in breach of the rules, consideration can be given to halting payments from the EU's structural funds or suspension of their voting rights. Pushing countries out of the Euro Area is a bridge too far and would oblige them under the Treaty to withdraw from the EU as well. In addition, it should be made crystal clear that no country should in the future be allowed to adopt the euro for mainly political reasons. And lingering doubts about involving the IMF in bailouts of Euro Area countries should be overcome. While the Fund's role as an additional source of money is welcome, its presence is particularly important to ensure that borrowers' economic programs are well designed and that policy conditions are adequate.

All in all, despite much muddling through and hand-wringing, the Euro Area has proved to be more resilient than often thought. Pronouncements from political leaders that they will "do what it takes" to keep the euro bloc together no longer sound hollow.[17] And, since any country leaving the Euro Area will face very high economic and political costs, a breakup of the Euro Area is highly unlikely; an opinion shared by many astute observers, such as Willem Buiter, the chief economist of Citibank and former member of the BoE's monetary policy committee.[18]

11
Saving the System

The international financial system required frequent firefighting from the 1980s onward. In reaction to the global firestorm that flared up in the summer of 2007, a raft of measures was taken, although many of them still need further elaboration. While new legislation and rule-making on both sides of the Atlantic have fallen short of what many observers regard as necessary for a more permanent effect on the system, the changes agreed upon have materially reduced the risk of another major financial crisis in coming years. But the global *financial* system represents only part of the *international financial and monetary architecture*. The financial part can be compared to the superstructure of a building, including the roof, walls, floors, and wiring, all of which can cause serious problems when damaged. By contrast, the international *monetary* system can be compared to the fundament of the building, which, if it crumbles, requires a complete restructuring. During the financial turmoil of recent decades the monetary system has remained largely unscathed. There is no reason for complacency, however, as vulnerabilities and imbalances have gradually increased. Were the system to come under severe pressure, drastic measures would be needed to save it from collapsing. Some preventive action has been taken in recent years in the scope of IMF and G20 deliberations, but more needs to be done to further reduce the possibility of a breakdown which would surely have grave consequences for global welfare.

International monetary crises have, fortunately, been infrequent. Apart from the demise of the obsolete gold standard in the 1930s and the dollar crisis of the early 1970s, the global monetary system as a whole has not been severely endangered. Large fluctuations in the dollar–deutschemark exchange rate during the mid-1980s were surmounted in a timely fashion through international cooperation (the Plaza and Louvre accords, described in the Prologue). Moreover, despite concern about excessive currency fluctuations during the worst of the crisis of 2007–09, the dollar did not plunge, as it served as a *safe haven*, attracting inflows from investors who sought the protection offered by

US Treasury bills. In addition, *global imbalances*, as reflected in the large US current account deficit – which reached a peak of more than 6 per cent of GDP in 2006 – mirrored by large surpluses in China and oil exporting countries, narrowed substantially (the US deficit fell to 3 per cent of GDP in 2009), but a renewed increase in global imbalances could emerge rather quickly. The political difficulties of bringing down the American budget deficit, as well as China's continued unwillingness to free its exchange rate, point in that direction.

Two contrasting views have dominated the debate on global imbalances. On the one hand, Dooley and others have maintained that a Bretton Woods II system has evolved, with China content to keep exporting much more than it imports to create jobs and the US at ease with running large trade deficits that allow it to continue living "beyond its means." The "deal" involves China financing the US deficit at low interest rates.[1] On the other hand , the IMF and other observers have frequently issued warnings about the vulnerability of a situation in which the United States has been absorbing a very large share of world savings while its domestic savings have continued to be too low.

Whither the dollar?

While the American twin deficit has been financed smoothly over the years – the capacity of the US to borrow in its own currency has greatly contributed to this process – the probability that this borrowing streak could suddenly end has increased. The debt problems of a number of European countries should serve as a warning signal in this respect. But many Americans, both public and politicians, do not seem unduly concerned about the chances and dangers of a rapidly falling dollar. Just how dangerous would a sudden steep reduction in the value of the dollar be? First, a plunge of the world's major trading and financial currency could severely disrupt both goods and financial markets. With many commodities, like oil and various metals, priced in dollars on world markets, a hefty dollar depreciation would hurt commodity producers. Trading partners of the United States would lose competitiveness and could be tempted to take protectionist measures. The catastrophic experience with trade protection of the 1930s is a lesson that has, fortunately, not yet been forgotten, at least by policymakers, and trade measures have been few in recent years.[2] But such positive behavior cannot be taken for granted, especially if recovery from a deep recession is slow, coupled with stubbornly high unemployment. Global financial markets, conducting the most of their business in US dollars, would be roiled if the dollar were to fall rapidly. While some cross-border financial transactions are hedged in one form or another, very substantial amounts remain uncovered, either because hedging is expensive or because it is not available for certain types of transactions. And hedge funds do not, in fact, hedge, their whole strategy being built on taking open positions. A particularly problematic practice is known as the *carry trade*. It entails borrowing in currencies with low interest rates and investing the proceeds in high interest rate currencies without hedging. A profit is made when the interest rate differential exceeds any loss due to exchange rate movements. For instance, many investors have borrowed heavily in yen and Swiss francs at low interest rates, but also in dollars obtained at near-zero rates. They then proceed to place the money at high interest rates in countries such as Brazil, Korea, and Thailand. Countries on the receiving end of the carry trade often experience unwanted appreciation of their currencies and risk painful reversals in case of a sudden stop. They have from time to time taken measures to discourage large capital inflows, including capital controls. And they have complained to the United States and others about their easy monetary policies causing investors looking for higher yields to "carry" capital in large volumes to their domestic markets. There have even been apocalyptic warnings of *currency wars* as the Fed's policy of *quantitative easing* (money creation in a situation where interest rates are at rock bottom in an attempt to stimulate the economy) has been interpreted by some as a way of pushing down the dollar. This is despite regular pronouncements by the US Treasury, which decides on exchange rate policy rather than the Central Bank, that a strong dollar is in the interest of the United States.

What constitutes a strong dollar has, understandably, never been defined. Assuming that it implies avoiding a serious undervaluation of the dollar (the IMF has judged the American currency to be somewhat overvalued or in the right range in recent years), what can be done to maintain a "strong" dollar? The first, but rather weak, line of defense is *open-mouth policy*, consisting of reassuring pronouncements about the strength of the currency. Obviously this approach only works if the mantra, such as "a strong dollar is in the interest of the United States," is judged to be credible. A second line of defense consists of erecting an extensive network of *swap arrangements* between central banks (currencies are lent for short periods and then reversed), allowing rapid support to deal with sudden, reversible capital flows. If the problem turns out to be more persistent, the Fed can support the dollar through large-scale *intervention* in the foreign exchange market. But, since US foreign exchange reserves are relatively small (around $60 billion), it will need to obtain currencies like euros and yen by issuing bonds in foreign currencies.[3] Intervening in concert with the likes of the ECB, the Bank of Japan, and the Bank of England would be much more effective than going it alone. But currency intervention, especially for advanced countries with their voluminous foreign currency markets, is often seen as ineffective after a while. Still, the experience of China, which has managed to keep the appreciation of the *renminbi* very limited (perpetuating its undervaluation) by amassing a staggering amount of $3 trillion of official foreign exchange (around one-third of global reserves), demonstrates that, if there is a willingness to conduct gargantuan and indefinite interventions, the value of a currency can be very significantly influenced, or manipulated, as is regularly claimed. And, among advanced countries, Switzerland has aimed at keeping its exchange rate from rising rapidly by purchasing large amounts of foreign currencies. But such extreme action comes at a considerable cost in view of the risk of dollar (or euro) depreciation. Moreover, sterilizing the monetary effects of such large purchases to avoid inflation can be expensive.[4] There has so far been only one instance of modest intervention in the dollar–euro exchange market (in 2000, to support a then flagging euro). And Chinese-scale purchases, whether of dollars or euros, are highly unlikely to occur elsewhere.

One more instrument is available to counter unwanted movements in exchange rates, which is clearly the most effective, but also the one with the strongest side effects. Gearing *monetary policy* towards defending the currency value is acceptable only under certain conditions. During the Asian crisis it was necessary to push up interest rates, as the costs of a collapsing currency in countries like Korea and Indonesia outweighed the costs of foregone growth (see Chapters 2 and 3). Sharp, but short-lived, increases in interest rates were able to stabilize the won and the rupiah at the time. But this is not a policy that can be maintained for a long period because of the damage to the domestic economy. And, under a system of floating rates, the larger the country the less likely it is to sacrifice domestic objectives for external stability, as under the classical gold standard. It is, therefore, hard to envisage either the US Treasury or the ECB redirecting its focus on the exchange rate in the conduct of monetary policy, except under truly unusual conditions. At the same time, the global financial crisis has taught us to be able to "think the unthinkable." For example, if the US, while failing to bring its fiscal deficit back to sustainable territory, gets embroiled in a serious military conflict in the Middle East or Northern Asia, the result could be a run on the dollar which could force the Fed to raise interest rates when domestic conditions do not call for policy tightening.

Reforming the monetary system

The IMF, as its very name implies, has a special responsibility for overseeing the international monetary system, but it could have done a better job over the last four decades. Little analytical work has been done in this area by its staff since the 1970s, and for many years there was hardly any discussion of the functioning of the system in its Executive Board.[5] It was only after the United States accused the Fund of being "asleep at the wheel" with respect to exchange rate issues, reflecting its unhappiness with China's resistance to letting its exchange rate float freely,[6] that Fund management took new systemic initiatives. Rodrigo de Rato, a former Spanish Minister of Finance, who had succeeded Köhler as the IMF's Managing Director in 2004, first proposed to reduce global imbalances through a process of *multilateral consultations*, bringing together five main players in the world economy (the United States, the Euro Area, China, Japan, and Saudi Arabia). But the aim of having the five parties agree on a set of policies that would reduce both the US balance of payments deficit and the counterpart surpluses elsewhere was not realized, as the US and China did not agree to take the talks to the ministerial level. Another initiative developed at the IMF under Rato was an attempt to strengthen the Fund's grip on countries' exchange rate policies. This initiative has so far also proven to be ineffective.

The international monetary system consists of five main parts: the international adjustment process, the exchange rate system, international liquidity, international capital flows, and the role of the IMF in managing the system. A while after the global crisis broke out, the Fund staff produced a number of useful analytical and policy-oriented papers on the monetary system,[7] while John Lipsky, the IMF's second in command, spelled out the position of the Fund's management.[8] Progress has been made on reforming several elements of the monetary system, but important gaps remain. These gaps constitute a risk to the smooth functioning of the system and have to be plugged to save it from serious disruption such as a "disorderly unwinding of global imbalances," to use the euphemistic language of the IMF. The international adjustment process, or the course required to bring back global imbalances to sustainable territory, is closely related to the exchange rate issue, as well as that of the demand for international liquidity. And the role of the IMF is to steer the international monetary system in such a way that it fosters international trade and economic growth at low rates of inflation.

Adjustment and financing of balance of payments deficits need to go hand in hand. Abrupt adjustment is bad for growth, and financing is needed to smooth the necessary reduction of too large deficits. What is too large (unsustainable) is an old discussion. For instance, in the 1970s adjustment issues were frequently discussed at the OECD (then the leading forum for analysis of global economic issues). Industrial countries' current account balances were scrutinized, and suggestions for bringing down deficits and surpluses put on the table. At the same time, discussions on adjustment mechanisms took place at the IMF as part of a comprehensive effort to reform the international monetary system in the wake of the collapse of the Bretton Woods system.[9] But no consensus could be reached on what was not sustainable or on a mechanism that would reduce payments imbalances. Attempts to influence countries' policies to better achieve international balance with the aid of a system of indicators, developed at the IMF in the 1980s, were also unsuccessful in improving the adjustment process.

Following the conflagration of 2007 and beyond, the G20 developed a number of initiatives to collectively foster strong, sustainable, and balanced economic growth. Such a process implies a reduction of global imbalances.

The G20 embarked on a *Mutual Assessment Process* (MAP) intended to measure progress toward members' commitment, made at their Pittsburgh Summit of September 25, 2009, "to develop a process whereby we set out our objectives, put forward policies to achieve these objectives, and together assess our progress."[10] The IMF has been tasked to provide the necessary analysis to evaluate how countries' policies fit together. In the final stage, alternative policy scenarios are drawn up by the Fund staff whenever national policies do not add up to achieve the best global outcome. The exercise is, no doubt, a useful one, but for it to lead to significant policy adjustments that deviate from individual countries' initial objectives would require a rare level of international cooperation. Moreover, the G20 is too large a body to achieve a true give and take on national policy objectives. A better way to achieve some kind of a tradeoff in national policies would be to discuss the issues in a small group of the most important players on the world scene. But, rather than the five participants brought together in the multilateral consultations of 2006, it would make more sense to work with eight: the United States, the Euro Area, Japan, China, the United Kingdom, India, Russia, and Brazil (in line with the size of new IMF quota shares), with the possible addition of Saudi Arabia when energy is high on the agenda.

At the Seoul G20 meeting of November 11–12, 2010, the US Secretary of the Treasury proposed a broad approach to global imbalances, with current large current account deficits and surpluses serving as a trigger for closer examination of a country's policy mix. The suggested number for an external imbalance was 4 per cent, but with country-specific factors taken into account. At the 4 per cent level the United States would not at the time have qualified as "a country of interest," a category which, among G20 members, would include only the surplus countries China, Russia, Saudi Arabia, and Germany,[11] with South Africa and Turkey on the deficit side. But excluding the US, with its current account deficit (measured in dollars) still large, is hard to justify. Lowering the bar to 3 per cent of GDP would add the US, Japan, and India.

The American proposal was primarily an attempt to break away from the stalemate in the debate between the United States and China on the renminbi exchange rate. But it did not carry the day, as China and Germany did not support Secretary Geithner's approach. History repeats itself: all previous attempts at finding a mechanism to improve the international adjustment process and bring down global imbalances have met with limited success at most. As long as no sanctions apply and no conditional credit is sought, there is only a slim chance of countries adjusting their policies when this is not in their immediate national interest. One ray of hope is that it cannot be ruled out that global players with large imbalances can be convinced that it is in their longer-term – or enlightened – interest to take measures contributing to greater global stability. And there is an important task for the IMF: to produce analyses and recommendations to achieve such possible breakthroughs.

Exchange rate initiative stymied

Exchange rates are central to the Fund's mandate, but since the switch to floating rates by major countries in the early 1970s it has struggled to define its proper role in this domain. Currency depreciations and appreciations can play an important role in reducing external imbalances, but care has to be taken to avoid overshooting, as occurred during the Asian crisis. At the same time, resistance to correct currency overvaluation (Argentina in the early 2000s is a clear example) or undervaluation (China in recent years) can both damage the national economy and produce unwanted spillovers to other countries. The Fund's arsenal of tools to influence exchange rates is limited, and falls into the category of "soft law."[12]

In recognition of this unsatisfactory state of affairs, the IMF proceeded to strengthen its rules on exchange rate and related policies, resulting in a scheme to publicly assess the appropriateness of countries' exchange rates. The most controversial part was that it enabled the Fund's Executive Board to designate a member's currency as "fundamentally misaligned."[13] While no sanctions apply to this label, apart from "naming and shaming," a verdict of gross undervaluation can trigger retaliatory action by a country's trading partners. China voted against the decision, fearing that it could lead the United States to denounce China as manipulating its currency's value, allowing Washington to introduce trade measures against Beijing. In response, China refused to allow Fund staff to perform the standard annual examination of its economy. IMF management bravely tried to have some small countries' currencies labeled as fundamentally misaligned, beginning with the tiny Maldives, but got nowhere. After a flurry of diplomatic activity, the new IMF Managing Director, the savvy former French politician Dominique Strauss-Kahn, who resigned under a cloud in May 2011, quietly dropped attempts to use the "offensive" label. Instead, he spoke of a "substantial undervaluation" of the renminbi. This tactical retreat may help to encourage China to play a constructive role, outside the glare of publicity, in the G20 or in a smaller group of economic powerhouses.

Closely related to exchange rate issues, the size and composition of *international liquidity* has become a hot topic again. The IMF has the obligation to monitor the adequacy of international reserves, defined as resources which are available at all time and without conditions. Besides reserves, international liquidity consists of conditional liquidity, mostly the credit facilities of the Fund. In recent decades little work was done on reserve adequacy, partly because countries with access to international financial markets could easily replenish their reserves by borrowing. And *special drawing rights* (SDRs) – an artificial reserve asset that can be issued with a 85 per cent majority of the votes by the IMF – could be created when there was a shortage of global reserves.[14] But dollar reserves expanded so rapidly in the early 1970s that there was little concern about any scarcity. The Asian crisis, however, demonstrated that the reserves of some countries had been too small to support their currencies from taking a nosedive. And the IMF was slow to develop benchmarks or metrics for judging reserve adequacy. It clung to such obsolete rules of thumb as maintaining reserves of no less than three months' worth of imports. In a world with hugely increased and mobile capital flows, new approaches were needed. With this gap in mind, I tried my hand at developing an operational benchmark to assess countries' reserve adequacy.[15] The benchmark is based on a distinction between potential *external* drains of reserves, measured by the volume of a country's short-term external debt, and potential *internal* drains, using a certain share of the money supply as a proxy. Applying this benchmark – which has been used in a number of IMF country reports – I concluded at the start of the 2000s that several emerging countries were holding too few reserves. Among these were Argentina, Brazil, Mexico, Hungary, Russia, South Africa, and Turkey.[16]

By contrast, countries' accumulation of reserves in more recent years has frequently exceeded prudent levels of self-insurance. This can be expensive, as the net costs of holding foreign exchange reserves (measured as the return foregone on investments that could have been undertaken with those resources, minus the – much lower – yield enjoyed by investing reserves in liquid assets) can be quite high. Calculations based on 2005 data indicated that Malaysia was already "losing" 8 per cent of GDP in this way at the time, China 6 per cent, and Russia (which went from having puny reserves to a flood in just half a decade) 4 per cent.[17] Five years on, many more countries, including Asian countries as well as Brazil, had accumulated very large reserves. Rising reserve levels had become "too much of a good thing."[18] This was borne out by experience during the global firestorm, when most emerging countries were able to ride out the crisis without dipping deeply into their reserves. Early in the crisis, however, there were justified concerns that some large capital importers could get into serious trouble if the flight toward safe havens continued for too long. To prevent this, world leaders took resolute action. IMF funds available for lending were doubled to $750 billion, and in a surprise move it was decided by the G20 to have the Fund issue new SDRs (for the first time in thirty years) to the tune of $250 billion, nicely topping up the total package to an awe-inspiring $1 trillion. Simultaneously, the Fund revamped its various lending facilities (further discussed in the section on the role of the IMF). These swift actions helped to prevent the global crisis from spreading to emerging countries, which soon returned to enjoying impressively high growth rates, while the advanced countries were mired in stagnation and experienced a slow recovery. In addition, capital flows to many emerging countries (Eastern Europe being the main exception) became so plentiful that the countries faced difficult monetary policy choices. Countries like Brazil could either let their currencies appreciate, but face a serious loss of competitiveness, or they could add to already ample reserves or lower interest rates, which would further stimulate an already booming economy. But they could also introduce capital controls.

Capital controls reexamined

As explained in Chapter 2, the worldwide liberalization of capital movements came to an abrupt halt at the time of the Asian financial crisis. But, although pleas for reintroducing *capital controls* were widespread in the aftermath of the crises in emerging countries, few restrictions were actually put in place. Policymakers realized that controls on capital outflows could damage future inflows, as investors do not like the prospect of being stuck with a "mousetrap currency." Moreover, as many emerging countries were flooded with inward capital after a period of successful adjustment, the debate shifted to restrictions that would discourage inflows. This seemed to be the least unfavorable option to a number of countries swamped by "hot money." They rightly argued that these inflows were not caused by their own actions but stemmed from excess liquidity caused by expansionary monetary policy in advanced countries. These conditions were ideally suited to the carry trade, as interest rates fell to close to zero in the United States and other advanced economies at the same time as much higher yields could be enjoyed in places like Brazil and Korea.

Not only were such large capital movements complicating economic policy in well-run emerging countries, but they also posed a danger of abrupt reversals of "hot money." This led a number of countries to introduce measures to slow down the influx of foreign capital. Measures such as reserve requirements on local banks' foreign borrowing and the requirement to deposit imported short-term capital in interest-free accounts were put in place. Some observers, often those who had been critical in the past of the Fund's approach to capital controls (which was often misunderstood), applauded these actions. Others showed understanding, but cautioned against regarding such measures as a cure-all. Past experience with controls on unwanted inward flows is mixed. Often their effects are short-lived, as circumvention becomes widespread after a while, especially where sizable administrative bureaucracies have not (yet) been put in place. Europe's experience in the early 1970s, when it received a glut of capital fleeing from the dollar, is not very encouraging. More recent episodes in emerging countries show mixed results. All in all, controls on capital inflows can bring relief in the short run, but are usually undermined over time. The existence of a large volume of "footloose" money remains a threat to the smooth functioning of the international monetary system. As a first step toward achieving a more stable flow of cross-border capital, close monitoring of such flows is highly desirable. In addition, guidelines for dealing with disruptive capital flows could be developed. The IMF is the obvious organization to work on these issues.

The role of the IMF

The Fund has enjoyed a spectacular comeback and silenced those critics who labeled it as having become an obsolete institution. It reacted promptly to the threat of balance of payments crises and sudden stops in emerging countries during the near-meltdown of the international financial system. This was especially helpful with respect to Eastern Europe, but also enhanced confidence in Latin American countries. IMF resources were drastically increased and its credit facilities streamlined. And its Executive Board – after too long a delay – actively debated ways to reform the monetary system. Among the major topics were a possible resurrection of the SDR, as an important reserve asset, and its governance. And, as mentioned in the previous section, a discussion has started on involving the IMF in dealing with unwanted capital movements.

SDRs were introduced in the late 1960s in reaction to concerns that the world could face a shortage of reserves. But the role of the SDR rapidly decreased as a surfeit of dollars flowed into the reserves of Europe and Japan in the 1970s. The new asset, slated to become the "principal reserve asset" as enshrined in the IMF's Articles of Agreement,[19] was rapidly evolving into a kind of monetary *Esperanto*. Renewed interest in the artificial asset emerged with the revival of the debate on the international monetary system. Diversification of reserves had in the meantime become an important topic, especially after the creation of the euro. A spontaneous gradual increase in the euro's share in international reserves raised questions about the ideal composition of reserves. And, with concerns rising in 2007 about the stability of the dollar, followed in 2010 by fears over the position of the euro, the SDR reappeared on the stage after a very long absence. But the decision to allocate $250 billion in SDRs in 2009 was the wrong way to increase its role. There were two flaws involved: the first was to create unconditional liquidity in a world with excess reserves; the second was that new SDRs are distributed according to IMF quota shares. This is akin to carrying coals to Newcastle, as neither advanced countries nor China had a need for more reserves. But the desire to present a package of $1 trillion in new IMF-related resources (see above), and the ease of not having to involve the US Congress in deciding on SDR handouts, made this an attractive option for G20 leaders. Another flawed idea that has emerged is to promote the role of the SDR by issuing the artificial currency on a regular basis. At present the share of SDRs in global reserves is less than 4 per cent. To achieve principal asset status, stupendous amounts of SDRs (at least the equivalent of $5 billion) would have to be created, which would not only be reaching the wrong countries, but would also be potentially inflationary. A better, tailor-made, route to provide liquidity or credit lines to countries with large current account deficits or capital outflows is to provide large-scale *conditional* IMF credits. As long as conditionality is strong enough, inflationary consequences need not be feared. An important exception has been made for countries following "sound policies" by providing them with access to very large credit lines (FCLs) without upfront (or *ex ante*) conditions. Colombia, Mexico (initially $46 billion, later increased to $74 billion, the largest IMF commitment ever made to a country), and Poland have entered into FCL agreements which serve to give markets confidence about the potential borrowers' ability to withstand sudden stops. But what happens if the Fund considers that a country no longer follows sound policies? Markets are likely to react negatively when a country loses its FCL eligibility. According to Age Bakker, who was an IMF Executive Director from 2007 to 2011, such a scenario makes the Fund very reluctant to go that route.[20]

Finally, the *governance* of the Fund has been revamped to reflect the increased importance of emerging countries in the world economy. A shift of 6 per cent in quota shares from advanced countries to emerging countries has been agreed without reducing the voting power of low-income countries. In addition, European Union governments have agreed to give up two of their seven Executive Director chairs for the benefit of emerging countries. These are useful changes, but are to some extent a sideshow to please countries like China and Brazil, whose quotas will increase substantially but who will still operate in an Executive Board of twenty-four persons. A truly deep-seated change would consist of having a single chair for the Euro Area, but for now there is insufficient political support for this step. It has also been agreed to move away from the unwritten rule that the managing director always hails from Europe (and the president of the World Bank from the United States). This could be taken further by also no longer automatically appointing an American as the Fund's number two. But there should, of course, be a sound balance between geographical areas in the IMF management team of four persons. Management appointments are now made for five-year, renewable terms. In order to discourage any attempts at chair-clinging, a onetime, non-renewable term of eight years, as exists for the Executive Board of the ECB, would be better. A delicate, still to be resolved, governance issue revolves around the respective roles of the G20 and the IMFC (the Fund's ministerial committee). So far the G20 has gained in influence at the expense of the IMF. But there will always be an important role for the Fund, given its remarkable expertise.[21]

Unfinished business

It is imperative to make the international monetary system stronger in order to minimize the risk of serious damage to the system. In addition to the steps taken so far by the IMF/G20 as well as in Europe to bolster the euro, three areas deserve particular attention: international reserves, the carry trade, and private sector involvement. Moreover, erosion of central bank independence needs to be prevented.

The unbridled accumulation of *international reserves* by China and elsewhere in Asia has been a by-product of keeping the exchange rate undervalued, with the aim of stimulating export-led growth. Reserve levels compatible with self-insurance have long been surpassed. Large reserve holdings, traditionally kept mostly in dollars, can lead to sizable losses when exchange rates fluctuate sharply. To reduce this risk, central banks have gradually diversified the composition of their reserves, reducing the share held in dollars (still around 65 per cent) and increasing that held in euros (between 25 and 30 per cent).[22] Sudden shifts between foreign currencies held by central banks, or merely rumors of such a move, can unsettle markets. While the direct exchange rate effect of central banks reducing the dollar share in their reserves need not be very large, market reaction could be strong, interpreting the move as a lack of confidence in the primary reserve currency.

It is possible to reduce the risks of diversification and foster the role of the SDR at the same time. The SDR can provide a low-risk alternative investment avenue to the dollar and the euro. As the SDR is composed of a basket of currencies (the dollar, the euro, the Japanese yen, and the pound sterling, and in future probably also the renminbi), its value is more stable than those of individual currencies. But it is not a full-fledged currency that can be used directly in interventions. It first has to be converted into dollars or euros before it can be used to support a weak currency.[23] The suggestion of creating new SDRs is not the answer to the diversification issue, since, as was explained in the previous section, this would only add to the global excess of reserves. The solution is putting in place an SDR *Substitution Account* (SA) whereby central banks could exchange part of their dollars (and perhaps euros) into SDRs.[24] An SA would be administered by the IMF, but legally separated from it. As conversion into SDRs would not pass through the foreign exchange markets, the rate of the dollar or the euro would not be affected. The SA would only be allowed to place the dollars it receives in deposits with, for instance, the Bank for International Settlements. And the SA would be explicitly prohibited from intervening in foreign exchange markets, as this is not an activity the IMF should undertake at all.

A crucial question concerning a Substitution Account is how to share any exchange rate losses that it may incur. Disagreement on this matter at the last minute scuppered a proposal already agreed upon by the IMF Executive Board in 1980 to establish an SA, with an eye to removing the dollar overhang that existed at the time. But this problem can be overcome by combining a limited burden-sharing scheme with the use of some of the IMFs gold as a backstop. Simulations by Peter Kenen, a longtime scholar of the international monetary system, show that, if the United States were to assume the exchange rate risk of the SA on its own, it would not lose money under a base scenario, but would have to make substantial payments in a worst-case scenario.[25] The problem could be solved by sharing the burden of any losses with other IMF members or by charging a fee to users of the Account. In addition, a portion of the Fund's gold could be earmarked to provide a backstop in case losses surpass a certain (unlikely) level. Earlier opposition to selling Fund gold has diminished in recent years, and this ought to be acceptable as a way to make the international monetary system more stable.

Not only would an SDR Substitution Account – which can be established without a time-consuming amendment of the IMF's statutes – reduce shocks to the international monetary system, but it would also offer something for everyone. First of all, China and other large holders of dollar reserves would be provided with an attractive alternative investment opportunity. Not surprisingly, the Governor of the Chinese Central Bank, Zhou Xiaochuan, has expressed interest in a Substitution Account.[26] The United States would benefit by being protected from a hard landing of the dollar as a result of diversification, while Europe would be better shielded from excessive fluctuations of the euro. And, as Fred Bergsten, Director of the Peterson Institute for International Economics, points out, a Substitution Account would contribute to greater stability of the international monetary system by reducing the international role of the dollar, which he considers also to be in the interest of the United States. This would benefit all members of the international community. Bergsten sees creating an SA "as a big step psychologically."[27] Finally, using IMF gold as a means to strengthen the international monetary system by acting as a backstop would be at least as worthwhile as using it for supporting the Fund's income and providing grants to the poorest countries (something that is not within the remit of a monetary institution), as has happened in recent years.

Constraining the carry trade and other potentially disruptive capital movements would also bring more stability to the international monetary system. How to do this without too many side effects is another matter, but should not be evaded. Giving the IMF a bigger role in monitoring cross-border capital flows would be a useful first step. And some of the financial reforms set in motion in the wake of the global firestorm should have some effect on the carry trade, such as the Volcker rule (see Chapter 9), an approach that should be adopted worldwide. More directly, strengthening supervision on banks' currency mismatches would be helpful. A particular problem arises as far as hedge funds are concerned. Their business models are based precisely on taking speculative positions, and as far as their clients are concerned *caveat emptor* applies. But, since their activities can create problems for national economies, some degree of oversight is needed. It remains to be seen whether the rules designed in the US and Europe will be of much help in this regard. What could be more effective is special scrutiny by supervisors of the – sometimes very sizable – lending by banks to hedge funds. For countries on the receiving end of the carry trade, capital controls, including macroprudential measures, could bring temporary relief, but in the end they might need to adjust their monetary policy. And, as mentioned before, the IMF could play a role in developing guidelines for a proper response to disruptive cross-border capital flows.

Letting private banks and investors share part of the burden of bailouts (*private sector involvement*) has a mixed history, as previous chapters have borne out. Moral hazard remains a major issue, especially on the creditor side. There are several ways in which private creditors can be part of the solution rather than part of the problem when sovereigns become overextended. To leave debt restructuring entirely to the debtor country on one side and banks and bondholders on the other can result in a disorderly and damaging process, as seen in Argentina in the early 2000s. The voluntary code on sovereign debt restructuring (described in Chapter 8) has so far been applied only to small countries where the stakes are very low for private creditors. It is doubtful that the code will produce an optimal outcome when (much) larger amounts are involved. Incorporating collective action clauses (CACs) in sovereign bond contracts (treated in Chapter 8) is a much more promising approach. This route has also been chosen by the Euro Area members in the future European Stability Mechanism for dealing with their partners who are facing a solvency crisis. Private creditors will have to accept haircuts of some kind and should take the experience to heart, reducing moral hazard. The IMF and the Financial Stability Board should urge all countries that have not yet done so to adopt CACs. While the application of CACs solves the problem of holdouts that can frustrate a deal, they do not guarantee a satisfactory outcome, as the majority of creditors and the debtor may continue to disagree on the size of the haircut. This possibility calls for a *CAC plus* approach, with the IMF providing its authoritative debt sustainability analyses and serving as an honest broker to bring the negotiating parties closer. A case can also be made for a Brady plan approach, followed for Latin American countries in the 1980s and described in the Prologue, which allows gradual rescheduling to smooth the process of debt relief. A full-fledged sovereign debt rescheduling mechanism, as discussed in Chapter 8, is not needed under a CAC plus or Brady-type approach and has been rejected by Euro Area members for the ESM.

While solvency crises can be dealt with in an orderly manner, it is, of course, much better to try to prevent them. That is why, when a country is facing a liquidity crisis, the IMF should be called in at an early stage – although early action is seldom taken – and private creditors pressured to maintain their exposure to countries facing a liquidity crisis. The Vienna Initiative is an excellent model in such situations and has also been endorsed by the Euro Area's future ESM. This should also push back moral hazard, since most creditors are likely to realize that if they do not play along CACs will come into operation and haircuts will become inevitable.

Protecting *central bank independence* in a system of checks and balances is crucial for maintaining the stability of the international financial and monetary system. The world's major central banks earned respect for their unorthodox actions to save the global banking system from disaster and helping, in tandem with exceptional fiscal stimulus, to prevent another Great Depression. At the same time, stubbornly high unemployment as a result of the deep recession and opposition to huge bailouts amplified ever-present criticism of the Fed, mainly from populist quarters. Calls for reducing the American Central Bank's autonomy have been politicized. The ECB and the Bank of England have also been exposed to attacks from some quarters over their handling of the crisis. And it is to be expected that central banks will face more political pressure in the future as they raise interest rates to avoid inflation taking hold, especially when unemployment is still higher than before the crisis. Moreover, the Fed and the Bank of England have been formally given a bigger role in maintaining financial stability, while the ECB, which does not have a formal role in this domain, has taken on the task of calming financial markets. This course of events has drawn major central banks into the politically risky business of dealing with troubled banks. And conducting monetary policy with an eye also to asset price inflation (bubbles in the housing and equity markets), as advocated by some policymakers and many observers,[28] could prove to be quite unpopular. All in all, the signs are that the rather comfortable lives led by central bankers before the global crisis will not return anytime soon and that attacks on their independence could escalate. Since reduced central bank autonomy would be a big backward step in terms of maintaining monetary and financial stability, responsible politicians and the Financial Stability Board, as well as the IMF, should counter unfair and poorly informed criticism.

Epilogue

The financial world is a dangerous place, and has become more so since the mid-1990s. One emerging country crisis followed another, culminating in a near-meltdown in advanced countries after 2007. A complete catastrophe was only averted by the resolute action of central banks, treasuries, and the IMF. Has the shock of this narrow escape been sufficient to jolt the major players in the global financial system to adjust their behavior so drastically that systemic crises will be a thing of the past? Surely not. But much will already have been gained if the frequency and depth of financial firestorms can be reduced. What has become abundantly clear is that financial markets cannot be left largely to their own devices. Both the rational expectations and the efficient market theories, the underpinnings of the light-touch approach to regulation, have been found wanting.[1] The challenge for policymakers is to fix what is broken and prevent future conflagrations as much as possible, while avoiding unduly stifling the operation of financial markets.

So what is to be done? Experience with past crises, as covered in this book, demonstrates that several of the remedies applied have worked and that some lessons have been learned, but that others were not learned or were ignored. On the positive side, regulation and supervision of the financial system have been tightened and anchored in major legislation passed in the United States and new rules adopted by the European Union. Although these reforms fall short of what is really needed, they should reduce the riskiness inherent in the system; that is, if they are swiftly and comprehensively implemented and not undermined by uncooperative politicians unduly influenced by pressure groups. Another positive development is the restoration of the IMF's role as the centerpiece of the international monetary system, as well as the very substantial increase in the Fund's lending capacity. But care should be taken not to weaken Fund conditionality too much in an attempt to lessen the "stigma" attached to asking for IMF financial support. At the same time, the role accorded to the Fund in dealing with Euro Area crises is most welcome, but has proved to be very challenging. At the time that final corrections to the manuscript were made (June 2011) the greek sovereign debt marathon was still being run.

International cooperation in fighting the global firestorm has been impressive, but is subject to erosion as calm returns to markets and economic recovery becomes self-sustaining. While the G20 has proved to be a useful forum for high-level discussions, it is too big to achieve real breakthroughs in changing national economic policies. A smaller group, bringing together the world's major economic players, is likely to produce better results. American leadership in international financial and monetary matters, often successful but sometimes experienced as too politically inspired, should remain important, but should be subjected to stronger challenges. Global initiatives are unlikely to originate in Europe as long as it continues to punch under its weight. Only if the Euro Area succeeds in speaking with one voice can the old continent play a major role once again in shaping the future of the international financial and monetary architecture. (Great Britain will probably continue to side more with the US than with the rest of the EU.) As the emerging countries are spectacularly increasing their share in the world economy, their influence in the international arena is growing commensurately. As a result, the advanced countries will more often have to support compromises in the IMF and other forums.

While many initiatives have been taken to strengthen the system, unfinished business remains in several areas. Global imbalances are likely to grow again as the United States continues to rely excessively on foreign capital for financing its budget and its external deficit and China keeps the value of its currency too low. Major countries working in a small group might be able to break the impasse. As reserve diversification could push the dollar too low, an SDR Substitution Account administered by the IMF should be established. And, while long-term capital flows contribute significantly to global welfare, short-term flows, especially the carry trade, can cause serious disruptions. Though difficult to remedy without causing too many side effects, the issue should not be ducked. Moral hazard has not been pushed back to an acceptable level, although new initiatives in the Euro Area for dealing with sovereign debt problems envisage a larger role for the private sector in the future. Finally, it is worrisome that central bank independence is again under attack, especially in the United States. Leaving the existing autonomy of the world's major central banks intact is vital for maintaining financial and monetary stability. Responsible politicians and the IMF should be very clear on this point.

Notes

Preface

1. *New York Times* (1995) Western Allies Rebuff Clinton in Mexico Vote (February 5).
2. Brau and McDonald speculate that modesty could explain this reticence, with individuals wishing to avoid taking credit for successes by the Fund, as these are team efforts. But it could be that describing failures is even more unattractive. Eduard Brau and Ian McDonald (eds.) (2009). *Successes of the International Monetary Fund: Untold Stories of Cooperation at Work*. Basingstoke and New York: Palgrave Macmillan, pp. 3, 4.
3. I was in a position to observe these crises closely as well, as I worked at the Netherlands Bank and the IMF during these periods.

Prologue

1. Charles P. Kindleberger (1989). *Manias, Panics and Crashes: A History of Financial Crises* (revised edition). Basingstoke: Palgrave Macmillan, p. 3.
2. Moral hazard is a concept that originated in the insurance industry. For instance, a person can be tempted to burn down his or her house when he or she is insured for more than the actual value of the house. In the financial world, moral hazard refers to banks and countries taking excessive risks in anticipation of a bailout by the public sector.

1 Tequila and *Tesobonos*

1. J. Onno de Beaufort Wijnholds, Sylvester C. W. Eijffinger and Lex H. Hoogduin (eds.) (1994). *A Framework for Monetary Stability*. Dordrecht: Kluwer Academic Publishers.
2. For a comprehensive treatment of the causes of the Mexican crisis, see Mario I. Blejer and Graciana del Castillo (1998). "Déjà vu all over Again? The Mexican Crisis and the Stabilization of Uruguay in the 1970s." *World Development*, Vol. 26, No. 3 (March).
3. Fischer had been a brilliant academic and a high official at the World Bank.
4. See Robert E. Rubin and Jacob Weisberg (2003). *In an Uncertain World: Tough Choices from Wall Street to Washington*. New York: Random House.
5. Alan Greenspan (2007). *The Age of Turbulence: Adventures in a New World*. New York: The Penguin Press, pp. 159, 160.
6. Kafka, born in Prague and a nephew of the famous author Franz Kafka, served for a record 33 years as an IMF executive director.
7. In the Board of Governors all members of the IMF are represented at the level of ministers of finance or central bank governors. It is involved only in the most important decisions, such as quota increases or the issuance of SDRs.

2 From Miracle to Panic and Back: The Asian Crisis

1. Gunnar Myrdal (1968). *Asian Drama: An Inquiry in the Poverty of Nations*. New York: Twentieth Century Fund.
2. World Bank (1993). *The East Asian Miracle: Economic Growth and Public Policy*. Oxford: Oxford University Press.
3. This episode was never made public.
4. Robert Rubin and Jacob Weisberg (2003), *In an Uncertain World: Tough Choices from Wall Street to Washington*. New York: Random House, p. 220.
5. Later ousted in a military coup amid accusations of corruption.
6. A famous photograph shows the Indonesian president signing the document while seated, with Camdessus standing nearby with his arms folded "like a Dutch colonial master," according to some commentators.
7. *International Herald Tribune* (1998). Ms Sukarnoputri herself later became president of Indonesia (March 12).
8. Fourth annual economic conference organized by the National Bank of Croatia. I attended a large number of these excellent conferences.
9. Independent Evaluation Office (2003). *The IMF and Recent Capital Account Crises: Indonesia, Korea, Brazil*. International Monetary Fund.
10. The Paris Club may conjure up thoughts of entertainment, but it is a body chaired by the French Treasury in which creditor governments work out deals on debts owed to them by developing countries.
11. Joseph E. Stiglitz (2002). *Globalization and Its Discontents*. New York: W.W. Norton & Company.

3 The Korean Christmas Crisis

1. Construction was going on everywhere, and the country was quickly gaining a foothold in shipbuilding, car manufacturing, and electronic products. This industrial takeoff was later followed by China and other Asian countries.
2. Anne O. Krueger and Jungho Yoo (2002). "Falling Profitability, Higher Borrowing Costs, and Chaebol Finances during the Korean Crisis" in David T. Coe and Se-Jik Kim (eds.), *Korean Crisis and Recovery*. International Monetary Fund and Korean Institute for International Economic Policy.
3. Paul Blustein (2001). *The Chastening: Inside the Crisis That Rocked the Global Financial System and Humbled the IMF*. New York: Public Affairs.
4. Robert Rubin and Jacob Weisberg (2003), In an Uncertain World: Tough Choices from Wall Street to Washington. New York: Random House, pp. 228–41.
5. Brau and McDonald (2009), p. 37.
6. Hubert Neiss, Wanda Tseng, and James Gordon (2009). "The Korean Crisis Ten years Later; A Success Story" in Brau and McDonald (2009).
7. Ukraine defaulted in 1998.
8. *International Herald Tribune*, December 5, 1997.
9. Such candor was not common. Board members sometimes had difficulty in obtaining sufficient information from IMF staff and management. Only after considerable pressure did we receive all the facts necessary to reach well-reasoned positions. Tom Bernes, the diplomatic Canadian Executive Director, succeeded in getting management to report on Korea at every Board meeting.

10. On the Treasury side, expert officials like Timothy Geithner and Ted Truman were deeply involved, but had to deal with the outspoken political views of the State Department.
11. Rubin and Weisberg, (2003), pp. 240–1.
12. Robert D. Novak (1997). "Befuddled by The Bailout." *Washington Post,* December 29, 1997.
13. Padma Desai (2003). *Financial Crisis, Contagion, and Containment: From Asia to Argentina.* Princeton University Press, p. 219.
14. Jeffrey Sachs (1997). "Power unto Itself." *Financial Times* (December 11).
15. Stanley Fischer (1997). "IMF – the Right Stuff." *Financial Times* (December 17).
16. Shailandra Anjaria (1997). "Criticism of IMF based on faulty analysis and off the mark." *Financial Times* (December 17).
17. These intentions, which were *not* formal conditions, included opening the Korean money and bond markets to foreigners and allowing foreign borrowing by corporations.
18. Age Bakker and Bryan Chapple (2002). "Advanced Country Experience with Capital Account Liberalization." *Occasional Paper* No. 214, International Monetary Fund.
19. Pierre-Olivier Gourinchas and Olivier Jeanne (2004). "The Elusive Gains from International Financial Integration." *Working Paper* No. 04/47, International Monetary Fund.
20. Rawi Abdelal (2007). *Capital Rules: The Construction of Global Finance.* Cambridge, Massachusetts: Harvard University Press.
21. O'Donnell later became Secretary of the British Cabinet of Ministers.
22. Jonathan Ostry and others (2010). "Capital Inflows: The Role of Controls." *Staff Position Note SPN/10/04.* International Monetary Fund (February 19). www.imf.org/external/publ/ft/spn/2010/spn1004.pdf
23. Independent Evaluation Office (2005). *The IMF's Approach to Capital Account Liberalization.* International Monetary Fund.
24. Alan Greenspan (1997). Speech delivered at the Economic Club of New York. Reported in *International Herald Tribune* (December 4).

4   Indonesia with Nukes: The Russian Crisis

1. At its lowest point, life expectancy for Russian males fell below 60 years.
2. Martin Gilman (2010). *No Precedent, No Plan: Inside Russia's 1998 Default.* Cambridge Massachusetts: MIT Press.
3. John Odling-Smee (2006). "The IMF and Russia in the 1990s." *Staff Papers,* Vol. 53, No. 1, pp. 151–94. International Monetary Fund.
4. *New York Times* (1996). "IMF Head: He Speaks, and Money Talks." Interview with Michel Camdessus (April 2).
5. The success of these outings and the (lack of) enthusiasm from Camdessus's side is not known, but, since he had served in the French Army as a junior officer in the 1950s, the Fund's Managing Director most likely could shoot straight.
6. Odling-Smee (2006), No. 40, p. 173 .
7. I first met Chubais around 1990, when he was still an academic from Leningrad visiting the Netherlands and gathering ideas for transforming the Russian economy. But by 1998 he had become a central figure in an enfolding drama that had the international financial community on tenterhooks.
8. Sergei Kiriyenko, who had taken over from Chernomyrdin in March 1998, was given his marching orders after the default. President Yeltsin wished to bring back

Chernomyrdin as prime minister, but did not succeed, as his candidate was twice voted down in the *Duma*.

9. Author's interview with Mozhin, May 4, 2009.
10. The Bulgarian currency board, introduced in 1996 in the midst of a severe currency crisis at the insistence of the IMF, did deliver stability. The Argentine scheme had already been in place for seven years and was deemed a great success at the time.
11. Rubin recalled that, after the LTCM mishap, he frequently discussed these problems with Larry Summers and Alan Greenspan. Rubin's position – which differed from that of the others – was that the use of derivatives and high levels of leverage could pose problems, mentioning also that "many people who used derivatives didn't fully understand the risks they were taking" (p. 288). While these words were to prove prophetic, one wonders whether Rubin could not have done more to limit the role of Citibank in risky business transactions when he became an influential strategist. Citibank's near-bankruptcy in 2008 posed a serious threat to the financial system.
12. Described in detail in David Owen and David O. Robinson (eds.) (2003). *Russia Rebounds*. International Monetary Fund.

5   Double Bailout for Brazil

1. Described in Gustavo H. B. Franco (2000). "The Real Plan and the Exchange Rate." *Essays in International Finance* No. 217. Princeton University (April).
2. The General Arrangements to Borrow had been concluded between the IMF and ten industrial countries (the Group of Ten) in the early 1960s, and negotiations were underway in the fall of 1998 to add more creditors to the list of lenders (the New Arrangements to Borrow).
3. Independent Evaluation Office (2003). *The IMF and Recent Capital Account Crises: Indonesia, Korea, Brazil*. International Monetary Fund, p. 23.
4. Rubin and Weisberg (2003), pp. 289–90.
5. Rubin and Weisberg (2003), p. 291.
6. Lorenzo L. Perez and Philip R. Gerson (2009). "Anchoring Policy Credibility in the Midst of Financial Crisis" in Brau and McDonald (2009), pp. 106–20.
7. Benchmarks agreed in an IMF financed program are the lightest form of conditionality. Missing benchmarks do not lead to a suspension of the credit, as is the case when performance criteria are not met.
8. My own position continued to be that Brazil should manage the float rather than leaving the real completely free to find its own level. This stance was a response to the so-called bipolar approach to exchange rate regimes, choosing either a hard peg or a free float. See Stanley Fischer (2004). "Is the Bipolar View Correct?" in Stanley Fischer, *The IMF in a Time of Crisis*. Cambridge, Massachusetts: MIT Press, pp. 227–54.
9. Morris Goldstein (2002). "Brazil's Unwatched Borrowing" *Financial Times* (August 27).
10. After a short stint with Citibank, Fischer became Governor of the Bank of Israel in 2005.
11. Fraga was succeeded as central bank governor by the dependable Henrique Meirelles, who had spent part of his career in the American private sector.
12. In its report on capital account crises in Indonesia, Korea, and Brazil, the IEO referred to one executive director arguing during the annual discussion of the Brazilian economy in 1997 that consideration should be given to allowing the exchange rate to float, so as to avoid a crisis of the real if investors lost confidence in Brazil. And,

in February 1998, "one Executive Director … expressed displeasure over the absence of a clear discussion of exchange rate options in the papers prepared for the Board by the staff." IEO (2003). *The IMF and Recent Capital Account Crises: Indonesia, Korea, Brazil.* International Monetary Fund, p. 123.
13. IEO (2003). , p. 138.
14. Colin Powell, a former Four Star General and US Secretary of State, favored overwhelming the enemy with more than the necessary number of troops; a strategy that worked well during the Gulf War of 1990.

6 The IMF Fails: The Argentine Drama

1. Argentina does not score very well in international comparisons of educational standards.
2. The law that established the currency board. Strictly speaking, this was not a full-fledged currency board, as it allowed some leeway for lender of last operations by the Central Bank.
3. The peso was to move with both the US dollar and the euro in equal weights, once the euro reached parity again with the dollar. In the event, the dollar appreciated further against the euro, raising expectations of a devaluation of the peso.
4. Michael Mussa (2002). "Argentina and the Fund: From Triumph to Tragedy." *Policy Analyses in International Economics* No. 67. Washington D.C.: Institute for International Economics (March), p. 12.
5. Estimates of the volume of assets held abroad by Argentines were as high as $100 billion. *The Economist* (2002). "A Decline without Parallel" (2 March), p. 28.
6. O'Neill had been CEO of the aluminum giant ALCOA, and Taylor was an outstanding economist who had been a professor at Stanford University. O'Neill was "relieved of his duties" by President George W. Bush after less than two years, while Taylor served from 2001 to 2005.
7. See Ron Suskind (2004). *The Price of Loyalty: George W. Bush, the White House, and the Education of Paul O'Neill.* New York: Simon and Schuster, p. 173.
8. The IEO mentions in its excellent report on Argentina that "noneconomic considerations" played an important part in this regard. See Independent Evaluation Office (2004). *The IMF and Argentina: 1991–2001.* International Monetary Fund, p. 5.
9. Since there was considerable irritation concerning my position, the Dutch Ambassador in Buenos Aires was summoned to receive a formal complaint.
10. My position is mentioned in Paul Blustein (2005). *And the Money Kept Rolling in (and out).* New York: Public Affairs, pp. 154–5.
11. The laminated cards are reproduced in John B. Taylor (2007). *Global Financial Warriors: The Untold Story of International Finance in the Post 9/11 World.* New York: W.W. Norton and Company, pp. 72, 90. Taylor also mentions playing golf with Anne Krueger at the IMF country club, p. 117.
12. Taylor (2007), p. 92.
13. *Clarin* (2002) (December 13). As quoted in the IMF Morning Press.
14. *Financial Times* (2003) Comment and Analysis (January 21).
15. *Financial Times* (2003) "IMF chief happy to gamble on debt-laden Argentina." (September 15).
16. In nominal terms, not in present value terms, which would have implied a haircut of 85 per cent.
17. As reported by Argentine news agency *Telam*, March 6, 2005.

18. Rato took over from Köhler in May 2004, when the latter was elected as president of Germany.
19. Described in Tomas J. T. Baliño and Charles Enoch (1997). "Currency Board Arrangements: Issues and Experiences." *Occasional Paper* No. 151. International Monetary Fund (August).

7 Turkey Stumbles

1. During a widely publicized confrontation between the Turkish President, Ahmet Sezer, and the Prime Minister, Bulent Eçevit, a copy of the Turkish constitution was thrown back and forth.
2. The process is described in detail in Hugh Bredenkamp, M. Josefsson and C. J. Lindgren (2009). "Turkey's Renaissance from Banking Crisis to Economic Revival" in Brau and McDonald (2009), pp. 43–84.
3. Taylor (2007) p. 168.
4. Taylor (2007) p. 171.
5. Taylor (2007) p. 179.

8 Lessons Learned, Not Learned or Ignored

1. For small investors the lesson was to be cautious about investing in bonds issued by most emerging market countries.
2. Peter B. Kenen and Alexander K. Swoboda (eds.) (2000). *Reforming the International Financial and Monetary System.* International Monetary Fund. My contribution was called "More Private Sector Involvement and Less Official Financing," pp. 277–84.
3. Anne O. Krueger (2002). *A New Approach to Sovereign Debt Rescheduling.* International Monetary Fund.
4. Raymond Ritter (2009). "Transnational governance in global finance: the Principles for Stable Capital Flows and Fair Debt Restructuring in Emerging Markets" *Occasional Paper* No. 103. European Central Bank (April). www.ech.int/pub/pdf/scpop8/ecbocp103.pdf
5. Proposals for introducing CACs go back to a post-Mexican crisis report prepared under the chairmanship of Jean-Jacques Rey: Group of Ten (1996). "The Resolution of Sovereign Liquidity Crises: A Report to the Ministers and Governors Prepared under the Auspices of the Deputies." Basel; Martin Wolf was an early supporter of CACs, as was I, which is reflected in our contributions to the 1998 conference at the IMF. See Kenen and Swoboda (2000), pp. 282, 296.

9 A Global Firestorm

1. White first warned of the "inherently pro-cyclical" nature of the financial system in Claudio Borio and William R. White (2003). "Whither Monetary and Financial Stability? The Implications of Evolving Policy Regimes." Jackson Hole: Federal Reserve Bank of Kansas City (August). www.kansascityfed.org/publicat/Sympos/2003/pdf/BorioWhite2003.pdf. Other clear warnings are contained in William R. White (2006). "Is Price Stability Enough?" *BIS Working Papers* No. 205. Various annual reports of the BIS, which bore White's imprint, expressed similar concerns.

2. Raghuram G. Rajan (2005). "Has Financial Development Made the World Riskier?" Jackson Hole: Federal Reserve Bank of Kansas City (August). www.kansascityfed.org/publicat/Sympos/2005/pdf/rajan2005.pdf.
3. Author's interview with Papadia, July 12, 2010.
4. Other important central banks, such as the Bank of England, took similar measures.
5. Paul Volcker (2008). *Speech* before the Economic Club of New York, April 8, 2008.
6. Henry M. Paulson, Jr. (2010). *On the Brink: Inside the Race to Stop the Collapse of the Global Financial System.* New York: Business Plus, p. 117.
7. The term is ascribed to the Prussian military analyst Carl von Clausewitz, according to *Wikipedia.*
8. In one of history's strange twists, the Governor of the State of New York, Eliot Spitzer, was reported to have played a critical behind-the-scenes role in saving the monoline insurer Ambac (*Financial Times,* March 10, 2008) the day before admitting to having visited a professional escort, which led to his resignation.
9. Paulson (2010), p. 161.
10. Paulson (2010), p. 180.
11. Paulson (2010), p. 225.
12. *Financial Times,* September 2, 2010.
13. Lehman's total assets were $600 billion, as compared with $2.3 trillion for Bank of America and somewhat less for JP Morgan and Citibank.
14. Paulson (2010), p. 229.
15. Paulson (2010), p. 224.
16. Paulson (2010), p. 241.
17. Martin Wolf in rejecting the doctrine that some banks are too big or too interconnected to fail argued that "[no] normal profit-seeking business can operate without a credible threat of bankruptcy." "Do Not Learn the Wrong Lessons from Lehman's Fall." (*Financial Times,* September 16, 2009).
18. In private, some Western senior policymakers entertained the thought that government purchases of equities, as had taken place in Hong Kong during the Asian crisis of 1997, would calm markets by halting the slide on stock markets. Russia followed that course of action, but others did not.
19. Gordon Brown (2010). *Beyond the Crash: Overcoming the First Crisis of Globalization.* New York: Simon & Schuster.
20. Peer Steinbrück, who was adamantly opposed to conducting stress tests on European banks, described the checks on US banks as "worthless" (*Financial Times,* May 14, 2009). A little more than a year later the new German government agreed to release the results of stress tests for German banks.
21. Analyzed in Chapter 11.
22. In a more fundamental vein, Rajan traces the fault lines of the latest crisis to a world economic system overly dependent on American overconsumption and related indebtedness to drive global economic growth. See Raghuram G. Rajan (2010). *Fault Lines: How Hidden Fractures Still Threaten the World Economy.* Princeton University Press.
23. Risk management issues have been lucidly explained by Matthew Valencia in *The Economist,* February 13, 2010.
24. Pietro S. Nivola and John C. Courtney (2009). "Know Thy Neighbor: What Canada Can Tell Us about Financial Regulation." Washington D.C.: Brookings Institution (May 11). Australia's well-supervised banking system also suffered little from the crisis. (April 23). www.brookings.edu/papers/2009/0423_canada_nivola.aspx
25. Clear examples are provided in Independent Evaluation Office (2011). *IMF Performance in the Run-Up to the Financial and Economic Crises.* International Monetary Fund.

26. Ben Bernanke (2010). *Remarks* to the American Economic Association (January 2).
27. Reinhart and Rogoff have shown that financial crises over the centuries share many elements. See Carmen M. Reinhart and Kenneth S. Rogoff (2009). *This Time Is Different: Eight Centuries of Financial Folly*. Princeton University Press.
28. Named after Paul Volcker, the respected former chairman of the Fed, who served as special economic advisor during the first two years of the Obama administration.
29. Author's interview with Foot, July 30, 2010.
30. Timothy Geithner and Larry Summers (2009). "A New Financial Foundation." *Washington Post* (June 15).
31. A similar conclusion is reached by Morris Goldstein and Nicolas Véron (2011). "Too Big to Fail: The Transatlantic Debate." Peterson Institute for International Economics, *Working Paper Series* WP 11–2, Washington D.C.
32. Institute of International Finance (2010). www.iif.com.
33. Financial Stability Board and Basel Committee of Bank Supervisors (2010). *Assessment of Macroeconomic Impact of Stronger Capital and Liquidity Requirements*. Basel.
34. The IIF and FSB/BCSB estimates are not directly comparable because of methodological differences.
35. Author's interview with Foot, January 14, 2011.
36. Adair Turner (2009). Interview. *Prospect* (August 27).
37. Mervyn King (2010). *Speech* at the Buttonwood gathering organized by *The Economist*. New York (October 25). Simon Johnson and James Kwak (2010). *13 Bankers: The Wall Street Takeover and the Next Financial Meltdown*. New York: Pantheon Books; reach a similar conclusion with respect to American banks.

10 Europe's Turn

1. For an in-depth analysis of the processes at work see Bas B. Bakker and Anne-Marie Gulde (2010). The Credit Boom in the EU New Member States: Bad Luck or Bad Policies? *Working Paper* 10/130. International Monetary Fund.
2. B. Bakker and I. Vladkova-Hollar (2006). "Asia 1996 and Eastern Europe: Deja-Vu All Over Again?" Mimeo. International Monetary Fund.
3. Officially known as the *Joint IFI Action Plan in Support of Banking Systems and Lending to the Real Economy in Central and Eastern Europe*.
4. European Banking Group Coordination Meeting for Hungary. *Concluding Statement* by participating parent banks, Brussels, May 20, 2009.
5. When I first visited Kiev in 1992 with a Dutch delegation seeking to enlist Ukraine as a member of the constituency led by the Netherlands in the IMF and WB, I was struck by the deep lack of understanding of Western economics and policymaking. Technical assistance by the IMF and other IFIs proved helpful, but was needed for a very long time.
6. Åslund describes how in 2004 a sense of hubris prevailed, with the "elite" thinking "that they could get away with anything." Anders Åslund (2009). *How Ukraine Became a Market Economy and Democracy*. Washington D.C.: Peterson Institute for International Economics, p. 164.
7. Independent International Experts Commission (2010). *Proposals for Ukraine: Ukraine 2010 – Time for Reform*. Kiev.
8. Brian Sturgess (2010). "Greek Economics Statistics: A Decade of Deceit." *World Economics*, Vol. 11, No. 2. (April–June).
9. Chancellor Angela Merkel (2010). Transcript of *Statement* to the Media. Berlin (April 28).

10. The process is described lucidly in Patrick Honohan (2009). "Resolving Ireland's Banking Crisis." *The Economic and Social Review*, Vol. 40, No. 2, pp. 207–31. See also Klaus Regling and Max Watson (2010). *Report on the Sources of Ireland's Banking Crisis.* Dublin: Government Publications Office.
11. Surprisingly all the Landesbanken passed, although narrowly.
12. Comprised of the ministers of finance of the Euro Area. Meetings are chaired by Jean-Claude Juncker, Prime Minister of Luxemburg. The president of the ECB also attends the meetings.
13. A senior American official described Trichet to me as a magician who knows exactly which buttons to push and which levers to pull.
14. Lorenzo Bini Smaghi (2010). "The Financial and Fiscal Crisis: A Euro Area Perspective." *Speech* held for Le Cercle: Brussels (June 12). www.ech.europa.eu/press/hey/date/2010/html/sp200618_1.en.html.
15. *Statement* by the Eurogroup, Brussels, November 28, 2010. www.consilium.europa.eu.
16. It is surprising that CACs were not introduced in all EU countries following the agreement on such clauses in the IMF in 2002 and their subsequent widespread adoption by emerging countries.
17. Kierkegaard has stressed that Europe's leaders are credible when they pledge to do what it takes to save the euro and the Euro Area, but that the process could be messy: Jacob F. Kierkegaard (2010). "How Europe Can Muddle through Its Crisis." *Policy Brief* No. 10–27. Washington D.C.: Peterson Institute for International Economics. www.piie.com/publications/pb1027.
18. Willem Buiter (2011). "The Debt of Nations." *Global Economic Review*. New York: Citibank (January 17).

11 Saving the System

1. Michael Dooley, David Folkerts-Landau and Peter Garber (2003). "An Essay on the Revised Bretton Woods System." *Working Paper* No. 9971. National Bureau of Economic Research.
2. The existence of the World Trade Organization, in which trade disputes are discussed in a multilateral forum, has undoubtedly helped in this regard.
3. This was done both in the 1960s and in the 1970s, but is unlikely to be repeated.
4. Estimates are provided in J. Onno de Beaufort Wijnholds and Lars Søndergaard (2007). "Reserve Accumulation: Objective or By-product?" *Occasional Paper Series* No. 73. European Central Bank (September). www.ecb.int/pub/pdf/scpops/ecbocp73.pdf
5. During my tenure at the IMF Board I brought up this matter a few times, but received little response.
6. The message was relayed by Tim Adams, then Undersecretary for International Affairs at the US Treasury: Timothy D. Adams (2005). "The US View on IMF Reform." *Speech* presented at the conference on IMF reform. Washington D.C.: Peterson Institute for International Economics (September 23).
7. Isabelle Mateos y Lago, Isabelle, Rupa Duttagupta, and Rishi Goyal (2009). "The Debate on the International Monetary System." *Staff Position Note* 09/26. International Monetary Fund (November 11); www.imf.org/external/pubs/ft/spn/09/spn0926.pdf "Reserve Accumulation and International Monetary Stability" (2010). Prepared by the Strategy, Policy and Review Department. International Monetary Fund (April 13). www.imf.org/external/up/pp/eng/2010/04130.pdf

8. John Lipsky (2010). "Reconsidering the International Monetary System," *Panel Presentation*, Jackson Hole Federal Reserve Bank of Kansas Symposium (August 28). www.imf.org/external/np/speeches/2020/082810.html.
9. A special high-level committee was established to report on reform of the international monetary system. This Committee of Twenty reflected the 20 constituencies represented in the Fund's Executive Board at the time, and should not be confused with the G20, which was created in 1999. The report of the C20 covers several of the issues still on the agenda 40 years later: Committee on Reform of the International Monetary System and Related Issues (Committee of Twenty) (1974). *International Monetary Reform: Documents of the Committee of Twenty*. International Monetary Fund.
10. Group of Twenty (2009). *Leader's Statement*: The Pittsburgh Summit (September 24, 25).
11. Russia and Saudi Arabia are special cases, being large oil exporters. Germany is part of the Euro Area, which as a whole is roughly in external balance. Current account imbalances within a monetary union are less worrisome than those outside the union, but, as Greece and Ireland have demonstrated, can still cause serious problems if they become very large.
12. The IMF *Articles of Agreement* include certain obligations for its members to collaborate with the Fund "to assure orderly exchange rate arrangements and to promote a stable system of exchange rates" (Article IV, section 1), but, apart from a – seldom issued – verbal rap on the knuckles, no sanctions apply.
13. International Monetary Fund (2007). *Decision on Bilateral Surveillance over Members' Policies*. International Monetary Fund.
14. Special drawing rights were introduced in 1969. They can be exchanged against strong currencies of IMF members through a process of designation.
15. J. Onno de Beaufort Wijnholds and Arend Kapteyn (2001). "Reserve Adequacy in Emerging Market Economies." *Working Paper* No. 01/143. International Monetary Fund.
16. The Fund staff improved the Wijnholds/Kapteyn benchmark approach ten years later: International Monetary Fund (2011). "Assessing Reserve Adequacy" *Paper* prepared by the staff (February 14). www.imf.org/external/np/pp/eng/2011/021411c.pdf
17. Estimates by de Beaufort Wijnholds and Søndergaard (2007).
18. Graham Bird and Ramishen Rajan (2003). "Too Much of a Good Thing? The Adequacy of International Reserves in the Aftermath of Crises." *World Economy*, Vol. 26, No. 6, pp. 873–91.
19. Article VIII, section 7 and Article XXII.
20. Author's interview with Bakker, January 25, 2011. Poland's CFL was increased in 2010 while it was running a budget deficit of 8 per cent, which stretches the notion of "sound policy."
21. Lombardi sees either the two bodies coexisting or the G20 becoming the global steering committee and the IMF acting as its executive arm. Domenico Lombardi (2009). "The G-20 and IMF: The Future Role of the International Monetary System" in *G-20 Summit: Recovering from the Crisis'* Brookings Institution Washington D.C. (September 17).
22. Information on the currency composition of foreign exchange reserves is incomplete, as China, unlike the majority of other countries, does not provide a breakdown of its holdings.
23. This reduces the attractiveness of the SDR. Before they can be used directly in interventions, the private sector should be allowed to hold officially issued SDRs, and a market in them should be created.

24. The idea of an SDR Substitution Account goes back to 1974. See Committee of Twenty (1974), pp. 41–2.
25. Peter B. Kenen (2010). "The Substitution Account as a First Step toward Reform of the International Monetary System." *Policy Brief* No. 10-6. Peterson Institute for International Economics. www.piie.com/publications/pb1006.
26. Zhou Xiaochuan (2009). "Reform the International Monetary System." *Speech.* Peoples Bank of China (23 March).
27. Author's interview with Bergsten, April 7, 2011. Bergsten, a longtime supporter of an SDR Substitution Account, was the chief negotiator for the United States when the modalities for an SA were worked out in 1979.
28. The debate on asset price inflation and central banks is described in detail in Howard Davies and David Green (2010). *Banking on the Future: The Fall and Rise of Central Banking.* Princeton University Press.

Epilogue

1. George A. Akerlof and Robert J. Schiller (2009). *Animal Spirits: How Human Psychology Drives the Economy and Why It Matters for Global Capitalism.* Princeton University Press.

Index

No separate entries are included for the Executive Board, the Managing Director, management and staff of the International Monetary Fund as references to these are to be found throughout the book. Individuals belonging to these categories can be searched by name.

AAA rating, 134, 138
Abdelal, Rawi, 64, 65
Adams, Timothy, 200
African National Congress, 28
Agency paper (US), 137, 138
Akerlof, George, 202
AK Islamic Party (*see* Turkey)
Albania, 157
Alfonsin, Raul, 95
American International Group, 138, 140, 144, 150
Anjaria, Shailandra, 194
Argentina, 86, 94–109, 120, 181, 182
   Austral Plan, 95
   banking system of, 103
   causes of the crisis in, 120
   Central bank independence in, 97, 99, 103, 105
   corralito, 101
   currency board of, 75, 99, 103–106
   debt rescheduling by, 103–105
   default of, 99, 101, 104, 107
   devaluation by, 97–99, 107
   fiscal policy of, 96–106
   IMF financing of, 98, 100, 103–104
   Plan Primavera, 95
   political instability of, 94–95, 101
   reserves of, 97
   structural policy of, 106–107
   United States' role in, 100, 102, 106
Armenia, 10
Asian Development Bank, 30, 36, 57
Asian financial crisis, 25–69
Asian Monetary Fund, 39
Åslund, Anders, 199
Asset backed securities, 134, 145, 150
Asset price inflation, 189
Attatürk, Kemal, 110

Australia (*see also* Banks), 36, 125
Austria (*see also* Banks), 174

Babaçan, Ali, 114
Bail-in (*see* Private sector involvement)
Bail-out (*see under* Argentina, Brazil, Greece, Hungary, Indonesia, Ireland, Korea, Mexico, Romania, Russia, Thailand, Turkey, Ukraine)
Baker Plan, 6
Bakker, Age, 185, 194
Bakker, Bas, 157, 199
Baliño, Thomas, 196
Bank Bali, 45
Bank for International Settlements, 5, 12, 125, 132, 186
Bank Indonesia (*see* Indonesia)
Bank of America, 138
Bank of England, 134–136, 142, 154, 177
Bank of Japan, 177
Bank of Thailand, 29–30
Bankruptcy court, international, 22
Bankruptcy mechanism, international (*see* Debt restructuring)
Banks
   American, 59, 143–146, 149
   Australian, 198
   Austrian, 157
   Benelux, 142, 145–146, 168
   British, 141, 145
   Canadian, 144
   European, 140–144, 149–157, 168–169
   fail, too big to, 145
   French, 169
   German, 140–142, 157, 168
   Greek (*see* Greece)
   interconnected, too, 149

Banks – *continued*
  Irish (*see* Ireland)
  Japanese, 9, 11, 37, 51, 104, 153
  regulation and supervision of, 145–146,
    149–155, 190
  save, too big to, 165
  Spanish, 169
  Swedish, 157
Banque de France, 9, 129
Basel II, III, 150, 153–154
Basel Committee of Bank Supervisors,
  149, 152–153
Bear Sterns, 136–140
Beattie, Alan, 103
Belgium, ix, 126, 141
Belize, 129
Bergsten, Fred, 187
Bernanke, Ben, 135, 139–140, 146
Bernes, Thomas, 82, 193
Bidaya, Thanong, 29
Bini Smaghi, Lorenzo, 173
Bird, Graham, 201
Blejer, Mario, 103, 192
Blustein, Paul, 55, 193
Bolivia, 43
Bonds (*see also* Collective action clauses),
  188
  holders of, 20, 74, 104, 151, 166
Bonus culture, 157
Borio, Claudio, 197
Brady Plan, 6–7, 188
Brau, Eduard, 192
Brazil, 5, 27, 34, 70, 80–93, 120, 180, 182,
  185
  Banco Central do Brasil, 80, 85
  banking system of, 56
  capital flows, from and to, 65, 84, 87, 177
  causes of the crisis in, 120
  exchange rate of, 81–85
  external debt of, 81, 84, 88, 91
  fiscal policy of, 84–86, 90–91
  IMF credits, 83, 88
  monetary policy of, 84–85, 87
  private sector involvement in, 84, 91–93
  reserves of, 81–84, 86, 89
  rollover ratio for, 83–85, 91
  structural policy of, 84, 88, 91
  surveillance of, 89, 95
  United States' role in, 90
Bredenkamp, Hugh, 197

Bretton Woods II, 176
Bretton Woods system
  breakdown of, 1–3, 129
BRICS, 89
Brown, Gordon, 142, 154
Buiter, Willem, 174
Bulgaria, 41, 75
Bush, George W., 77, 87, 100, 114, 141

Camdessus, Michel, ix, 9, 15–16, 23, 38,
  42, 44–46, 53, 54, 58–61, 64–65,
  72–75, 78, 85, 86, 90–92, 126
Cameron government, 154
Canada (*see also* Banks), 83, 90, 135
Capital flows, 156–184
  carry trade, 177–183, 186–188, 191
  controls on, 177, 183
  hot money, 173
  liberalization of, 63–67, 122
Capital requirements (*see* Basel II, III)
Cardoso, Fernando, Henrique, 80–84,
  87–88, 90
Carry trade (*see* Capital flows)
Carstens, Agustín, 19, 130
Cavallo, Domingo, 95–102
Central and Eastern Europe, 156–161
Central banks, independence of,
  189, 191
Chaebols (*see* Korea)
Chapple, Bryan, 194
Chechnya, 76
Chernomyrdin, Viktor, 71, 73, 75
Chiang Mai Initiative, 39
Chile, 65
China (*see also* Global imbalances), 25, 27,
  30, 33, 57, 89, 147, 182, 185, 187
  central bank of, 138
  exchange rate of, 176–178, 181
  reserves of, 65, 176, 184, 186
  SDR Substitution Account, interest in,
    187
Chippa, Roberto, 101
Chubais, Anatoly, 73, 77
Citibank (Citigroup), 5, 138, 143
Clausewitz, Carl von, 197
Clinton, William Jefferson, ix, 14, 16, 38,
  42, 72, 83
Collective action clauses (*see also* Bonds),
  129–131, 173, 188–189
Colombia, 185

Committee of Twenty, 200
Connally, John, 2
Contagion, 5, 80, 100, 102
Contingent Credit Line (*see* IMF)
Cote d'Ivoire, 129
Countercyclical capital buffer
  (*see* Basel II, III)
Courtney, John, 198
Cowen, Brian, 166
Credit default swaps, 138, 152
Credit rating agencies (*see* Rating agencies)
Crisis
  causes of, 119–122, 143–146
  lessons from, 119–131
  liquidity, 135, 172–173, 188
  management (*see* IMF)
  prevention of, 20, 22, 124
  resolution of, 20, 22 ,59, 124
  solvency, 136–141, 172, 173
  systemic, 1
Croatia, National Bank of, 10, 193
Crockett, Andrew, 125
Currency board (*see* Argentina, Bulgaria,
  Hong Kong)
Currency wars, 177

D'Amato, Alfonso, 14
Davies, Howard, 202
De Beaufort Wijnholds, Onno, 192, 200,
  201
Debt restructuring, 22, 23, 127–131, 173,
  188
De Larosière, Jacques, 6, 9, 20, 59, 124, 152
De la Rua, Fernando, 101
Del Castillo, Graciana, 192
Deng Xiao Ping, 25
Deposit guarantees (*see also* Indonesia,
  Korea, Thailand), 152
De Rato, Rodrigo, 105, 178, 179
Derivatives, 144, 150
Derviş, Kemal, 112, 114
Desai, Padma, 61
Deutsche Bundesbank, 54, 169
Devaluation (*see* Exchange rates)
Dodd, Christopher, 140
Dodd-Frank Act, 149–152
Dollar (US)
  and international monetary system,
    175–178, 183, 187
  as reserve currency, 182, 186–187

as safe haven, 175
  vulnerability of, 176
Dooley, Michael, 176
Dornbusch, Rüdiger, 12, 20
Dow Jones industrial index, 141
Draghi, Mario, 153
Dubai, 104
Duhalde, Eduardo, 101, 103
Duisenberg, Willem, 16, 134
Duttagupta, Rupa, 200

Eastern Europe, 59, 127, 183–184
East-Timor, 44
Eçevit, Bulent, 192
Ecuador, 27
Efficient market hypothesis, 190
Eijffinger, Sylvester, 192
Enoch, Charles, 196
Esdar, Bernd, 59
Euro, 9, 162–164, 167–170, 173–174, 177,
  184, 188
Euro Area, 156–174, 179–180, 188, 191
Eurogroup, 170
European Central Bank (ECB), 16, 125,
  163, 165, 171, 177–178, 185
  bond purchases by, 168
  collateral requirements of, 163, 168
  Council of, 134
  independence of, 189
  interest rates, coordinated cut of, 135,
    142
  joint missions with EC, IMF, 172
  liquidity support by, 134–137, 165
  long-term repo facility of, 135
  open market policy of, 135
  swap line with Fed, 135
European Commission (EC), 161, 166,
  172, 174
European Exchange Rate Mechanism
  (ERM), 8
European Financial Stability Facility
  (EFSF), 165–167, 170–172, 189
European Monetary Union (EMU),
  8, 53
European Stability Mechanism (ESM),
  170–174, 188–189
European Supervisory Authority, 152
European Systemic Risk Board, 152
European System of Central Banks
  (ESCB), 134

European Union (EU), 8, 119, 152, 154–155, 163, 190
Exchange rates (*see also* Dollar, Euro, Global imbalances), 124
  executive board decision of 2007, on (*see* IMF)
  fixed, 21, 122
  floating, 122
  fundamentally misaligned (*see also* China, Maldives), 181
  overvalued, 181
  undervalued, 179–181
Exchange Stabilization Fund (*see* United States)

Fannie Mae, 137–138, 151
Federal Deposit Insurance Company (FDIC), 149
Federal Reserve Bank of New York, 76
Federal Reserve System (Fed) (*see also* Bernanke, Greenspan), 14, 132–135, 140–143, 146, 149, 155, 177
  AIG, rescue of, 140
  Bear Stearns, rescue of, 136
  commercial paper market, support of, 141
  financial crisis, role in, 134–135, 139–141
  independence of, 189
  interest rates, coordinated cut of, 135, 142
  liquidity support by, 134–135
  quantitative easing by, 177
  stress tests, studied by, 143
  swap lines, extended, 135
  term auction facility of, 135
  term securities lending facility of, 135
Financial crisis (*see* Crisis)
Financial Oversight Council (*see* United States)
Financial Services Authority (United Kingdom), 154
Financial Stability Board (FSB), 125, 149, 152–153, 188–189
Financial Stability Forum (FSB), 125, 145
Finland, 174
Fischer, Stanley, 13, 40, 42, 48, 59, 62, 74, 82, 85, 87, 90, 92, 100, 102, 113, 124, 127
Flexible Credit Line (*see* IMF)
Folkerts-Landau, David, 200

Foot, Michael, 151, 153
Foreign exchange reserves (*see* International reserves)
Fox, Vicente, 18, 19
Fraga, Arminio, 85–87
France (*see also* Banque de France), 141
Franco, Gustavo, 81
Franco, Itimar, 84
Freddie Mac, 137–138, 151

Gaidar, Yegor, 71
Garber, Peter, 200
Geithner, Timothy, 88, 139, 143, 150, 152, 180
Geraschenko, Viktor, 76
Germany (*see also* Deutsche Bundesbank), ix, 38, 43, 70, 93, 104, 141, 162, 166, 170, 172, 174, 180
Gerson, Philip, 195
Gilman, Martin, 194
Ginandjar, Kartasasmita, 40
Gingrich, Newton, 14
GKOs (*see* Russia)
Global imbalances (*see also* China, IMF, United States), 147, 176, 179, 181, 191
Goldman Sachs, 138, 141
Goldstein, Morris, 88–89, 199
Gordon James, 193
Gore, Albert Jr., 77
Gourinchas, Pierre-Olivier, 194
Government Sponsored Entities (*see* Fannie Mae, Freddie Mac)
Goyal, Rishi, 200
Gramlich, Edward, 145
Greece, 156, 161–167, 170, 173, 190
Greenspan, 14, 48, 66–67, 145, 148
Greenspan Put, 146
Group of Four, 126
Group of Seven (G7), 8, 20, 38, 54, 59, 70, 80, 88, 100, 103–104, 114, 116, 119, 125, 130, 141–142
Group of Ten, 195
Group of Twenty (G20), 52, 125, 135, 141, 149, 152–154, 160, 175, 179–182, 185–168, 191
Gulde, Anne-Marie, 199

Habibie, B.J., 40, 44–45
Haircuts (discount on loan principal), 78, 103–104, 166, 173
Hanke, Steve, 41–42

Hedge funds, 145–146, 152
Herd behavior of banks, 143
Hong Kong, 25, 27, 29, 53, 125, 198
Honohan, Patrick, 199
House prices (*see* United States)
Hungary, 9, 27, 34, 157–158, 182
Hypo Real Estate, 142

Iceland, 165
Independent Evaluation Office (*see* IMF)
India, 25, 180
Indonesia, 25, 27, 33–50
Inflation targeting, 122, 149
Ingves, Stefan, 113, 115
Institute of International Finance, 199
Inter-American Development Bank, 83, 98
Internal devaluation (*see also* Greece), 146
International adjustment process (*see also* Global imbalances), 23, 179
Internationale Nederlanden Groep (ING), 169
International financial system, 21, 149–150, 170, 175, 191
International liquidity (*see also* International reserves), 179, 181
International Monetary and Financial Committee (IMFC), 26, 142, 185
International Monetary Fund (IMF)
    access rules of, 15, 63
    and Argentina, 94–109
    Articles of Agreement of, 2, 184, 187, 201
    Board of Governors of, 24
    capital flows, role with respect to, 34, 63–66, 184, 188, 191
    and Colombia, 49
    conditionality of, 5, 17, 23, 185
    Contingent Credit Line (CCL) of, 125–126
    early warning system of, 22
    Extended Facility of, 166
    Flexible Credit Line (FCL) of, 127, 157, 185
    fundamental misalignment, declaration of, 181
    gold of, 187
    governance of, 185
    and Greece, 161–164
    and Hungary, 157–159
    Independent Evaluation Office of, 43, 66, 77, 92
    and Indonesia, 33–50

and Ireland, 166–167
and Korea, 51–69
and Mexico, 11–24
Multilateral Assessment Program (MAP) of, (*see also* G20), 180
Multilateral Consultations of, 178
ownership, of borrowing countries, 20, 36, 48–49, 57
quotas, increase in, 4, 23–24, 34, 185
and riots, 6, 39
and Romania, 158–159
and Russia, 70–79
and South Africa, 28
Special Data Dissemination Standard (SDDS) of, 126
stigma experienced by borrowers, 127, 190
Supplemental Reserve Facility (SRF) of, 57, 83
Systemic Transformation Facility of, 9
and Thailand, 28–33
and Turkey, 110–118
2007 decision on bilateral surveillance of members' policies of, 181
and Ukraine, 159–161
World Economic Outlook of, 26
International monetary system, 121–131, 138, 175–191
International reserves
    accumulation of, 79–186
    adequacy of, 122, 182, 185
    diversification of (*see also* SDRs), 191
    self-insurance, 182
Intervention, in foreign exchange markets, 43, 123, 177
Iraq, 114
Ireland, 130, 164–167, 170, 172–173
Isarescu, Mugur, 158
Italy, ix, 8, 104, 105, 141, 174

Japan (*see also* Bank of Japan, Banks), 29, 30, 36, 39, 55, 68, 73, 83
Jeanne, Olivier, 194
Johnson, Simon, 199
JP Morgan Chase, 136
Juncker, Jean-Claude, 199

Kafka, Alexandre, 15
Kapteyn, Arend, 201
Kemp, Jack, 61
Kenen, Peter, 187, 197

Kiekens, Willy, 126
Kierkegaard, Jacob, 200
Kim, Dae Jung, 58
Kindleberger, Charles, 1
King, Mervyn, 154
Kirchner, Christina Fernandez de, 105
Kirchner, Nestor, 104–105
Kiriyenko, Sergei, 194
Kohl, Helmut, 42, 72
Köhler, Horst, 86, 88, 100, 103–104,
    112–113, 178
Kok, Willem, 45
Korea, 25, 26, 35, 51–69, 91, 120, 177, 183
    capital account liberalization by, 63–67
    causes of crisis in, 120
    chaebols in, 52, 66, 68
    exchange rate of, 52–53, 58, 62, 68
    financial system of, 52–53, 60
    financing, by IMF, 56–57
    fiscal policy of, 67–68
    Grand National Party of, 57
    liquidity crisis in, 54
    monetary policy of, 58, 62, 67–68
    ownership of, 58
    private sector involvement in, 59
    reserves of, 52–54, 61
    rollovers by banks, 58
    second line of defense for, 57, 60
    structural policy of, 67–68
    surveillance, of IMF, 52, 62–63
Kremers, Jeroen, 103
Krueger, Anne, 52, 87, 102, 127–129, 192
Kuchma, Leonid, 75
Kwak, James, 199
Kwon, Okyo, 55

Landesbanken (Germany), 169
Latin America, 4–6, 11, 80, 147, 184, 188
Latvia, 158, 164
Lavagna, Roberto, 120
Lehman Brothers, 139–141
Leveraging, 134, 141
Liberia, 129
Lim, Yeal Chang, 55
Limbaugh, Rush, 14
Lindgren, C.J., 197
Lipsky, John, 179
Lipton, David, 57
Liquidity crisis (*see* Crisis)
Liquidity requirements (*see* Basel III)

Lissakers, Karen, 40, 65
Living wills
    of banks, 149–150
Lombardi, Domenico, 201
Long Term Capital Management (LTCM),
    70, 75, 125, 146, 149
Lopes, Francisco, 85
Lott, Trent, 40
Louvre Accord, 8, 175
Lula, Luiz Inacio da Silva, 86–89

Maastricht criteria, 161
Mahathir, Mohammed, 27
Malan, Pedro, 82, 85, 87, 90, 93
Malaysia, 25–26, 28–29, 36, 182
Maldives, 181
Mandela, Nelson, 28
Mateos y Lago, Isabelle, 200
McDonald, Ian, 192
McDonough, William, 76
McNamara, Robert, 137
Meirelles, Henrique, 195
Menem, Carlos, 95
Merkel, Angela, 163, 170–172
Merrill Lynch, 138
Mexico, ix, 5, 11–24, 81, 86, 91, 120, 126,
    130, 182, 185
    banking system of, 12–13, 17, 19
    capital outflows, 13
    causes of the crisis in, 120
    current account of, 12, 13, 18
    devaluation by, 12, 13, 17, 20
    Europe, role of, 15–16, 18, 20, 22
    Exchange Equalisation Fund, financing
        from (*see also* United States), 15, 17, 18
    fiscal policy of, 13, 19
    foreign debt of, 18
    IMF, involvement of, 12–21
    monetary policy of, 17, 19
    Partido Revolucionario Institucional
        (PRI), 12
    reserves of, 13, 15
    structural policies of, 19
    surveillance of, 20
    tesobonos issued by, 13, 17–18, 20, 22
    United States, role of, 14–20
Monetary policy (*see also under* Brazil,
    European Central Bank, Federal
    Reserve System, Indonesia, Korea,
    Mexico, Russia, Turkey), 146, 178, 189

Monoline insurers, 137
Moral hazard, 7, 17, 20, 21, 23, 54, 68, 74,
  76, 78, 92, 108, 114, 119, 123, 139,
  142, 146, 148, 172–173, 188, 191
Morgan Stanley, 138, 141
Mozhin, Aleksei, 75–76
Multilateral Assessment Process (*see*
  IMF)
Multilateral consultations (*see* IMF)
Mussa, Michael, 97
Myrdal, Gunnar, 25

Nederlandsche Bank, De, 16
Neiss, Hubert, 40, 45, 58, 193
Nemtsov, Boris, 73
Netherlands, ix, 14, 44, 93, 113, 125, 126,
  141, 174
Newly industrialized countries, 25
Nivola, Pietro, 198
Nixon, Richard, 2
Non-governmental organizations (NGOs),
  49
Nordic countries, ix, 93, 126
Northern Rock, 136, 154
North Korea, 51
Novak, Robert, 194

Obama, Barack, 149, 168
Obama administration, 152
Odling-Smee, John, 72–73, 77
O'Donnell, Augustine, 65
Oil shock, 19, 23, 34
O'Neill, Paul, 87, 100, 128
Open mouth policy (*see* Intervention)
Organization for Economic Cooperation
  and Development (OECD), 52, 55,
  110, 179
Organization of Petroleum Exporting
  Countries (OPEC), 3, 35, 50
Ortiz, Guillermo, 15, 19
Ostry, Jonathan, 194
Ottoman Empire, 110
Owen, David, 195
Ownership (*see* IMF)
Özal Turgut, 110

Papadia, Francesco, 134
Papandreou, George, 162
Paris Club, 44
Paulson, Henry Jr., 136–141

Perez, Lorenzo, 194
Peron, Juan, 94
Philippines, 26, 29, 35
Plaza Accord, 8, 175
Portugal, 162, 164, 166–169, 172
Portugal, Murillo, 91
Powell, Colin, 92, 167
Primakov, Yevgeni, 72, 76
Private equity funds, 152
Private sector involvement (PSI), 48, 59,
  68–69, 84, 91–92, 118, 123–124,
  172–173, 188–189
Pronk, Jan, 44–45

Quarles, Randal, 130
Quotas (*see* IMF)

Rajan, Raghuram, 133, 198
Rajan, Ramishen, 201
Rating agencies, 134, 145, 151–152
Rational expectations theory, 190
Recycling oil money, 4
Redrado, Martín, 105
Regling, Klaus, 199
Reinhart, Carmen, 191
Renminbi (*see* China, Exchange rate)
Rernchai, Marahanonda, 130
Reserves (*see* International reserves)
Rey, Jean-Jacques, 197
Risk management, 4, 144, 148
Ritter, Raymond, 197
Robinson, David, 30, 194
Rogoff, Kenneth, 198
Romania, 157–159
Roubini, Nouriel, 132
Rubin, Robert, 14, 15, 48, 55, 59, 82
Ruckauf, Carlos, 103
Russia, 9, 27, 56, 69–79, 102, 126, 138,
  141, 160, 180, 182
  capital flight from, 73–74
  causes of crisis, 120
  collapse of, 73–76
  default by, 70–74, 76
  devaluation by, 74, 76, 78
  Duma of, 76
  fiscal policy of, 71–78
  GKOs issued by, 74
  and Group of Seven, 72–74, 76, 78
  IMF credits granted to, 72–73, 76
  monetary policy of, 71, 73, 76, 78

Russia – *continued*
  oligarchs in, 71
  privatization in, 71
  reserves of, 77
  structural policy of, 78
  surveillance of, 77–78

Sachs, Jeffrey, 61, 71
Sakakibara, Eisuke, 39
Sarkózy, Nicolas, 142, 170, 172
Saudi Arabia, 125, 179, 180
Schäuble, Wolfgang, 163, 172
Schiller, Robert, 202
Schweitzer, Pierre-Paul, 2
SDRM (*see* Debt restructuring)
SDRs, 2, 181–182, 186–187
SDR Substitution Account, 186–187, 191
Securities and Exchange Commission
  (SEC), 145
Securitization, 144
Self insurance (*see* International reserves)
Serbia, 158
Sezer, Ahmet, 192
Shadow banks, 145
Short selling, 152
Singapore, 25, 29, 36, 125
Singh, Anoop, 48, 103
Slovakia, 14
Smithsonian agreement, 2
Sócrates, José, 166
Soft law, 129, 181
Solvency crisis (*see* Crisis)
Søndergaard, Lars, 200
Soros, George, 8, 27, 85
South Africa, 27–28, 180, 182
South Korea (*see* Korea)
Sovereign debt (*see* Debt)
Soviet Union, 9
Spain (*see also* Banks), 98, 164, 167–169, 172
Special drawing rights (*see* SDRs)
Special purpose vehicle, 144, 171
Spitzer, Eliot, 198
Stability and Growth Pact (SGP), 161, 174
Standstill (*see* Crisis)
Stark, Jürgen, 59
Steinbrück, Peer, 198
Stiglitz, Joseph, 46–47
Stigma (*see* IMF)
Strauss-Kahn, Dominique, 65, 163, 181
Stress tests, 143, 169

Sturgess, Brian, 199
Sudden stop, 159
Suharto, 33–41, 44, 46–47
Sukarno, 35
Sukarnoputri, Megawathi, 39
Summers, Lawrence, 14–15, 38, 48, 152
Susskind, 196
Swap arrangements, 177
Sweden (*see also* Banks), 164, 166
Switzerland (*see also* Banks), 93, 125–126,
  135, 141–142, 178
Swoboda, Alexander, 197

TARP (*see* United Sates)
Thailand, 25–33, 91, 177
Tietmeyer, Hans, 26, 54, 125
Toxic assets, 138, 143
Trichet, Jean-Claude, 129, 134, 142, 163,
  170, 174
Tseng, Wanda, 193
Turkey, 27, 100, 110–118, 121, 164, 180,
  182
  AK Islamic party of, 114
  bilateral US loan to, 112
  causes of crisis in, 121
  devaluation by, 112
  and European Union, 111, 118
  external debt of, 117
  financial system of, 33, 113, 115, 117
  fiscal policy of, 111–112, 115–116
  IMF credits granted to, 111–114
  liquidity crisis in, 111
  monetary policy of, 116
  rollovers by banks, 113
  surveillance of, 116–117
  United States' role, 114
Turner, Adair, 154

Ukraine, 10, 27, 55–56, 72, 156–157,
  159–161
United Kingdom (*see also* Bank of England,
  Banks: British), ix, 8, 53, 59, 104, 133,
  141–142, 145, 154, 166, 173, 186, 191
United States (*see also* Banks: American,
  Dollar, Federal Reserve System,
  Global imbalances, G7, G20, Living
  wills, Rating agencies)
  and Argentina, 100, 102, 106
  balance of payments deficit of, 133,
  147, 176, 191

United States – *continued*
  bankruptcy code of, 127
  and Brazil, 81–83, 90–93
  budget deficit of, 176
  campaign financing in, 151
  Comptroller of the Currency, 150
  Consumer Financial Protection Bureau,
    150
  exchange rate (*see* Dollar)
  filibuster in, 151
  financial crisis in, 133–145
  Financial Crisis Inquiry Commission,
    139
  housing crisis in, 132–134
  and Indonesia, 36, 38, 40, 46
  and Korea, 55, 57–58, 60, 68
  leadership of, 191
  levy on bank profits in, 151
  and Mexico, 14–20
  and multilateral assessment process (*see*
    G20, IMF)
  and multilateral consultation (*see* IMF)
  Office of Thrift Supervision of, 150
  quota in IMF of, 119, 126
  representation in IMF/WB of, 185
  Republican Party in, 149
  reserves of, 177
  and Russia (*see also* G7), 70
  stress tests in, 143
  and Thailand, 29–30
  Toxic Assets Relief Program (TARP) of,
    138
  Treasury Department of (*see also* Baker,
    Brady, Geithner, Paulson), 38, 58–59,
    82, 100, 149, 177–178
  treasury securities of, 137, 176
  and Turkey, 114
  Wall Street Reform and Consumer
    Protection Act (*see* Dodd-Frank Act)
Uruguay, 87

Valencia, Matthew, 198
Value at Risk (VAR), 148
Van Houtven, Leo, 16
Van Rompuy, Herman, 170
Venezuela, 6
Véron, Nicolas, 199
Verwey, Maarten, 171
Vienna Initiative, 158, 172–173
Volcker, Paul, 136
Volcker rule, 150, 187

Wachovia, 138
Wahid, Abdurrahman, 45
Wanniski, Jude, 61
Washington Mutual, 138
Watson, Maxwell, 199
Weber, Axel, 168
Wellink, Aernout, 153
White, William, 132, 148, 197
Whittome, L. Alan, 12, 21
Witteveen, H. Johannes, 3–4, 60
Wolf, Martin, 197, 198
World Bank (WB), 25–26, 30, 34, 36,
    46–49, 57, 67, 70–71, 77–78, 83,
    98, 104, 110, 112, 116–117, 141,
    159, 185
World Economic Outlook (*see* IMF)
World Trade Organization (WTO), 200
Wriston, Walter, 5

Yakusha, Yuriy, 56
Yamaichi, 55
Yeltsin, Boris, 72–73
Yoshimura, Yukio, 39
Yugoslavia, 9

Zalm, Gerrit, 99
Zapatero, José Luis, 168
Zedillo, Ernesto, 13, 19
Zhou Xiachuan, 187